"At last we have an indispensible guide that covers the subject of publicity. Written by a professional publicist, *The Publicity Kit* answers all the questions . . . from concept to implementation in both the print and electronic media."

Gus Boyd
Boyd Marketing Communications

"The public relations area has always been a mystery to me until reading and using the principles presented by Jeanette Smith. Even a beginner can follow *The Publicity Kit* with confidence."

Kenneth E. Giddens
Chief Financial Officer
Saber Software Corporation

"Jeanette Smith has done a terrific job of translating her work experience into one of the most sensible how-to books I have read on the subject of media relations and story placement. As practical as it is enjoyable to read."

Ray J. Artigue, APR
President
Evans/Artigue Public Relations

"A marketing communications diamond. Should be incorporated as an intricate part of any business plan. It could literally mean the difference between success and failure."

Raymond J. Champney
Champney Associates
Advertising, Marketing,
Public Relations

" . . . the most thorough foundation-setting and specific practical example book of all books I've encountered in PR."

John Gillan
President
Practical Public Relations

"*The Publicity Kit* is the most valuable book in my library. I strongly urge all business persons to take advantage of the wealth of information contained here. Particularly useful to professionals who need exposure, but may elect not to advertise."

Wanda Grasse
Attorney at Law
Monterey Park, California

"*The Publicity Kit* is remarkable . . . Essential for the beginner and the seasoned professional. Get this book and keep it handy."

L.R. Ward
Manager, Employee Relations
TU Services

"Useful and complete, *The Publicity Kit* is the definitive how-to reference for anyone involved in organizational communications."

George Arnold
President
Evans/Dallas
Advertising, Marketing,
Public Relations

The Publicity Kit

A Complete Guide for Entrepreneurs, Small Businesses, and Nonprofit Organizations

JEANETTE SMITH

John Wiley & Sons, Inc.
New York • Chichester • Brisbane • Toronto • Singapore

Library of Congress Cataloging-in-Publication Data

Smith, Jeanette,
    The publicity kit : a complete guide for entrepreneurs, small businesses, and nonprofit organizations / by Jeanette Smith.
        p.   cm.
    Includes bibliographical references and index.
        ISBN 0-471-54586-4 (alk. paper) —ISBN 0-471-54587-2 (pbk. : alk. paper)
        1. Industrial publicity—United States.   2. Small business—United States—Management.   3. Publicity.   4. Corporations, Nonprofit—United States—Management. I. Title.
    HD59.S52   1991   91-10451
    650—dc20

Printed in the United States of America.

10   9   8   7   6   5   4   3   2

Printed and bound by Courier Companies, Inc.

Text Credits
pp. 2, 22, 50, 51, 56, 69, 85, 109, 110, 134, 152, 190: Reprinted with permission of *The Dallas Morning News*; p. 10: Bill Hosokawa, "Readers Representative." Reprinted with permission of the *Rocky Mountain News*; p. 30: Bob Greene, the *Chicago Tribune*. Reprinted by permission: Tribune Media Services; pp. 72–73: Reprinted by permission of *Editor & Publisher* magazine; pp. 59, 85, 171, 175, 202, 210, 215, 218, 219, 221, 224: Copyright © 1990 by The New York Times Company. Reprinted by permission.

Preface

The reasons for wanting to produce effective publicity are as varied and individual as the businesses and organizations that desire it. There are, however, two common goals:

- A need to publicize something specific: a new service, a fundraising event, the announcement of a new official, or a merger, for example.
- A need to build general credibility and to enhance an image that will result in added business or increased fund raising results.

Faced with this agenda, your organization may not have anyone on staff who is trained to handle publicity, and may not even know how to get started. It is for this reason that *The Publicity Kit* has been written. Here is a "ground zero" guide to steer the inexperienced, untrained person through the process of planning, writing, and producing publicity, with success and ease. It covers everything required to produce publicity for your company or organization in an exemplary, professional manner. And it presents methods, procedures, and techniques by which you can construct a custom-designed information program.

You probably have an immediate need for publicity. Therefore, *The Publicity Kit* presents the essential information first followed by step-by-step guidance for writing and submitting publicity releases that look professional and reflect well upon you and your company or organization. You may wish to flag key sections of the book so they are easily accessible as your publicity or advertising needs develop and expand.

Although each chapter is designed to teach you about handling specific types of publicity, it would be preferable for you to read the entire book so you can gain a better understanding of *why* you are directed to do things in sometimes seemingly uncommon ways. And because newspapers are such an important vehicle for successfully distributing your message, this book will also help you to better understand how newspapers operate.

You will also learn how to generate the highest return on your efforts by expanding a simple release into other, highly productive, perhaps less costly, forms of publicity. For example, your news release may qualify for wire-service distribution that will save distribution costs that would have been incurred if you had to send the release to each recipient individually. It may qualify as broadcast news, or, by attaching a fact sheet or enclosing a press kit, you may provide reporters with information that leads to expanded coverage.

As you discover the benefits of *good* publicity, you may wish to expand your efforts; *The Publicity Kit* can show you how to carry out an extended campaign program to fit your needs, goals, and resources. And, in the unlikely event that your company or organization is the focus of "bad press," you will have the information and guidance to turn the problem around and to attract positive attention. This book will also show you how to design and write advertising when the message you want to distribute doesn't qualify as news.

In the Appendixes you will find sample news releases, a sample photo-release form and photo guidelines, information about how to define your publicity objectives, the basics of brainstorming, and where to find additional resources. There is also a Glossary that translates the hybrid, specialized language of the news industry into understandable English.

Contents

The Yes and "Know" of Publicity

What publicity is; why organizations need it

Publicity Defined

It has been said that publicity is nothing more than doing the right thing and telling about it.

Miami was virtually unknown before the late publicity master, Steve Hannagan, brought it to world prominence with a publicity program that focused on using the dateline, "Miami," in publicity stories describing good, fun things happening there and the benefits from visiting, working, and living in the Florida beach town.

Simply, *publicity* is the principal tool used in wooing and winning *public* opinion to achieve good *public* relations. Notice the prominence of the word *public*? A good public image, established through positive publicity, shows up on the profit side of the ledger.

Publicity tells the story a person or an organization wants the *public* to know. It is the face your organization presents, through media, to the *public*.

Public Image

Trump, Tylenol, Perrier, Exxon, and more recently, Sudafed. If this were a word-association test, what would come to mind? You might immediately recognize that each name has attracted enormous publicity—the kind a small business or nonprofit group hopes never to acquire.

It is far easier and much more pleasant to produce beneficial, productive publicity than it is to turn an image from poor to better. The latter task, however, is also a function of publicity.

"Remember this," cautioned the late public relations counsel and publicity director, Herb Baus, "What is *believed* about an organization can be more important than what is true about an organization."

The "Minimax" Technique

At the start of the August 1990 Iraqi crisis, when oil once again became an international concern, *The Dallas Morning News* gave the following headline:

**Big Oil Once Again Strains Credibility by Hiking Gas Prices
at Start of Crisis**

Then the newspaper told its readers: "The U.S. oil industry has a way of shooting itself in the foot."

Shooting themselves in the foot is the most common difficulty many organizations have. So, something else to remember might be stated by misquoting the late comedian, Ed Wynn, who said, "A bachelor is a man who never makes the same mistake once." In other words, the person who does publicity for an organization should be a person who never makes the same mistake once.

Shortly after General Manuel Antonio Noriega's capture, a story in *The Chicago Tribune* offered answers from some of the country's foremost public relations experts about how each might design a positive media campaign on behalf of one of the nation's most notorious jail inmates.

According to the news story, one PR specialist questioned had as his clients such big names as former baseball owner George Steinbrenner, real-estate baron Donald Trump, and slash-and-burn media mogul Rupert Murdock. Not the most saintly stable of do-gooders around.

Most answers were strictly tongue in cheek, such as one public relations specialist's suggestion to get Imelda Marcos named as General Noriega's legal guardian and release Noriega to her custody. Another specialist would call for "disclosure that, while hiding out in the papal nuncio's house in Panama City, General Noriega found religion, canned the voodoo act, and was speaking daily to Mother Teresa."

What all this adds up to is that publicity is used to build a good image. Scientists might call it a *minimax* situation: Minimize the poor; maximize the good. Obviously, it is a far easier job when the image isn't already tarnished.

Technically, publicity is a message purposefully planned, executed, and distributed through selected media to further the particular interest of an organization or an individual, *without payment* to media.

A Publicity Crisis

The New York Daily News, when faced with a crippling, perhaps deadly, labor dispute, decided not to chance shooting itself in the foot. It called in a publicity expert.

The specialist is a publicity and public relations professional who specialized in nuclear power and had fronted for GPU Nuclear Corporation, responsible for the worst nuclear power accident in U.S. history at Three Mile Island. She became the most visible face of *The Daily News* management and seems to have prevented what was at the time the second-largest metropolitan daily newspaper in the United States from shooting itself in the foot. She also seems to have followed the minimax principle of minimizing the negative while maximizing the positive to keep *The Daily News's* best possible face before the public.

The Necessity for Publicity

Publicity is a critical part of an effective, productive, and successful nonprofit operation. If your constituency is ignorant of your existence, it will be impossible for you to provide service to them. And no matter how well organized and well managed your organization is, it will fail to accomplish its mission. Furthermore, positive publicity helps establish credibility, an essential ingredient for nonprofit organizations in attracting grants, donors, and volunteers.

The success of for-profit organizations also depends on potential customers' and clients' awareness of the organizations' existence and on their receptiveness to it. These businesses, however, have greater access to advertising to help attract public awareness, because they usually have greater incomes and larger operating budgets. Advertising, publicity, and public relations should be regular operating expenses for for-profit organizations.

It is just as true for for-profit organizations as it is for nonprofit organizations: good publicity helps to establish credibility. And credibility establishes trustworthiness and reliability, along with the feeling that the organization is worthy of confidence. That kind of reputation is worth money in the bank.

The Media as Publicity Channels

Media are the communications channels used to present your organization's story to the public: print, electronic, and word-of-mouth. The most popular media are newspapers, radio, television, and direct mail. Print media can also be magazines, flyers, brochures, and newsletters.

Don't discount the effect of print-media choices because, as the publisher of *Family Weekly* magazine stated, "Television may have become our eyes and ears and our public meeting space, but print continues to be our memory." Memory can't be trusted; and your customers, clients, and constituents can't get from television or radio spots (as they can from print sources) hard-copy clippings of your telephone number and address to tuck into a pocket or an address book. Nor can television and radio give them a coupon to mail-order something you are offering. Furthermore, printed stories are collectible proof that can later become the base for a documented background or history of the organization. (See Appendix E for information about subscribing to a clipping service.)

Publicity's Function, Task, and Job

The *function* of publicity is to win as much goodwill for an organization as is possible. The *task* of publicity is to promote the good and true and to have the public reject what is untrue. The *job* of publicity is to tell the story through a variety of media.

Just as different tools are used to construct a building, publicity requires a variety of media to further the particular interest or image of an organization or to solve a publicity problem.

Publicity Is News

Publicity is *news* of interest to many people. It can create an image for a personality, an organization, or a city (as in the case of Miami)! There is even a hotdog stand in Los Angeles that has its own paid publicity agent; and, because so many celebrities patronize the place, the publicity circulated is news of interest to many people.

Publicity in Every Organization

Basically, publicity is news. So your work boils down to examining the countless human-interest stories and information found right in every group of people and in every organization. These stories are waiting to be dug out, properly dressed up, and made available to news media.

As you gain practice, you will find yourself looking at every event, person, and experience with the question, Would this be interesting to enough readers to make it a good publicity story? You also will be looking for the unusual and the unexpected for possible feature stories.

Feature stories? News stories? There are differences, but both can produce publicity for your group. (The differences between the two and how to write each are covered in Chapters 6 and 7.)

The Differences Between Publicity and Public Relations

Publicity is part of an overall public relations plan—often the most visual part. So take a short detour here and look at what public relations is, in particular as compared to publicity.

The facetious explanation given in *Orben's Current Comedy* is as follows: "Public relations is the fine art of making sure that something is no sooner done than said."

At a recent regional meeting of the Public Relations Society of America at Southern Methodist University's School of Continuing Education, the first handout of the session provided 34 definitions of public relations! Obviously, there is little consensus among professionals in the field. That's because "PR deals with an intangible, hard-to-define commodity—information," according to Dr. Roy Busby, professor of journalism at the University of North Texas.

Jeffrey Goodell, a New York-based business writer, acknowledges the problem of defining public relations in an article in *The New York Times Magazine*. The story is about Hill & Knowlton, one of the two biggest public relations companies in the world according to Goodell. Goodell wrote:

> Given the fact that even people who have been in the business for years can't agree on what to call their profession, it's no surprise that outsiders often misunderstand how public relations works. . . . The distinction between journalism and public relations is sometimes blurred.
>
> Many public relations professionals are, in fact, former journalists who have been lured to the other side of the fence (usually by a hefty increase in salary).

When you speak of publicity, a person readily understands that you are telling your story through some form of media. But when you use the term *public relations* to many this also means *publicity*.

PR, however, is a great deal more.

Public Relations Defined

Public relations can be a speakers' bureau or public polls and surveys to create credibility and goodwill. It can be open houses; telephone-answering techniques; personal contacts by representatives; training institutes for staff; policy interpretations; newsletters; employee, client/customer, grantsmaker, or pressure-group relations; audio-visual presentations; direct mailings; fund raisers; and more!

The Hard Sell and the Soft Sell

Public relations has two sides, as Jeffrey Goodell points out in *The New York Times Magazine* article: "The hard sell and the soft sell. . . . The softer, less glamorous side of public relations is full of mundane tasks like writing newsletters and annual reports. . . . The hard sell is typified by what is known as 'crisis management' and is one of the most lucrative aspects of the business.

The hard sell brings in the big bucks because it not only covers no-holds-barred corporate warfare with millions of dollars on the line, but it also includes accidents and scandals. The hard sell also pays the highest salaries because the job is spelled "S-T-R-E-S-S"—in capital letters. A joke going around in the industry states that one crisis management specialist was fired because his ulcer healed, and his boss thought he'd lost interest in his job.

In an article titled "PR Superstars: 100 of the Brightest," in *Public Relations Quarterly,* the principal criterion was not earnings (although most of these superstars are believed to earn more than $100,000 a year), but successful results. The article says, "They succeed at doing what many other PR people don't even think to try."

Public Relations as Publicity

Of course, public relations includes publicity, which often is a major portion of PR and usually is the most highly visible part.

Properly utilized, public relations can reinforce advertising, expand message reach, establish or add credibility, generate excitement and support, tell the whole story, reach distinct and special audiences, and create public acceptance.

"The public relations professional must be listener, interpreter, and communicator. He or she must know WHAT to say. WHO to say it to. HOW best to say it, and WHY it ought to be said. He must possess the instincts of the businessman, the skills of the journalist, and the foresight of the psychologist." That excellent description was given by Herbert H. Rozoff in *Public Relations Journal*. It says a good deal about the importance of public relations.

Publicity and PR as Distinct from Advertising

Public relations reinforces advertising. And though advertising can be public relations, public relations is *not* advertising. Nor is publicity advertising.

Publicity may be confused with or thought of as advertising by the uninitiated. Most certainty it is not—although you might stretch your definition to say it is advertising you cannot buy! However, please *never* think of publicity as free advertising. There is no money value to publicity space. In fact, money cannot buy it under any circumstances.

Another point along the same line is that people tend to give greater value to something that is purchased. The value of good publicity, however, which is free, is immeasurable. Not only do readers tend to put more trust in printed news than in advertising, but publicity can be one of your most cost-effective marketing tools.

Newspaper *advertising* is sponsor-purchased space in which you present your message to attract public attention or patronage to a product, an organization, or an idea.

Newspaper *publicity* is a message—about a product or a service, an organization, or an idea—that is prepared strictly within the parameters of newspaper news and distributed to the editorial news department (instead of to an advertising department) of a daily or weekly newspaper, *without payment* to the newspaper.

Don't Try to Disguise Advertising as "News"

An editor receives hundreds of publicity stories each day, most of them labeled "News." A goodly portion of these march briskly across the desk and into a wastebasket because the editor considers them an attempt to get a free ad that should have been bought and paid for. Advertising, after all, pays most of his salary and of the newspaper's bills.

People sometimes mistakenly regard a newspaper as purely a public service, operating solely to provide information to readers. Information is *one* of its services, but a newspaper is strictly a free-enterprise business that must make a profit to survive. It won't be around long if it doesn't. (For a better understanding of newspapers, see Chapter 16.)

Revenue Sources

Newspaper revenues come, basically, from two sources:

1. *Circulation* (sale of copies);
2. Advertising (sale of space).

In almost all cases, ads provide more than half of the revenue, usually about two-thirds.

Although broadcast media do not use as large an amount of publicity as do newspapers, don't ask or expect radio or television to use, as news, information that belongs in a paid commercial. Radio and television media do, however, provide time for public service announcements (PSAs). (Preparing and distributing PSAs is dealt with in Chapter 14.)

Questions for Your Public Relations Plan

Every for-profit or nonprofit organization has public relations—either good or bad PR.

The late public relations counsel and journalist Herb Baus advised, "Everything that the organization can do to improve its public relations will improve its ability to get results and realize the objectives for which it exists."

In developing a plan and policy for achieving *good* public relations, it is essential to ask and to answer three simple questions:

1. What impression and effect do you want to make on the public?
2. What do you want the public to do?
   - Respect the organization's credibility and integrity?
   - Respond more positively to sales messages?
   - Link the organization's name with its product or service?
   - Give money?
   - Volunteer time and skills?
   - Hire the handicapped?
   - Demand better nursing-home conditions for the aged?
   - Support training for the retarded?
   - Provide counseling for juvenile offenders?
   - Support legislation?

3. What specific actions must be taken by the public if you are to achieve your objectives?

These questions must be given adequate thought and research. The answers are essential to achieving a successful publicity campaign.

Publicists as Newspaper "Staffers"

How much of the published news and feature material in newspapers comes from publicity sources? A study conducted among newspaper editors by Ury-Sigmond Public Relations indicated that 21 percent of the nonadvertising contents of newspapers comes from publicity sources. However, the study also produced the statistic that 81 percent of the news and feature material from these sources is *rejected.* Only 6 percent is used as written.

A sizeable number of newspeople—print and electronic—look upon publicity people as extensions of their staffs, covering news areas that the medium could not otherwise afford to cover. When you hand a legitimate news story to an editor, he or she appreciates it. The editor knows that the lifeblood of a newspaper is news, but that there is no way the staff, no matter how large, can cover everything that happens.

So, in effect, you become a member of an editor's reporting staff, *if* the editor can rely on you as a dependable and discriminating news source. The other side of the coin is that the editor can fire you as a reporter by tossing your material into the wastebasket if he or she has reason to doubt your integrity or accuracy.

Tale of a Publicity Default

Of all sad words of tongue or pen, what of the job well done that might have been! The story that follows details how those concerned with providing information to the public let everyone down. In the "Readers' Representative" column in the Denver *Rocky Mountain News,* Bill Hosokawa detailed what can happen to an important news story when the organization's responsible parties don't provide sufficient information to the newspaper.

The event was the Hispanic Annual Salute (HAS) Award Dinner, with 16 organizations acting as cosponsors and more than a thousand people attending. Total coverage was six paragraphs on page 28 the day *after* the function.

Hosokawa stated that there was "no denying the event was worthy of this newspaper's attention and was undercovered." Then he explained why it happened, after questioning the newspaper's city editor. The editor had the following to say:

> In researching how this story came to be, I find that we received only a routine news release telling us the salute was going to be held. Neither the assistant city editor who assigned the story, nor the reporter who covered it, remember anything about the news release that indicated the event was anything out of the ordinary. It would have been immensely helpful to have had complete information in advance. We had no communication from [HAS] individuals or others that would have told us this was an important event. In fact, our ongoing effort to be sensitive to events and issues that directly affect minority readers was responsible for our covering the salute at all.

The chairman of HAS contended that a press kit about the event, with photographs of the honorees, was sent to the *News* some weeks before the banquet. Hosokawa believes, however, that "the matter unfortunately fell between the cracks or, more accurately, was buried under the mountain of material that arrives daily."

That this example (of what can happen on both sides of the publicity fence) was made public is unique. Seldom does a company or a nonprofit organization know why its releases aren't used, and it tends to place the blame on the newspaper. In this case, the matter was given public attention through the "Reader's Representative" column. A disgruntled reader had written to the column to question the newspaper's coverage of such an important event within the Hispanic community.

What this incident says to anyone and everyone who prepares publicity for his or her organization is that there can be no relaxation in following the guidelines on publicizing a staged event. (See Chapter 12.) And it shouts the advice most loudly to nonprofit organizations who depend so heavily upon volunteers to perform their important jobs.

Something else this story says is that the publicity was highly important to the entire Hispanic community and especially so to HAS and to the volunteers who did all the work in preparing and carrying out the event. What is even more disheartening for them is that the newspaper would have done considerably more in recognition of its Hispanic readership, if only it had known about the event in advance and if only the publicity job had been properly handled!

So, try not to shoot yourself in the foot. Stay on top of things all the way through to the end of a story. Newspapers *want* your news!

The Yes and "Know" of Being a Publicity Representative

The preceding story illustrates that, to be your group's publicity representative, you must do the job to the best of your training and ability, or you let the group and a lot of people down. This book is the road map to your destination. However, *you* must be the vehicle to get your organization there.

If you are the owner or chief executive of the organization, you have incentive to do the best possible job so that the results will show up in profits. As an entrepreneur, you may have no desire whatever to use the knowledge and expertise you are acquiring to produce publicity for any reason other than to benefit your own organization.

There are other users of this book, however, who were appointed by their employers, or were selected as volunteers in a nonprofit organization, to do the job. Someone once said that there is no limit to what the boss can do if he or she puts someone else's mind to it! It is to these people (rather than to the owners or top-management executives) we now give information about the benefits that come from learning how to be a publicity practitioner and from doing an excellent job of it.

Your Personal Benefits

No matter how you acquired the job—by election, by appointment as chairman of the publicity committee, or by the boss's pointed finger and, "You do it"—you are lucky. Ultimately, the more and the better you know the field of publicity, the better you serve your own ends. There can be personal good fortune in this appointment.

Over time, you will learn things and make contacts that can last and profit you for a lifetime. You may even decide you like the job well enough to add it to your career skills. It certainly never hurt a resume to list publicity writing and production as skills. Employers often see them as added helpful abilities that can be deciding factors over competitors who have otherwise equal abilities. Nonprofit organizations actively seek out these skills from among their volunteers. In other words, don't discount this opportunity. It can turn into a rewarding, even gainful, activity.

Some who progress through this book from enthusiastic beginner to competent paraprofessional may wish to seek full-time employment in the field. For them, publicity might be likened to a penthouse with a great view of the entire field of communications: A solid background in it equips a person to work in any medium.

If you have no desires to enter the field, publicity work produces another asset that can be highly worthwhile in a climb up the career ladder. Concise, clear communication, an absolute necessity in publicity writing, is the mark of an effective communicator, which, in business, is a first requisite for success. David Ogilvy, in his book, *The Unpublished David Ogilvy*, tells how important this ability is. (Ogilvy & Mather is one of the nation's well-known advertising firms.)

- *If everybody in our company took an exam in writing, the highest marks would go to the 14 directors.*
- *The better you write, the higher you go in Ogilvy & Mather. People who THINK well, WRITE well.*
- *Wooly minded people write wooly memos, wooly letters, and wooly speeches.*
- *Good writing is not a natural gift. You have to LEARN to write well.*

If you decide you want to explore publicity as a career, there is one more rewarding achievement: It is one of the higher-paying branches of print journalism.

No matter whether you look to publicity as a vocation or an avocation, your job is similar to a medical doctor's except that your *first* dedication is to *increase* health. Your job description would call for you to do the following:

- Solve problems
- Observe symptoms
- Diagnose causes
- Prescribe solutions

In the case of illness of your organization, you must also alleviate pain to the best of your ability!

Your Qualifications as a Publicist

As a publicist—volunteer, appointed, or paid—what qualifications must you have? Basically, there are only four:

1. Nose for news
2. Ability to present news

3. Energy to do the work

4. Integrity

Nose for News

Nosing out the news for a publicity release merely takes a little thought. But fleshing out bare-bones facts to present a meaty, interesting news release requires hunting for unusual angles, adding an original twist, and sometimes digging deep for information beyond obvious facts.

It will surprise you to see how soon you will begin to develop a news sense and to know instinctively when a happening is news and when it isn't. One of the best ways to develop this sense is to study your newspapers. Notice kinds of stories used and which ones go on special pages (page one; community-news page; family, club, sports, and business pages; etc.).

As you study the different types of news and the different styles of newspapers, start a collection of examples of various types of news stories. Paste them into a scrap book or file them in a system that makes them easily accessible for future reference and study. When you are ready to send out a release, you can imitate the style and construction of an article or column that already has appeared in the particular paper or papers to which you will submit your release.

Ability to Present News

Ability to present the news requires knowledge of the mechanical production of copy to certain specifications. Anyone able to correctly use and type the English language can follow these specifications. (It's all spelled out in Chapter 8.)

Energy to Do the Work

Energy to do the work encompasses sheer stamina for digging out and collecting the news—then typing, typing, and more typing. (A publicist must have a typewriter, a word processor, a computer, or someone to do the typing. This is essential.)

Integrity

Integrity is the most important quality you must have. If an editor does not have faith that the information you give him or her is true and correct in details and that it will not backfire on him or her when printed, the editor cannot be expected to use the material. Your job is to win public confidence for your organization through publicity. If the information in the release is found to be incorrect, untrue, or inaccurate, you will destroy credibility and confidence in your organization. At the same time, you will destroy your own credibility with the publication that you are hoping will use your information.

The Copycat Method

The kind of mind that is geared to being a first-rate publicist loves planning and executing a campaign and enjoys digging for the news angles and getting them accepted and used by media.

It also helps to be a "jack-of-all-media," because, for better-than-ordinary results, you must be able to adapt your writing style to suit the medium that will use your release. The less the editor has to alter the material, the more likely it is that it will be used.

This is a relatively easy skill to acquire; it merely means being a copycat. Call it "using OPB"—using Other People's Brains! It can be the secret to a beginner's success. Each time you have a release to write, find a newspaper or magazine story similar to the one you want to write. Just change it to fit your circumstances. In other words, you don't have to reinvent the wheel each time, and you don't have to be a trained writer.

Disadvantages of Publicity Work

Although you may be able to start with very few qualifications, publicity work isn't an easy job. You seldom will be completely satisfied with the job you do, no matter how well you perform. You'll know you could have done more, if you had more of the following:

- • Help
- • Time
- • Money

You'll rarely and probably never have the satisfaction of receiving a byline or even of getting the credit for a story that may appear word-for-word as you wrote it. The story may even appear under someone else's byline!

There are benefits, though. If you take your job seriously and approach it as a learning experience, there is much that will serve you well, if ever you wish to enter the for-pay business of professional publicity.

2

Analysis of a News Story

How different types of news require specific styles of writing

What you see is news,
what you know is background,
what you feel is opinion.
  Lester Markel, American editor (1894–1977)

Straight News as Facts

Early in Mark Twain's training as a news reporter, he was warned to keep strictly to fact and to never report anything that he couldn't verify personally. Shortly after receiving this warning, he was assigned to cover an important social event, and this was his account:

> A woman giving the name of Mrs. James Jones, who is reported to be one of the society leaders of the city, is said to have given what is purported to be a party yesterday to a number of alleged ladies. The hostess claims to be the wife of a reputed attorney.

The main purpose of news is to present information. News is the reporting of facts. The first precept of good newswriting is to make things easy for the reader. The trick is to flesh out bare-bones facts with descriptive detail that makes the reader see and feel the story.

There are, basically, three kinds of articles in newspapers: news stories, feature stories, and editorials. An editor will appreciate submission of the first two as publicity releases, but not of the third. Read the paper's editorials, but don't submit them.

Editorials as the Newspaper's Domain

Editorials are the exclusive domain of the newspaper's management in which to present its own opinions and advice. With tongue firmly in cheek, Ralph Schoenstein in *Saturday Review* demonstrates the primary purposes of editorials: to stimulate thinking, stir discussion, and arouse action. "Journalists have been writing editorials," Schoenstein wrote, "since the *Eden Examiner* said:"

> *Things have come to a pretty pass when it's unsafe to walk on the Garden's fashionable East side.*
> *It is hoped that the Power-That-Be will do more than merely deport Mr. Cain and others of his ilk. May we therefore suggest that remedial legislation also be forthcoming from Him to curb this shocking outbreak of terror that poses an ever-present threat to the security of the entire fallen world.*

Newspapers rarely use editorials that are not staff-written or solicited as guest editorials. (Of course, there is no rule against getting to know the editor and suggesting that he or she write the editorial you have in mind!)

Publicity Releases as News

Most publicity releases fall into the news-story category. Every news item that enters a newspaper office passes into the hands of the newspaper's editors—people with great responsibilities. The editors scan the reams of copy received daily to find the best and most interesting news stories for their readers. It is their job to sift, sort, trim, and—from all the news and features flowing in from all parts of the world—fashion a complete newspaper.

So before you go to all the trouble of writing a news release, think about what it will contain and whether or not it really is news, so that it can at least compete for placement in a newspaper's limited news hole (news space).

The Two Types of News Stories

Publicity, then, is news, of which there are two types: spot news and created news.

Spot News

Spot News is spontaneous, usually beyond your control, and certainly not of your making. An example might be the injury or death of a visitor at a company-sponsored event. The publicity derived would not be beneficial, so your principal functions as the organization's press contact would be to try to turn around the harmful impact from such an uncontrollable event and to assist the media in every possible way to do their jobs in covering it. An excellent guideline for your role here is to be helpful, obliging, and honest. Don't be a "suppress" agent!

Created News

Created News comes from a created event that produces controlled publicity: meetings, elections, appointments of individuals to higher organization positions, performances, or almost any kind of happening. Assignment of contracts, new services, new products, new programs, new projects, awards, or recognition of or by affiliates—all are material for news stories.

Truly created news may come from a strictly staged event: a benefit, an open house, a reception, a training program, a community-interaction accomplishment and so on. The main disadvantage to such a staged media event is that it is time-consuming for you and your organization. A lot of work must go into an event that will be so compelling that news teams will flock to your door. (See Chapter 12.)

The Basic Elements of News:
Names, Times, and Events

An editor looks at every release with one thing in mind: Is it legitimate news of interest to a large number of readers? You should ask yourself, to how many people is this story of interest? Then you can better understand the editor's problem of measuring the newsworthiness of each piece of copy submitted to him or her.

If you are looking for publicity for a commercial product or service, you must also ask yourself if the release really is a news item—or is it advertising? You can be sure that if the editor smells an attempt to pass off as news advertising that should be paid for, he or she will toss your release quicker than you can say, "Publicity is *not* free advertising."

Evaluation Test for a News Release

Here, roughly, are "test" questions to help you evaluate any information you plan to send as a news release:

- Is it of interest to at least 10 percent of the publication's readers or to the readers of that particular section to which you will direct it (e.g., business, sports, family, magazine, etc.)?

- Is it timely? Past events are history, not news. *The Wall Street Journal* says it best in one of its self-promotion ads: "Dedicated to the proposition that news does not improve with age."

- Does it include names of people? Better still, does it include names of well-known people? Experience has taught editors that people are their own favorite subjects, and that names, names, and more names help build circulation. People not only like seeing their names in print—in positive ways—but will buy extra copies of those editions. The greater the sale of papers, the higher the advertising rates and the greater the profits, some of which may become salary increases for editors.

- Does it have a local angle?

- Does it have a human-interest angle? *Human interest* is a hard-to-define element that has to do with events in human life. Human interest appeals to the emotions—the part of the consciousness that involves feeling or sensibility. Love, fear, sadness, and laughter are emotions that can provide human interest.

- Is it an ad? In the beginning, until you are totally familiar with how publicity differs from advertising, don an imaginary editor's hat and try putting yourself in his or her place. Examine the subject matter with a critical eye to decide whether it should go to the editor or to the advertising department. (For more information about advertising, see Chapter 15.)

Newspaper Space Limitations

Even if your news release passes all the above "test" questions, it still may not get printed. It may have to be forfeited because it arrives on a particularly heavy news day when there is little room for much else.

There is a space factor for newspapers, and reams and reams of releases come in each day, far more than can possibly be used in the allotted space. By way of proving this point, for a column she wrote for a relatively small Los Angeles-area newspaper, a reporter took all the press releases the newspaper received in one 24-hour period and pasted them together. They added up to the distance around 16 city blocks, and that didn't include wire-service copy and reporters' stories—only press releases!

To filter out the chaff along with the overload, editors screen stories through the exercise of experienced judgment. You may sometimes disagree with their judgment; you may feel space is wasted on items that do not interest you. But remember, the editors are attempting to meet the needs of *all* their readers—people of varying ages, occupations, incomes, and educations, and, hence, of varying interests.

Basics of a News Story

A news story should be all of the following:

- Factual. You naturally want every story you give to an editor to be as accurate and impartial as one prepared by one of his or her own reporters.
- Timely. This is one of the oldest newsroom sayings, so old it's reached cliche standing: Yesterday's news is history.
- Interesting. Try to appeal to the largest possible number of readers.
- Objective. Straight news must never include the writer's opinion.
- Written in an *inverted pyramid* format (as described in more detail in Chapter 6). Facts should be arranged in the order of importance; the most important facts are always stated first. Figure 2.1 illustrates the use of the inverted pyramid format in a short news story and a long news story.

Components of a News Story

In general, the structure of a news story (as illustrated in Figure 2.1) is the opposite of that for other literary forms. In a straight-news story, "it's what's up top that counts."

Former CBS newsman Walter Cronkite has often been quoted as saying that television news is a headline service. Instead of minimizing the depth and significance of television news reports, the statement actually recognizes the importance of headlines. In effect, a headline is a news bulletin. Each

FIGURE 2.1   News Story Structure

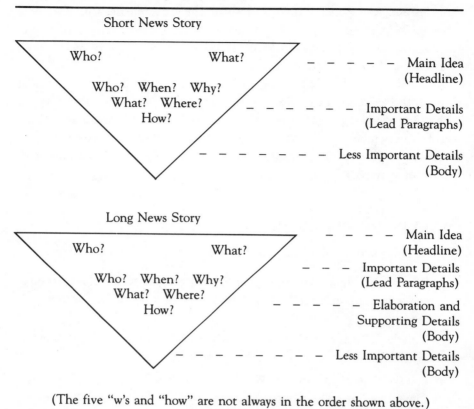

Short News Story

Who?   What?   — — — — — Main Idea
                                                  (Headline)
Who? When? Why?
What? Where?   — — — — — — Important Details
    How?   (Lead Paragraphs)

                        — — — — — — — Less Important Details
                                                  (Body)

Long News Story

Who?   What?   — — — — Main Idea
                                                  (Headline)
                                        — — — Important Details
Who? When? Why?   (Lead Paragraphs)
What? Where?
    How?   — — — — — Elaboration and
                                                  Supporting Details
                                                  (Body)

                    — — — — — — — — Less Important Details
                                                  (Body)

(The five "w's and "how" are not always in the order shown above.)

headline should be a summary of an article's contents, but it also can be a "commercial" to attract readers to the story.

Headlines are written so that busy people may glance through a book-sized newspaper and obtain the meat of the day's news within a few minutes. Headlines together with leads give readers the main points of news stories.

In a straight-news story there is no buildup to a climax as in feature writing. The writer boils down the story to its principal facts and lays them all out, right in the lead paragraphs, or lead (pronounced "leed").

The *body* of a news article explains in more detail the facts covered in the lead, and each paragraph diminishes in importance to the end. Paragraphs are short, usually no more than 50 or 60 words, because big blocks of type on narrow-width columns have a gray, dull look and are difficult to read.

There is no excuse for dullness in writing the story. A mere catalog of facts is not a news story. As pioneer newspaper publisher E. W. Scripps told young newsmen, "There is really no such thing as an uninteresting story. There are only reporters who do not know how to present it in an interesting manner."

Newspaper Writing Style

Before you sit down to write your first news release, study newspaper writing style. Learn a newspaper's usual style of abbreviation, capitalization, and spelling.

If you will submit only to local papers, the job is relatively easy. Study those local newspapers. If, however, you will be sending releases throughout a broader area, there also is an easy way to learn the style of most newspapers.

There are three "bibles" of style that will be found in virtually every newsroom in this country:

1. *The UPI Stylebook, A Handbook for Writers and Editors* is published by United Press International. (Address and ordering information is in Appendix E.) As the stylebook editor says in describing the book, "It is a set of consistent guidelines that reflect current usage. The primary purpose is to achieve consistency in spelling, capitalization, punctuation, and usage for newspaper wires." Because almost every newspaper subscribes to a wire service, most newspapers adapt to the wire service's style. It is easier to abide by this policy than to have to separate styles and have to change every wire story to fit the individual newspaper's style.

2. *Associated Press Stylebook and Libel Manual* is published by Dell Publishing. This book covers style information such as spelling brand names and place names; identifies the correct form for government agencies, military titles, ship names, and corporation names; and verifies correct punctuation, capitalization, and abbreviations. It also provides a libel section for people writing for newspapers, newsletters, or anything that goes to the public in print.

3. *The Elements of Style,* by William Strunk, Jr. and E. B. White is published by the Macmillan Publishing Company, Inc. This tiny booklet (4-by-7-inches, 71-pages) is more than a newspaper stylebook. It is also concerned with what is correct or acceptable in the use of English. It concentrates on fundamentals: the rules of usage and principles of composition most commonly violated. It should be in the hand of every person who must communicate in writing for any purpose.

Writing Principles

Many schoolbook writing rules are broken by practical reporters and editors who know that their product—the newspaper—must sell. To do that, the writing style must be alive and kicking. Good newswriting is vivid, clear, concise, and simple.

Accuracy, simplicity, and objectivity are essential in newswriting. It is equally important for the reporter and the publicity writer to keep personal opinions out of news stories; the expression of opinion is the privilege of the editorial pages. News columns must be kept as factual as the human element permits.

Errors in names haunt editors. A minor matter? Not to an editor whose readers say, "If they can't get the *name* right, can I believe anything they print?" Take that question to heart. Write it on your mirror where you'll see it every morning, and apply it to your releases—both news and feature. Remember, an editor will be asking, "If they can't get small facts right, can I count on any of the information they send me as correct?"

The Editor's Job

A major job of every newspaper editor is to select from the daily deluge of information what is significant enough to be printed and to decide on the amount of space to give each news item. So how can they—and you, in presenting your organization's news releases—know exactly what is news?

The magnitude of the question was aptly demonstrated in late August, 1990 shortly after Iraq's invasion and takeover of Kuwait. In a section one news story in *The Dallas Morning News,* under the headline "What is news, what isn't?" an attempt at evaluation was made. The story, in part, is as follows:

> When Saddam Hussein appeared Tuesday on American television with a new group of Western hostages, Patricia Hale of Spring, Texas, frantically watched for a glimpse of her husband, Ed. And then she felt angry and used.
>
> Of course, I watched, because I was hoping to see a picture of Ed," said Mrs. Hale, whose husband has been detained in Iraq since the Iraqi's Aug. 2 invasion of Kuwait.
>
> "He was not among the hostages appearing with the Iraqi president on a tape aired Tuesday morning on Cable News Network.
>
> "But afterward, you start wondering, isn't this propaganda? Isn't this playing into his (Mr. Hussein's) hand to air this?" she said. "I'd love to see a picture of Ed, but isn't this at the expense of something larger?"

"The question is hardly new. . . . The journalism community has faced this situation before. In past hostage crises, it didn't think it through particularly well, and then it just went on with its business as if it wasn't going to have to confront the question any more. Here we are again," said Kathleen Hall Jamieson, dean of the Annenburg School of Journalism at the University of Pennsylvania.

"If the news is on occasion pleasant, if the news is propagandistic, the American people will make up their minds by themselves. But they have to be given information," said Mr. [Marvin] Kalb [a former correspondent for CBS and NBC, and currently a professor at Harvard's Kennedy School of Government].

"The question you have to ask as a journalist: Am I being manipulated? In this case, the manipulation is clear," said Fred Friendly, a Columbia Journalism School professor and former president of CBS News.

Definitions of News

Editors admittedly can't precisely define what is news because it is far, far from a precise science. And making the determination in international crises situations is far more difficult than for local community circumstances. So, how do you make the determination?

There are no formula specifications; there is no categorical definition. As with the word *love*, there is no completely satisfactory definition for the word *news*.

It is almost easier to define what is *not* news: It is not gossip. It is not opinion.

An editor of the Palo Alto *Times*, Manchester Bodi, has this definition: "News is what everybody wants to know. It's what a lot of people should know, but they'd rather not. It's what some people don't want other people to know. It's what makes you wise, ignorant, happy, discontented, frustrated, satisfied. In other words, news is just about everything. Or nothing!"

Perhaps a better understanding of what is news comes from looking at the factors that guide reporters and editors in writing and editing it, as set forth by a journalism instructor, Dr. DeWayne B. Johnson, in a publication he wrote for the Santa Monica *Evening Outlook* that was used by area teachers in the *Evening Outlook*'s "Newspapers in Education" program.

Significance or consequence. The meaning of the news, the impact of the news, has a bearing on whether or not it is news. A peace feeler. A rumored entente. Editors look for meaning and so should readers. What is the long-range significance?

Magnitude. How big is it? In selecting news, editors are forced to gauge the "size" of the item, whether it be of a border clash, an auto crash, or an earthquake. An earthquake killing five in Timbuktu seems small in Southern California, but would seem big if it happened here on Wilshire Boulevard.

Proximity. The nearer the event, the more likely it is to be accepted here as news. Five dead in an auto crash in Timbuktu means nothing to readers on the Pacific Coast Highway. One fatality on a downtown Santa Monica street is worthy of notice.

Progress. An item indicating some small gain by the human race qualifies an item as news. A new serum, a more effective way of teaching, a landing on another planet, education, science. Progress enters the concept of what makes news.

Timeliness. News is an extremely perishable item—it is news because it is happening now. The "news peg" is the thing that makes it news today.

Unusualness. The quirks, the oddities, the rare situation. These make up news. News features, human-interest stories fall in this category and win a place in the "news hole" of the newspaper.

There are other ways of dissecting the news, but those in the above paragraphs are meant to provide you with a jumping-off place to help you understand, rather than to provide you with a definite answer.

3

Basic Steps to a Successful Publicity Program

What you need to know and do to get your publicity program off the ground

Publicity "Planagement" Program

Success for an organization could be spelled "p-l-a-n-n-i-n-g." "Business without profit is not business, any more than a pickle is candy," was a saying of American industrialist Charles F. Abbott. This chapter will help you set up your publicity "planagement" program to assure success and profit from your publicity efforts.

The first step toward a productive, profitable publicity program is to make the right decisions. So before you write one word of a news release, read the following sections to prepare yourself.

Step 1. Know Your Organization

If you are the entrepreneur or the head of an organization, you undoubtedly know the group intimately. If, however, you have been appointed to do the publicity job, then you should do research on your organization, its employees, and the people who serve and are served by it. Keep the information handy for reuse time and time again. Basic essential information includes answers to the following questions:

- Why was the organization formed? When? By whom?
- What has it accomplished?
- What is being done now?

- What are future plans?
- Who are the board members, management, and department heads (also staff, if the organization is a volunteer group)? List names, *correctly spelled*, addresses, geographic areas, and a bit of identifying information about each person, such as title, awards, former positions, community projects, or any other large or small claims to recognition. In the case of board members, name the person's company, corporation, government agency, or whatever place he or she earns a living. If the person is retired, give the name of the organization from which he or she is retired.
- Do you know and have handy (in written form) the company's slogan and upcoming projects or its goals and objectives if it is a nonprofit organization?

You will use portions of this information in every release you write. Having it easily accessible will save hours later when an editor or a reporter calls for additional information or verification.

Step 2. Lay Out a Plan

Get a plan. This is often the first advice given when you start a business, and it is no less important to the person starting a publicity program.

If you are an entrepreneur, perhaps you were given the "get a plan" start-up advice when you first began your company. Like thousands of others, you sat down at your computer and batted out something impressive. Then you filed it away, and you've been too busy to look at it since you got the company off the ground and flying. However, your publicity program plan should be a well-used road map that you refer to regularly to keep you on-route and to get you where you want to go.

All successful organizations have both short-term plans and long-term plans. A realistic first-time publicity program might be based on a one-year plan. After you get your feet wet and have a better understanding of how to do publicity, you can assure a successful publicity program by developing short-range, midrange, and long-range plans.

If you have been appointed to the job, you definitely will want to discuss, with the organization's management, exactly what your publicity program should accomplish. If you are the boss, you still may wish to put your program through your management committee for suggestions and endorsement. After all, this is the foundation of your entire publicity strategy, and your overall approach should be set to accomplish the goals of the entire organization. Others' brains can add perspective. Also, it is well known that involving subordinates by enlisting their help assures their greater interest and enthusiasm.

Publicity Budget. Our twenty-eighth president, Woodrow Wilson, is often quoted as follows: "The way to stop financial 'joyriding' is to arrest the chauffeur, not the automobile." Don't get arrested for not having a publicity budget or for not working within it! A budget is a very important part of a realistic publicity plan. Cost push and demand pull often create the bottom line in designing a practical publicity plan.

This is the time, then, to think about the help you will need. If yours is a for-profit organization, the subject of assigning the help you require is a cost factor that is a management decision. If you are head of your organization, you must realistically evaluate how much of your time you can devote to carrying out your plan and how much you must assign to others. Be prudent about the amount of additional time beyond your own that will be needed. If you represent a nonprofit organization and the help you require will come from volunteers, delegating tasks is not a budget matter.

Program Committee. Even if you feel you can handle the job alone for a nonprofit organization, it is wise to have an assisting committee from which succeeding publicity representatives may be chosen. No matter what others may tell you—for instance, that the best committee consists of three people, two of whom are absent—don't believe it. Serving on a committee permits others to gain a working knowledge of the procedures that will make for better representation in future years. As the late Dave Gottlieb, past president of the American Newspaper Publishers Association's Research Institute, quipped, "There ain't no one of us that's as smart as the all of us."

Brainstorming Sessions. Brainstorming with others who are knowledgeable about your plans and goals is almost always productive, and who could be better to conduct brainstorming sessions with than your special publicity committee? The team approach has many benefits. (Appendix D provides guidance in conducting brainstorming sessions.)

Other cost factors must be estimated and included in your budget: publicity-release distribution costs, photos, and so on. These cost estimates will be governed by your release schedule, which is detailed in "Schedule Releases."

Hand-Me-Downs.   There is one other item that any publicity plan for a nonprofit should provide: hand-me-downs! If you have ever served as a committee chair, you will understand the need to include pass-along items and information. When each new publicity representative starts a term of service with nothing from his or her predecessor, the work must be performed as if the organization had never been in existence before. These actions say to the media that the organization isn't very efficient.

Make plans to systematize your work into a notebook for your successor. Add to your media list (which you will learn to compile in Chapter 4), the "Who-to's," along with a few notes about each of the media people with whom you deal and their preferences (i.e., "He wants only local names, local angles," or "She won't use . . . ," and so on.)

As you send out each news release, file a copy in the back of the notebook. Not only your successor, but *you* will find it extremely helpful if you attach clippings or copies of the clippings of the final, published story to the original release. Your release together with the published story not only show the fruits of your efforts, but more importantly, they reveal how an editor changed your copy. This will help you adapt future releases to achieve greater acceptance and to know what types of releases were the most effective. This material becomes a ready-reference file and an efficient textbook and report to turn over to the next person who fills the position.

Step 3. Set Your Publicity Goals

A goal is a statement of broad direction or interest that is general, timeless, and always determined by needs. (Tips for writing effective goals and objectives are included in Appendix C.) Set down your publicity goals with the full knowledge, understanding, approval, and pledged support of management or leadership. Make sure that the purposes and desired achievements for your publicity program are clear.

Some of an organization's publicity goals might be as follows:

- To win recognition and public awareness of a specific service, product, project, event, program, or function that benefits the community.
- To gain prestige and dignity for the group; to establish, build, or improve image, reputation, and credibility.
- To attract attention to a program or a policy.
- To enlist volunteers.

- To bring a specific event or happening to the attention of the public and to enlist attendance.
- To give recognition to board members, executives, and employees for special activities outside the workplace or for awards won.

Step 4. Write Objectives

With your goals set, write objectives for each that define specific, measurable, and attainable end results. Objectives are different from goals in that the emphasis in the former is always on accomplishment. Write out your objectives to show what will be done, when it will be done, and what end result will be accomplished. (Tips for writing effective goals and objectives are in Appendix C.)

Be realistic! Set publicity objectives according to your available time and capabilities and those of your staff or committee, and also according to your budget. Answer the following questions before you begin writing your objectives:

- How much publicity does your group need? (The important word is *need,* not *desire.* Again, be realistic.)
- How much time can you invest in doing the work?
- How much budget do you have for mailing costs, photos, and staff?
- Is this a continuing, ongoing effort, or a one-shot event?
- Does the organization's need call for weekly, monthly, or only occasional releases?

Step 5. Schedule Releases . . . Including Photos

Reaching the public through publicity is often like trying to catch the attention of a hibernating dinosaur. Not only can the dinosaur seem to be sleeping so soundly that it cannot hear, but its skin can be so thick that it might need a number of nudges before it even notices the existence of a specific organization.

How quickly the "dinosaur" wakes up is directly related to the numbers and kinds of news releases an organization sends out. A single news item or feature story may reach a considerable number of people, but one print story, no matter how widely published, will not create a significant or lasting awareness. In other words, you must take the initiative, and initiative in publicity usually translates to mean news releases—a continuing, ongoing, regular schedule of news releases.

News Release Timetable.   Set a timetable for the year's publicity, including pictures for the print media. Make your schedules for releases and photos at the same time so that you can consult editors about assigning space for your important news stories. Some papers assign space for major-event stories with photos as much as six months to a year in advance. Plan to line up major layouts as early as possible. Keep in mind when planning your publicity schedule that the speed with which the public takes notice of your organization's work—no matter how important the work—is in direct proportion to the amount of the information you generate.

Press or Media?   In the *Chicago Tribune*, nationally syndicated columnist Bob Greene, gives some indication about the way newspaper people feel about getting lumped together with electronic-news people. He complains, "There was a time before the word *media* became a part of the national vocabulary, when you were a newspaperman or a television reporter or a radio guy, and you were considered part of 'the press.' "

Greene goes on to say that he thinks he knows exactly when this changed:

> In 1968, at the national political conventions, when reporters were given cardboard identification tags to wear around their necks, the tags had "Press" imprinted on them. At the 1972 national political conventions, however, the press tags were passed out—only they said "Media." The reason I recall this is that I remember being confused. I didn't understand what the word meant, and I didn't even know how to pronounce it. Other reporters were puzzled, too, but the forces behind the conventions explained that there were so many television correspondents and broadcast technicians on hand that the convention officials had decided to switch from "Press" to "Media."

Bob Greene's grumbling gives you a hint that it may be more expedient to identify newspaper people as the press and to identify radio and television people as the media.

(*Press release* is a term widely used by publicists, particularly those who come from newspapers. However, it implies the exclusion of electronic news people. Although you will seldom send publicity releases to radio or television because their time limitations rarely permit use of news items from small businesses or nonprofits, you may wish to use the more generic term, *news release.*)

When your schedule is outlined, evaluate it to decide what parts are of primary importance in overall organization plans, and arrange them according to priority. With the schedule set down, you now are able to intelligently discuss with editors your space requests and problems.

Step 6. Meet the Press

The next step is, Introduce yourself. In publicity, it's not only what you know, but also, sometimes equally important, who knows you!

A delightful "Ziggy" cartoon by Tom Wilson recognizes this "law." The cartoon says, "Business success is easy. . . . All you need is good old American know-who!"

Chapter 4 tells you how to make a media list—a "know-who" inventory of newspeople to whom you will introduce yourself. Chapter 5 presents in detail the ways and means to meet and work in harmony with the media.

A Letter or a Visit?   The manner in which you introduce yourself depends largely on the size of the newspapers and broadcast stations in your area. If you are working with smaller (suburban or rural) media, you may wish to introduce yourself in person. If your targets are large metropolitan dailies and television stations, it is a better idea to address letters to each one.

Draft a letter of introduction that you can send to everyone you plan to meet personally. However, for each person, make an individually typed, individually addressed letter. (To repeat this, send an individual, typed—not handwritten—letter to *each* person—not a carbon, not a photocopy. Each letter must be an original, to any editor or columnist on your media list whom you expect to contact for any reason during the forthcoming year.)

If you are the top executive, your letter can briefly state that you intend to send publicity releases, and that, at some point—when your schedule and the editor's schedule permit—you look forward to meeting him or her. You can also state that, in the meantime, you will appreciate any information that will help you conform your releases to his or her requirements. Mention that you are enclosing a self-addressed, stamped envelope (SASE) for his or her convenience. Follow the same procedure if radio or television publicity or public service announcements (PSAs) are included in your plans. (Details about producing radio and television copy are in Chapter 14.)

If you are a staffer or a volunteer, your letter should state that you are the new publicity representative for your organization and that you wish to learn anything and everything that will help you make your releases conform to the editor's requirements. Mention that you are looking forward to meeting him or her when you submit your first copy. Also mention that you are aware of deadline times and will arrange to arrive at a time when he or she is off deadline.

Contact Information.   Include with—or in—your letter of introduction, the addresses and telephone numbers where you may be reached. The letter itself should carry this information, but enclosure of a business card or a typed telephone index card for that person's file is a thoughtful gesture.

It never hurts to also give another name, address, and phone number of someone who is informed about your organization and who is familiar with its publicity program. For a news release, this can mean the difference between being used or being tossed if you are not available when there is need for verification or additional information by the newswriter.

Pertinent Data and Fact Sheets.   Attach to your letter of introduction a list of names: board members, major executives (with titles), and any other persons of importance in the organization. If you represent a nonprofit organization, this is an excellent opportunity to send an up-to-date directory of members. At the very least, send the names of new officers and committee chairpersons and their *correct* addresses and phone numbers.

Also enclose a brochure or a typed fact sheet about the organization. (A sample fact sheet is included in Appendix A; how to prepare a fact sheet is examined in Chapter 10.) Many editors keep files of such information.

In addition to the above items, add the *undetailed* schedule of publicity plans for the coming year, listed with the corresponding events that will be the basis for the news stories.

Follow-Up Contact.   After you have made your initial contacts, wait about a week or ten days, then give each person a call and request an opportunity to meet him or her. Actually, instead of sending a directory or a list of board members and major executives, you might carry it with you to use as a door opener.

In regard to a phone call, however, remember that you won't make any brownie points if you call when an editor is trying to get the paper out. So remember this general rule of thumb for newspapers: Evening papers are on deadline in the morning—actually not off the hook and a little relaxed until about 2:00 P.M.; morning newspapers have a reverse schedule—working afternoons and early evenings for a usual midnight deadline. Catch evening newspaper people in mid- or late-afternoon. Contact morning paper people before they start the deadline crunch.

There are no general rules for contacting radio and television news people because their operations differ so much from medium to medium and even from station to station.

4

Your Media List

How to ensure that your news will get to the right people

Consistent Flow of News Releases

Someone once said that a newspaper is the keyhole to the world. To misquote the quote: Your *media list* of newspapers is the world's keyhole to your organization.

A consistent flow of publicity releases establishes the fact that your organization is alive and active, and the law of percentages as to how many releases actually are used clicks into place. Salespeople know about percentage laws: one is that on average a certain number of calls produces a certain number of sales. Of course, factors such as the quality of the product influence percentages. Similar percentage laws will work for you, if the quality of your releases meets media requirements for content and format.

To accomplish your mission—to assure that a percentage of your releases is used—you must get your message out on a regular ongoing basis. A single article, no matter how lengthy, reaches a certain number of people but misses many others. One printed news story will not create a lasting awareness.

"Business is much too serious a thing to be left to chief executive officers," says Douglas K. Ramsey in *The Corporate Warriors*. Knowing the seriousness of this task, you may decide to assign the business of preparing your organization's media list to a member of your staff. Know, too, before you make the appointment, that the assignment is an essential part in developing a successful publicity program. It carries considerable responsibility.

A Key to Good Media Coverage

You cannot conduct a publicity program without a media list. It can be as small as a personal-contact roll call of a few people at a local newspaper plus, perhaps, a radio station or two; or it can be as extensive as a national or international mailing list.

The size of the media list is determined by your publicity program plans. The sophistication of its preparation can be decided by answers to a couple of questions: Is this a continuing, ongoing effort or a one-shot event? Does your publicity plan call for weekly, monthly, or occasional news releases?

Whether your media list is kept in a loose-leaf notebook, filed on index cards of a size that accommodates the information you catalog, or maintained in a computerized data bank, it is your personal directory of press and broadcast contacts. Not only is a well-maintained media list an essential component of a publicity program, but it saves time, energy, and resources.

As a publicity-release list, it should include every news outlet that will effectively reach the people you want your organization's message to reach.

Separate Lists for Releases and Advertising

If your media list or a portion of it will be used for placement of advertising, that portion must be separate and highly selective. For the greatest impact in advertising, placement in the media you select should be discriminating, frequent, and regular.

There are good reasons for keeping separate lists. Never, *never* send your publicity release through the advertising department of any publication, no matter how many ad dollars you spend with the publication. Often businesspeople who spend substantial amounts of advertising money feel that the expenditure should buy them some privilege in the editorial sections. The integrity of news judgment is a matter of great pride among editors and writers. There is deep resentment at the thought that anyone might attempt to influence the publication's decision as to what constitutes proper editorial matter.

Publicity Media List

The focus of media selection in this chapter is directed exclusively to uses for publicity purposes. Depending on the extent and diversity of the types of news and feature releases you expect to distribute, your media list can be arranged to meet selective, specific, differing needs and thereby save distribution time, energy, and costs.

The following sections not only assist you in decisions about who and what to include in your media list, but also give you mechanics for preparing and efficiently maintaining it.

Ready-Made Lists

Robert Frost laid it right out. He said, "The world is full of willing people; some willing to work . . . the rest willing to let them." But why do all that work yourself when someone else already may have done it for you? Try using OPB—Other People's Brains—which is just another way of saying, Why reinvent the wheel? If someone already has prepared a media list and it will fit your needs, why not use it? Or why not edit a ready-made list to fit your specific requirements?

Some cities have media guides, often published by the local public relations association or the chamber of commerce. You can learn if there is such a guide by calling these offices or that of a local public relations firm. If no guide exists, you may be able to get names from organizations you work with or from the PR department of a board member's company. If all else fails, you can develop your own list from scratch.

Media-List Name Resources

Most telephone book Yellow Pages give names, addresses, and phone numbers of area newspapers, some of which you may not be familiar with. Although you probably know the names of major area television stations, there may be radio stations you've never heard of.

If you plan to release to media beyond the range of your telephone book, other sources of information exist, each offering different kinds of information about various media. The best known directories are as follows:

- *Editor & Publisher International Year Book*
- *Bacon's Publicity Checker*
- *Standard Rate & Data Service, Inc.*
- *Gale Directory of Publications and Broadcast Media*

Your local library may have copies of one or more of the directories, but often they are not current editions, which means the data are outdated.

(Appendix E gives information on how these directories differ and how one or another can meet your information needs; it also provides listings of broadcasting directories and ordering information.)

Obviously, you will want to send your news releases to newspapers with readerships that are as large as possible and that are *appropriate* for your information. The same is equally true for broadcast media. However, don't hesitate to include them all if you are the least bit uncertain about their readership or listener bases. It is better to send information where it is not needed than to not send it where it may be used.

Large metropolitan areas such as New York, Chicago, Los Angeles, and Dallas may have more than one major metropolitan daily newspaper. Because these large papers serve the news interests of such broad geographical areas and cover international, national, and local events of areawide significance and impact, you may find it difficult to place news items that involve small companies or volunteer organizations. In these areas, it is important to include other newspapers on your media list. Rarely if ever will broadcast media use news items from small businesses. Smaller, independent stations, however, are more likely than large stations to use your nonprofit organization's public service announcements.

Suburban and Weekly Newspapers. If you plan to send publicity releases within a large metropolitan area, you undoubtedly will wish to include neighborhood and suburban newspapers that are published daily or weekly. In the Los Angeles area alone, there are more than 300 of these small papers. These papers, often family owned, are major sources of information to people outside of metropolitan areas. Often the owner is also the editor, and, sometimes he or she is a reporter and the advertising manager as well. Editors of smaller papers are searching for news items about people or happenings in their circulation areas, and they appreciate getting these items as the news or the events occur.

Beyond straight-news stories, other areas for publicity exist that clubs and charitable organizations should explore. In Southern California, for example, many metropolitan and community newspapers, weekly and monthly magazines and tabloids, and college and university newspapers offer organizations the opportunity to publicize events through community bulletin-board columns, calendar listings, business calendars, and society columns. A review of the media in your geographical area, to find the ways they can use your information, is well worth the extra effort.

Business Newspapers. The business-newspaper trade association, American Business Press, Inc., estimates that at least 8 out of 10 businesspeople in responsible positions regularly read one or more specialized business publications. According to the U.S. Small Business Administration, these readers are looking for new ideas, new equipment, new materials, new finished products, anything that will help them to do their jobs better and increase profits for their companies, whether they are owners or employees.

These newspapers can be important in getting your message to a highly vertical audience, and they may be receptive to your news releases. The newspapers have relatively small circulations, typically below 50,000, and some may distribute only a few thousand copies. But they provide intensive coverage of the industry, trade, or profession for which they are edited. It is likely that you will find one or a number of business newspapers in your field of interest.

School Newspapers and Newsletters. Don't forget to add to your media list the newsletters of other for-profit or nonprofit organizations as well as individuals who are in a position to spread the word.

Depending, of course, on the nature of your campaign and on the types and ages of the people you wish to reach, also consider including high school and area college and university newspapers.

Other Media. If you are setting up a new program in a school, or if your staff or employees are working with students in constructive ways, you may wish to check school-district information offices to locate parent-teacher organizations, most currently called PTOs, for bulletins or other such publications where you can get publicity. Churches distribute newsletters, bulletins, or small newspapers. If you anticipate releases that would be appropriate and appealing to members of such institutions, include them in your media list.

There are other special "communities" that have print means for communicating with their members or participants. It may take some digging to locate the names and addresses, but it also may be worth the extra effort.

Specific Contact Names and Titles

Read the newspapers, and follow radio and television news and talk shows to decide who would be the most logical person to contact at each of these. Call the various media, identify yourself and your organization, and find out who should be receiving your releases.

For area newspapers, pick up several copies of recent issues. A study of the newspapers, their content, and their mastheads usually provides the listing information you wish. A telephone call will get you specific names and titles. Create a file of these publications for future reference—not only for names of editors and columnists, but also for types of information they carry and the styles of writing they use.

The Newspaper Directory "Bible."   If you plan to work with other than local people and publications, go to the library and ask the reference librarian to direct you to a current copy of *Editor & Publisher International Year Book*. This book is the most complete and authentic directory of the newspaper business. It includes information about newspaper executives and departmental editors (business, financial, book, food, etc.) and listings for the following: news, picture, and press services; feature, news, and picture syndicate services; newspaper-distributed magazine sections; weekly and suburban newspapers; and much more. The July issues each year of *Editor & Publisher* magazine are devoted to syndicates and include a valuable directory of newspaper columnists.

When preparing your list of weekly newspapers, you may need to find out if some or all are published by a single company. (This information, too, is listed in *Editor & Publisher International Year Book.*) If so, all releases may be edited by one editor, and therefore only one copy may be required. However, each release should specifically set forth, in the top portion of the first page of the release, the names of the newspapers to which the release is directed.

On the other hand, each weekly may have its own editor and require a separate release to each paper. This is information you must dig out for yourself. It's not easily located in any directory.

General Titles.   If you are unable to find a specific name of an editor or reporter to whom to send your releases, the following generic list will suffice:

- City Desk, for daily newspapers. (City editors assign stories.)
- News Assignment Desk, for radio and television.
- Local News Desk, for wire services and periodicals.
- Political Desk, for newspapers and television.
- Business Editor, Financial Editor, Women's Editor, Sports Editor, or any other section editors who are appropriate recipients of your publicity news.
- Photo Desk, for newspapers, wire services, and periodicals.
- Editor, for weekly newspapers.

Verification and Spelling of Names

Some of the tips you will receive in Chapter 5, on how to get along with the media, stress getting media contacts' names right—and then spelling them correctly. This is just common sense. Every news contact wants to be addressed by his or her own name and title—not by his or her predecessor's—and no one likes to see his or her name misspelled. *Editor & Publisher International Year Book* lists names and titles of people who work for each publication. This information is correct at the time of the directory's publication deadline. However, there can be many changes in personnel, even after only a month or two. Check by phone, if you can, to verify the name and title and the correct spelling of both for each person on your media list.

Double-Planting

Another tip—no, a rule—is to never send the same release to more than one person at the newspaper. It is relatively easy to make enemies when two editors end up using the same story in different sections of one day's newspaper and check to find you sent the same release to each of them. This is called *double-planting*. If your list includes more than one person at each publication (city editor, business-page editor, woman's page editor, and others), be sure you remember to choose *one* individual to whom you direct each release.

Media-List Mechanics

For reasons that later will become apparent, it is best to separate your media list into separate categories—newspaper and broadcast. (One reason for this is that the format for each medium is totally different.) In this way, you can more easily eliminate broadcast media when they are inappropriate or send only to business editors, weeklies, high school and college newspapers, or any other individual category according to the nature of the information in each release. However, when the information is appropriate for all groups, the separate categories can easily be merged.

Start your media list (in separate sections) by filling in the blanks in Figures 4.1 through 4.3. After you have acquired the basics, you can refine each section of your list to precisely fit your organization's needs. Until you finalize each section, you may wish to keep individual outlets on file cards that can be shuffled or replaced as needed. Actually, if you keep a manual mailing list—as opposed to one compiled and printed by computer—it undoubtedly

FIGURE 4.1   Media-List Information Sheet (Newspapers)

Name of newspaper: _____

Address: _____

Telephone: _____

Name of editor/reporter/columnist interested in our operations:

_____

Other(s) to contact under other circumstances:

_____

_____

_____

_____

_____

Publication day (if a weekly or suburban): _____

Deadlines: _____

_____

_____

_____

_____

_____

_____

_____

_____

_____

_____

_____

_____

_____

_____

_____

From: *The Publicity Kit,* by Jeanette Smith © 1991 by John Wiley & Sons, Inc.

FIGURE 4.2 Media-List Information Sheet (High School and College Newspapers)

Name of newspaper: _____

Contact: _____

_____

Address: _____

_____

Telephone: _____

_____

_____

_____

_____

_____

_____

_____

_____

_____

_____

_____

_____

_____

_____

_____

_____

_____

_____

_____

FIGURE 4.3   Media-List Information Sheet (Broadcast Media)

Name of television or radio station: _____

Call letters and dial location: _____

Address: _____

Telephone: _____

Average age/format (radio only): _____

Public Service Director: _____

Preferred length/preferred material: _____

Public affairs program: Make arrangements to be on show through (name):

_____

_____

_____

_____

_____

_____

_____

_____

_____

_____

_____

_____

_____

_____

_____

_____

_____

_____

_____

_____

From: *The Publicity Kit*, by Jeanette Smith © 1991 by John Wiley & Sons, Inc.

will be easier to keep all entries on file cards for editing purposes. Personnel changes, even mergers and address changes, call for continuing updates.

Other types of information should be gathered for each broadcast station. For radio, identify and make note of each station's audience: its average age and format (e.g., all ages, contemporary, rock, news, sports, talk, etc.). For both radio and television, make note of the type and length of material they prefer:

> *Examples:*
> 15 seconds for community calendar
> 30 seconds for public service spots (PSAs)
> Copy with basic information for community calendar
> Scripts for PSA spots
> Two-week lead time for community calendar
> Six-to-eight-week lead time for PSA spots
> Prefers pretaped PSAs; does/does not tape
> Bulletin board program twice every hour during which PSAs are played; maximum time 10 seconds

(More information about broadcast publicity is presented in Chapter 14.)

Once you've developed your media list, it should be updated regularly with additions and deletions made as changes happen.

Efficiency Tips

Use the following tips to produce mailing labels:

- When your list is as complete as possible and if you type it manually, prepare it on carbon labels or copier labels.
- Create a copier master sheet of media and their addresses that can be reproduced onto pregummed pages of labels. (These can be readily applied to each envelope.)
- Make several sets of mailing labels. An emergency release can create a real crisis if you find that a set of labels must be manually typed.
- If you have access to computer-processed labels, put your media list on disk where it can be edited, corrected, or printed at a moment's notice.
- *Be sure* that every person's name and title and every publication's name and address are *correct*—no typos, no misspellings.

5

Media Relations

How and why you need to get along with the news media

Romance or Nightmare?

Getting along with the news media can be a romance or a nightmare. For example, there is no doubt that the media, particularly newspapers, has loved both tooting and touting Donald Trump as much as thumping and bashing him.

"He was riding high in April, shot down in May! Donald Trump's highly publicized financial woes have turned June into open season on the tycoon, with columnists and cartoonists lining up to kick the man while he's down," said The Associated Press, under a headline that trumpeted, "Writers Take Aim at Trump: The Target!"

Seldom is a small business the focus of bad press, and even more infrequently do broadcast media target small businesses. It is essential, however, for businesspeople to know how to avoid attracting negative attention and how to handle it if there are problems.

Good (and Bad) Media Relations

Some people seem to be born knowing how to get along with the news media: Walter Cronkite, Nelson Mandela, Mikhail Gorbachev, and Ronald Reagan (while he was in office).

Then there are those who have their problems: Kitty Kelley, Nancy Reagan's unauthorized biographer, who went from a media pet to being their target; top executives at Exxon during the 1989 Exxon Valdez oil spill; Donald Trump; and Jerry Jones, a man from Arkansas who skyrocketed onto the news scene when he purchased a football team that the people of Dallas have cherished for years.

So when a prominently displayed news story about the Dallas Cowboys football team began, "We need to have a little heart-to-heart, Jerry Jones," it was a clear indication that the team's new owner could use some coaching about how to get along with the news media. The story occupied substantial news space in *The Dallas Morning News* and offered Mr. Jones "a little constructive criticism on your public relations skills—or lack thereof." It went on to give "tips" from prominent public relations experts and image consultants: "We want to like you, Mr. Jones. . . . When you smacked down a few million dollars for our football team, you bought not only a bunch of big, sweaty guys, but also an important place in our community. We'd really rather like you than not.

"But gee, Mr. Jones, you're making it awfully hard."

Mr. Jones may have felt a little trampled on. He might have eased his offended feelings with a joke that has become popular among others who also seem to have trouble getting along with the press. Do you know why they bury reporters 26 feet under? Because deep, deep down, they're good people!

You can learn the basic principles of getting along with the news media better than the Dallas media believe Mr. Jones has. It is not that difficult. Really!

Benefits of the Media Partnership

It is essential that you learn how this affiliation with the media works. And you may have to know it well enough to teach others in your organization. It can provide vital benefits with which heads of for-profit and nonprofit organizations can build good relationships with the media. As the head of an organization, you can do the following:

- Build confidence in your organization's integrity.
- Build a recognition factor so that your press releases—on your organization's letterhead and with your name as contact—will be given the attention not given to unknown organizations and their executives.
- Establish a relationship that can show big returns if a not-so-positive happening involving your business occurs on which you wish to provide your viewpoint. If an editor or a reporter knows you, even if only casually, he or she will *listen* to what you have to say. This may mean the

difference in the media being able and willing to present your side of what otherwise might be an unbalanced report leaning heavily to the negative. Getting to know the news media can be a tangible investment in your organization's future.

Rules for Establishing a Good Relationship with News People

Although getting along well with reporters and editors is the very foundation of a productive publicity program, the entire subject can be covered in three short sentences:

- Know your organization; really know it.
- Do the publicity job efficiently, reliably, and credibly.
- Make the reporter's or the editor's job as easy as possible.

Having a great personality and other attributes are nice assets, but only the three things listed above really count.

To develop good relations with the news media, it is prudent to first accept the fact that you are helping newspapers and radio and television stations to do their jobs, which is telling their readers, listeners, and viewers as much as possible of what is going on in the world. News media, particularly understaffed press associations, can't do a full reporting job without the help of publicity practitioners.

Five "Commandments" for Good Media Relations

Good media relations are built on responsibility and regard for the truth, not on misrepresentation. A professional press agent's five "commandments" for achieving good media relations are as follows:

1. *Integrity.* Thou shalt not prevaricate, nor shalt thou exaggerate.
2. *Deadlines.* Thou shalt not procrastinate.
3. *Accessibility.* Thou shalt not build walls.
4. *Familiarity.* Thou shalt do thy homework.
5. *Honesty.* Thou shalt learn to say, "I don't know."

Integrity

The biggest thing you can have going for you is integrity. If the news media begin to question the reliability of a source, the person handling that publicity is better off selling used cars. Keep to the unvarnished truth. Tell it like it is. It works wonders.

This first "commandment" is validated by Jan W. Leemhorst, a Los Angeles public relations man who, in an article in the *Los Angeles Times*, gave the following advice and counsel to Richard M. Nixon during one of Nixon's times of strife.

> *Because truth is the key to good public relations as much as to good news reporting, there is no conflict between them; because public relations means easy access to certain information, it should lead rather than follow the news if it is properly practiced. When the news media consistently come up with startling disclosures, it is a certain sign that public relations has been mishandled.*

Another reporter, writing in the *Santa Monica Evening Outlook*, puts it a little more directly: [Covering the education beat] . . . "has taught me to respect those who neither hide nor even attempt to fight for stories which mislead the public by sugar-coating difficult issues."

Deadlines

Learn the deadlines of each of the media, and develop a newsperson's sense of urgency about meeting those deadlines. Remember, it's not just their deadline; it's yours, too. You can suffer only one consequence of procrastination with reference to getting your news to the media within the confines of their deadlines: death of that news.

There is a saying so old and overworked in newsrooms that it is a cliché: Yesterday's news is history. History—except as feature material—has no place in a news release. It is your responsibility to get your news to the media *before* the news happens, if possible, and *immediately* upon its happening, if you are unable to give advance notice.

Accessibility

This "commandment" is directed primarily to staff acting on behalf of an organization. If you are the head of the organization, there is an important message here for you, too.

A dangerous trap you can fall into is thinking you are the sole source of information for your organization. If you begin to build walls to prevent media from reaching other news sources within your organization, you can seriously restrict your publicity efforts. Any publicity representative worth his or her salt serves as a bridge between the media and the *best* sources of information within his or her organization.

It is a wise move for the top echelon of any organization to be in touch with media people, because the public and the media are people—and people respond to people. The public's perception of a business is in the personalities of the people they identify with that business. Being in touch also can be a definite plus if the media ever decide to report a problem concerning your organization.

Thomas Griffith, a former editor for *Life* magazine, writer for *Time* and *Fortune* magazines, and author of *How True: A Skeptic's Guide to Believing the News*, recommends that businesspeople meet the media:

> *Businessmen, who find their own activities under attack these days, seem increasingly inclined to take a dour view of the press—the agency through which those attacks are mainly registered. . . . And so they tend to be skeptical, wary, and critical of the press, ill at ease and generally defensive in their own encounters with it. Unfortunately, this posture only makes things worse. In their own interests, businessmen need to come to terms with the press.*

As the publicity representative for your company, whether you are staff or chief, you are the "advance man" or woman. When circumstances are appropriate and, definitely, when requests come from members of the media, be an easy bridge to facilitate access for the media to suitable members of your organization.

Familiarity

Know the people in your organization. Again, this is a "commandment" directed mainly to staffers or employees because the head of an organization, in most cases, not only knows his or her people, but knows about them.

News reporting and publicity relations are both "people" businesses: People talking to people make the news. Every group contains people who freeze up at the thought of talking to a reporter. Know who they are and hide them in a closet. Send them to Siberia. Put the knowledgeable and articulate people on display.

Honesty

It's tough on the ego to have a reporter ask a nice, simple question and to draw a complete blank in response. Go ahead and make an educated guess, but it's six to five you will be wrong. A couple of bad guesses and you've dug yourself some trouble. Just say, I don't know. Then get the answer—quickly.

You'd think that a 1990 gubernatorial candidate in Texas by the name of Clayton Williams would know this mandate. But the well-known businessman learned the lesson a little too late. Throughout the campaign, he earned a reputation of opening his mouth and putting both feet in it, and, as a result, he blew a 20-point lead, not to mention $8.5 million of his own money.

At his last press conference—the night he conceded the governor's race to his opponent—he was asked a question about the campaign. "He stumbled and fumbled for an answer before he finally did what some of his staff had wanted him to do all along," a news report in *The Dallas Morning News* said. Rather than blurt out something that could hurt him, the defeated candidate exclaimed, "Why don't I say, 'I don't know.'" Why didn't he do that all the way through the general election campaign, his aides wondered." Perhaps the lesson will serve him well as a businessman in his future relationships with the media.

Not even the owner or head of an organization always has all the answers! You do have advantages over staffers, however. You can ask for information from a vice president, a department head, or any employee for that matter; and you get it, pronto. It's not always that easy for those holding lesser ranks.

Even a "First Publicity Representative," former President Lyndon B. Johnson's press secretary, George Reedy (somewhat comparable to a vice president of Public Relations in a very large corporation) is on record with that complaint. "There were times," he said, "when I just couldn't get any information out of the White House. But I kidded no one. If I didn't know, I said I didn't know. I was never asked by the President to lie, and I wouldn't have. I would have quit first."

If you experience such difficulties, keep trying; or try another direction, another "tack," another information source. As a last resort, do as George Reedy did: Just say, "I don't know."

The "Know-Who" Factor

In publicity, it is not always what you know; it is often *who* you know! It is important to have at least a speaking acquaintance with the people you hope will use your releases. More importantly, these people should know you, know your integrity, and have faith in the integrity of the information you give them.

The editor and other people who work on a newspaper are no different from those who staff any business, except that they are more pressured. They live by deadlines that require them, in just a few hours, to write, edit, and print enough material to fill, on average, a 100,000-word book. They repeat this unbelievable task every day, day in and day out; they deserve your respect, for their abilities and for the demands upon their time; and they will appreciate your brevity, but not your curtness.

They also will appreciate your gaining an understanding of how they work and of the standards they must meet. (Chapter 16 gives you an in-depth view of newspapers that can help you gain an understanding that will make your meetings easier and better.)

The Importance of Sincerity

Back again to Dallas Cowboys owner, Jerry Jones, and his media troubles. "My gut reaction to the man is that he needs more sincerity," says an image consultant, speaking to a reporter for *The Dallas Morning News*. "There seems to be a plastered smile on his face."

The consultant advises, "Don't forget, Mr. Jones, you've taken stone-face Tom Landry's place in the public eye. He didn't smile often, but when he did—by God—you knew he meant it."

The message here is, be pleasant, but be sincere. Be honest about the content of your releases, but honest about yourself, too.

Emotional Restraint

Another lesson also comes through following Jerry Jones's early stumbles with media. *Dallas Morning News* columnist Blackie Sherrod puts it into perspective by comparing differences in the way that a previous Dallas Cowboys football team owner dealt with the press:

> Tex [Schramm] treated each utterance with the care of a mother driving a station wagon with baby in the front seat, ever on the lookout for chugholes. Tex is a natural master of semantics, omitting a word here, changing a verb there, which might—under careful scrutiny—alter the meaning or afford protection in case the statement was later questioned.
> Jones is—or was—a blurter. . . . He rushed in on his new Christmas bicycle, spouting enthusiasm, running from post to post like an eager puppy. Perhaps he didn't realize that in his new role, in his new critical spotlight, every

word or phrase would be rushed off to the microscope, there to be dissected and searched for meaningful intent or philosophy. This trap has caught more than one successful businessman thrust into media glare.

That's the lesson. When you have personal contact with the press, slow down your enthusiasm enough so that you don't give the impression of an eager puppy if the announcement is about an exciting company development. And if you are giving a reaction to negative publicity, keep your thinking cool so that you can watch your words in case a reporter does rush them off to be dissected for meaning or philosophy.

By way of an update on Jerry Jones's media troubles, the newspaper that in the beginning had so faithfully reported his many public image blunders has more recently acknowledged that Jones "has learned to smooth his rough edges." A lengthy article in the sports section of *The Dallas Morning News* gave reasons for Jones's initial missteps, reasons to which most businesspeople can relate.

> Jones never had a public profile before becoming the owner of the Cowboys. He was in private business, initially insurance and later oil and gas exploration, and he preferred to keep his business private. He rarely dealt with the news media, routinely turning down the few interview requests that came in. . . . Jones's strength as a businessman had been his ability to deal on a one-on-one basis with people. The smaller the group, the better he came across.
>
> The difference between the Jerry Jones of then [when he first purchased the Dallas Cowboys football team] and now [in December 1990] is in his delivery. He has as much to say now as he did a year ago, but there is more thought and sensitivity behind his comments. . . . It took a few hard hits before he started paying attention to the people who could help him [primarily the club's public relations directors].

Jerry Jones must have been highly gratified when he read that news story. Few businesspeople will ever receive similar media scrutiny—the newspaper stated that "no one in Dallas has been read and misread, understood and misinterpreted more than Jones." Jones's turnabout experience, then, is confirmation that the lesson of how to get along with the news media even under the most difficult circumstances can be learned.

A Stereotypical Image of a Reporter

You can always spot a reporter, right? Hat askew, cigarette clamped determinedly between his white teeth, pint flask within reach, and throat raw from ranting, "Stop the presses!" A swashbuckling, cocksure commando with notepad and pencil, more women friends than good sense, and an affinity for fisticuffs that makes world heavyweight champion, Buster Douglas, seem creampuffish by comparison.

This figure is, of course, a misconception made popular by those other-decade, late-night TV movies, and described in a Bell Telephone booklet, "A Nose for News is not Enough." It is not today's newspaper person, and a publisher quoted in the booklet explained why: "We couldn't afford him."

Tips for Assisting the News Media at Planned Events

None of the following tips are more than common-sense actions, but the list can be used as a reminder tally.

- When you schedule an event, make plans to invite the news media.
- Send complimentary tickets in advance. Make arrangements for them to be included as guests—individually seated with persons from your organization whom they know or would like to know.
- Assist them in every way in covering the event, or assign a capable staff person to do the job.
- Prepare a press release in advance if the occasion warrants.
- A day or so before the event, call the editor and ask if there are any special arrangements he or she may require—backstage pass, interview with a speaker, or contact with specific individuals who will attend. Do your best to make arrangements for all that is requested.

More Tips

Most of the following tips reiterate information presented elsewhere in this book. The list should be used as a checklist and memory jogger.

- Never send a story to an editor unless it is *newsworthy*.
- Use common sense and good taste in your news stories and in your relationships with news-media representatives.
- In your initial dealings with the press, arrange a convenient time with the editor to hand-deliver your news release, but after the first meeting, don't waste the editor's time with personal visits.
- Don't play favorites when distributing news releases. If there are several

media outlets in your area, make sure each has the information at the same time.

- If an editor uses your story, he or she has done so because it contained newsworthy material. There is no need for thanks, unless you know the editor well enough that he or she will not misunderstand your motive. It is, however, a gracious gesture to compliment a reporter on expert handling of a story.
- Never ask an editor to run a story as a favor to you.
- If a reporter contacts you for a story, don't provide, or "leak," the same story to other media.
- Treat the media fairly. If you promised an editor a story by a certain time, have it ready as promised.
- If an editor calls you after he or she has your release, provide the answers to his or her questions quickly and completely so he or she can complete the story.
- Don't ask to see—or hear—the reporter's story before it is printed. Reporters generally reject the notion of showing anyone outside the newsroom their stories before they appear. However, a good reporter will welcome an invitation to check back with you if the information gathered is not as clear as he or she would like it to be.
- Don't call the editor to complain if your story is not used in its entirety or if it is not used at all. Sometimes space and time limitations or reshuffled feature schedules can cause this. And, as a general rule, newspeople object to such questions as, When will this appear? or Will you give us a break on this story? or any similar suggestion that special favors are being solicited.
- If a serious error appears in your published or broadcasted story, call the appropriate reporter immediately. He or she usually will correct it. Complaining to the reporter's superior seldom produces anything except ill will for the future, without helping the present. Errors emphasize the desirability of being unmistakably clear in the first place.

Telephone Calls from Reporters

Working with the media is a two-way street. A reporter may contact you in response to a news release or for information regarding an unrelated story. When you do get such a call, find out who is calling and what news organization the individual represents. Find out what the specific questions are and how the information is being used. This will help you frame an answer to best suit the reporter's (and your) purpose. Tell the reporter you will get back to him or her "ASAP"—as soon as possible.

A Scripps-Howard News Service story explains that, "Because so much rides on anything they say to the media, PR people like to double- and triple-check the facts before giving an answer for the record." The story continues, "A PR man who left his newspaper job a while back for the awesome responsibility of filing a larger tax return, likes to tell this one: 'How many PR people does it take to change a light bulb? Answer: I don't know. Can I get back to you on that?'" The humor of the story tends to cover up what really is a backhanded compliment to publicity and public relations representatives who insist on being accurate and an acknowledgment of how hard and how often they try.

Answer only the questions being asked. Decide after the questioning if you want to go beyond the information that was asked for. There might be an opportunity to make the story more positive from your standpoint. If you do not have the information at hand, tell the reporter you will call back. Find out when the reporter's deadline is and get back to him or her before that time.

Imprudent or Evasive Answers

According to Joyce Haber, writing in the *Los Angeles Times*, "Actor Lorne Greene once said publicly, much to his credit: 'There are no indiscreet questions by reporters. There are only indiscreet answers.'" An old saying puts it another way: Many things are opened by mistake, but none as often as the mouth!

Know well the answers you wish to give—or ask for time to get them. Answering questions you are not equipped to answer only leads to trouble. Don't guess; call back. Conversely, to avoid answering a question that a reporter knows you are capable of answering also leads to trouble. It is damaging to claim ignorance. To say, No comment, is also harmful. If you wish to avoid a question, simply say that you believe a response at this time would be inappropriate.

It is as simple as the fact that reporters and their bosses don't like red tape, evasive answers, or standoff treatment. If they get it, what might have been a favorable story may never be written.

Most newspeople declare that the more unnecessary obstacles are placed in their way, the harder they will work to get their story, for getting it becomes a point of honor. They will almost always manage to print something on it, although such stories are bound to contain a high ratio of inaccuracies if the actual facts are denied to reporters by the very persons who are in a position to know the facts.

A Good Image Gone Sour

For many years, almost everything written about Exxon, the world's largest oil company, was positive. In addition to straight news of the company, there was complimentary news from and about Exxon's charitable foundation and its sizeable grants that assist a variety of nonprofits in the work they do.

Then, with the 1989 Exxon Valdez oil spill, it was almost as if Exxon became Chicken Little, and its sky appeared to fall in. An example of the harm that can be done by seeming to withhold information or by a seeming reluctance to offer it is shown in *The Dallas Morning News* story that follows. Read it, and learn from it.

> ### EXXON CLOSEMOUTHED ON MOVE: EXPERTS SAY OIL GIANT COULD HAVE USED NEWS TO BOLSTER IMAGE
>
> Whether it's an oil spill or a corporate relocation, Exxon Corp. doesn't want to talk about it.
>
> Exxon, sharply criticized for its closemouthed response after one of its tankers dumped a huge oil slick in Alaska waters in March, repeated the act Thursday when it announced it was moving its world headquarters from New York to Las Colinas [Texas].
>
> The news media were given a meager page-and-a-half release—and that was about it.
>
> No top executives were made available for interviews. No lengthy statements explaining the whys and wherefores of the momentous move were released. And the corporate public relations office closed as usual at 3:15 P.M. Dallas time—leaving instructions with the company switchboard not to forward any calls from reporters.
>
> All in all, experts say, Exxon missed a great chance to generate a little good publicity in its new hometown, especially in light of the beating it has taken in the wake of the Alaska oil spill.
>
> "It's certainly not in Exxon's best interest to make enemies in Dallas before it even gets there," Dean Rotbart [editor of the *Business Journalism Review*] said.
>
> "Instead of being the neighbor who moves in and invites you over for coffee and cake," [said Mr. Rotbart], "they're the neighbor who moves in and puts up a 'Beware of the Dog' sign."
>
> "So much of a company's success is based not on what a company does, but on what the public's perception is of what the company does," said Charles Marsh, an assistant professor of journalism at the University of Kansas.

"In the case of the oil spill," said Gerald Meyers [former chairman of American Motors who now advises executives on crisis management], "they really had two crises. One was the oil itself. The second was the crisis of public perception—and that one they brought on themselves."

Advance Research in Public Relations

Some years back, Esso decided to change its name to improve its image. The name ENCO was chosen—until the company learned that the word means "stalled car" in Japanese. Wouldn't that be a model example of a company shooting itself in the foot? Instead, the company changed its name to Exxon.

Advice on Handling Bad Press

There is no guarantee that everything ever written about your organization will be favorable. So what do you do after you've used up your personal 15 minutes of fame that artist Andy Warhol predicted for everyone? Is it possible that your 15 minutes will provide bad press? When this happens, take your media "black eyes" and work all the harder to keep further unfavorable situations from developing.

On telephone inquiries concerning controversial or otherwise difficult subjects, it sometimes pays to promise to call back in a few minutes and to use those minutes to develop an unmistakably clear reply. This may avoid misunderstandings, for while you know what you are talking about, not everyone understands terms and situations that are natural to you.

If you expect to be able to give the reporter the answers to his or her questions later, say so. When the time arrives, it is good business to make certain that you do answer those questions and that you don't volunteer the information to the reporter's competitors.

The more difficult the story, the more important it is to talk to the reporter in person, if possible. You might wish to write out a short statement and read it to the reporter to avoid mistakes. Naturally, there never is a reason or excuse for coloring or stretching the facts. A good reporter recognizes a "curve." Trite as it sounds, honesty is the best policy.

About the only circumstances that call for an official, formal reaction are when there are errors or gross misrepresentations of the facts. Here a letter to the editor is in order, stating the facts and making any corrections. Ask for a clarifying article or retraction; do not demand it. Mistakes do happen, and if the *editor* feels the mistake warrants a correction, he or she will have it made.

"Off-the-Record" Remarks

Occasionally, it is desirable to offer previously cleared background information, so that the reporter will be able to evaluate and interpret the facts you are presenting. Regardless of all that has been said and written on the subject, the phrase "off the record" is not universally understood. Some media people interpret this to mean that the information may be published if it is not attributed to the sources; others interpret it to mean the information cannot be published at all. If you encounter such a situation, it is wise to specify that what you say is not for publication. This may avoid embarrassing misunderstandings.

Your Role with the Media

The following points must be reemphasized. Your role with the news media is as follows:

- To be helpful
- To be obliging
- To be honest
- To avoid suppressing the news

The best reaction to criticism is to consider it. It might be valuable. If you are tempted to get into a battle with the media, remember, they always fire the last shot. Just continue working with them in the spirit of a free press.

The bottom line in how to get along with the news media is really nothing more than knowing how to get along with the PUBLIC: that's good publicity!

6

Newspaper Publicity Releases

What you need to know to successfully write a straight-news publicity release

Literature in a Hurry

Someone once said that newspaper writing is literature in a hurry. Alistair Cooke called it a sort of literature on the wing. Perhaps it is literature. Perhaps there are newspaper writers who produce literature; there certainly are scores of literary giants who began their careers as newswriters. (Some of the famous names in journalism are included in Chapter 16.) It is safe to say, however, that most newswriting is *not* literature; it *is* in a hurry, though.

David Holahan, in a feature story in *The New York Times*, states unequivocally that writing is hard. He quotes Red Smith, another writer, as saying, "There is nothing to it. Just sit down and open a vein." Then Holahan adds, "The gentlemanly Smith was too polite to add: If there is any blood left after the creation it will be shed when the editing is done."

Writing *is* difficult, but the tricks of the trade spelled out throughout this chapter make writing news releases relatively easy.

Newswriting Rules

It is as true of writing news releases as it is of learning Bridge, Monopoly, or any game: The *playing* is relatively easy and a lot more fun when you *know* the rules.

Focused Writing

Because the reader wants to know immediately what a news story is about, the summary of the story is placed at its beginning rather than at its end, where our grade school teachers taught us to summarize a story. Thus, the reader can get the gist immediately, decide if he or she wishes to read the rest, and, if so, hurry on through the entire story, all because of the unique style in which a news story is written.

News journalism rightly may be *information* in a hurry, but it is not a mere catalog of facts. As pioneer publisher E. W. Scripps told young newsmen: "There is really no such thing as an uninteresting story. There are only reporters who do not know how to present it in an interesting manner."

E. B. White's "Reminders"

No one wrote better rules for newswriting than William Strunk, Jr., coauthor with E. B. White of *The Elements of Style*. White calls the rules "reminders," and they appear as a chapter in the book that writers of every type enthusiastically testify is one of the tiniest, most powerful books around. You will do well to keep it alongside your typewriter or computer at all times.

Some of E. B. White's "reminders" are as follows:

- Write with nouns and verbs, not with adjectives and adverbs; in general it is nouns and verbs, not their assistants, that give good writing its toughness and color.
- Avoid the use of qualifiers (e.g., *rather, very, little, pretty,* etc.).
- Do not explain too much (e.g., "he said consolingly," "she replied grudgingly," etc). Let the conversation itself disclose the speaker's manner or condition.
- Avoid fancy words—the elaborate, the pretentious, the coy, and the cute (e.g., beauteous, curvaceous, discombobulate, tummy).
- Be clear. When you become hopelessly mired in a sentence, start fresh.
- Revise and rewrite. It is no sign of weakness or defeat if your manuscript ends up in need of major surgery. This is a common occurrence in all writing and happens to the best of writers.

Another book that is literally priceless because it is not available to the general public is *Learning in the Newsroom*. It was published by the American Newspaper Publishers Association Foundation and was compiled and edited by John L. Dougherty, Managing Editor of the Rochester (New York) *Times-Union*. Many newsroom supervisors have used it, and undoubtedly still do, as a valued manual for neophyte reporters. The following writing rules from the book are an edited version in the interest of space.

The Kansas City Star's Condensed Rules

An old *Kansas City Star* style sheet gives much of the same advice as does E. B. White's "reminders," but it says it more concisely:

- Use short sentences.
- Use short first paragraphs.
- Use vigorous English.
- Be positive, not negative.

Ernest Hemingway used this style sheet when he was a cub reporter for the *Star*. Hemingway said, "Those rules were the best I ever had for the business of writing."

Mark Twain's Rules

Mark Twain set down his own rules for writing. Most of them are appropriate today.

- Eschew surplusage.
- Say what you propose to say, don't merely come near it.
- Use the right word, not its second cousin.
- Don't omit necessary details.
- Avoid slovenliness of form.
- Use good grammar.
- Employ a simple and straightforward style.

Twain started his writing career as a newspaperman for a San Francisco paper, *The Alta Californian*. In the early 1860s, he was city editor of Nevada's *Territorial Enterprise*.

Ten Steps for Writing a Newspaper News Release

Is that plain, white, empty piece of paper staring back at you? Are you ready and willing to write your first news release, but still unsure how?

"There are shelves full of books on writing. But often you will experience, even after having read volumes, a terrible empty feeling when you sit

down to a blank sheet of paper to write a story." Those lines also are from
Learning in the Newsroom, a newsroom manual for beginning reporters, most
of whom have the advantage of being journalism graduates. This empty
feeling is recognized by anyone who writes. Don't let a bare sheet of paper
defeat you. What to do? Just use these ten steps (which are explained in the
sections that follow) to help you overcome your writer's block:

1. *Focus and clarity.* Know what you want to say.
2. *The lead paragraph.* Structure your story.
3. *News story body.* Flesh out the details.
4. *Imitation.* Follow the style and construction of existing articles.
5. *Completeness.* Cover all of the facts.
6. *Editorializing.* Don't give your opinion.
7. *Names.* Use proper style for spelling out of names.
8. *Closing.* Add a final paragraph.
9. *Editing.* Review your copy twice, then review it again.
10. *Accuracy.* Strive for a perfect news release.

Focus and Clarity

"Be sure you have an idea of what it is you want to say. Often when a reporter
asks a colleague for help with a lead paragraph," advises *Learning in the
Newsroom*, "he finds that he doesn't really know what it is he is writing about,
and as soon as he discovers what it is, the lead comes easily and naturally."

Outlines. Former Associated Press reporter, two-time Pulitzer Prize
winner, and book author, Don Whitehead, writes about his way of organizing
a news story in *Reporting/Writing from Front Row Seats*. He says, "Some
reporters have the ability to organize a story in their minds merely from
reading their notes. But my own method—in writing a news story or a book—
is to make an outline of the major points of the story and the sequence in
which I wish to present them."

The safest way to be sure of exactly what your story should include is to
make an outline of the major points of the story and the order in which you
will present them, from most important to least important.

One example outline might be as follows:

1. John Jones is named CEO of _____; (include company name and
identification)

2. Jones succeeds Joe Smith who resigned in February
3. Jones joins Bill Adams, company chairman
4. Jones's previous experience
5. Quotes from Adams regarding Jones's appointment
6. Quotes from Jones about his plans for employees
7. Information about the company and anything it is known for
8. Beginning date of Jones employment.

Another example outline might be as follows:

1. Brown will discuss why worker skills are declining.
2. At group meeting of _____; Briefly identify group.
3. Date and place of meeting.
4. Identify speaker and cite prominence.
5. Expand on topic to be discussed and purposes.
6. Include pertinent identifying information about sponsoring group.
7. Luncheon reservations are necessary and can be made by calling Jane Johnson at 000-1111, Ext. 123.

Interviews. Sometimes it is necessary to gather information for your news release, and you may need an interview with one or more individuals. The interview is a primary information-gathering technique of reporters and publicists, and it is the bedrock of journalism. Include it in your growing storehouse of "know-how" information.

In an interview, it always helps to know a little in advance about your subject's area of expertise. It also helps to make a list of questions you want answered; but keep the questions brief. Let your subject do the talking, and do not spend valuable time reciting lengthy questions. And always, always, ask only one question at a time.

A tape recorder can be a fundamental help when conducting an interview, particularly if you want exact quotes.

The GOSS Formula. Unlike a living-room conversation, an interview must have flow, direction, and intensity. A journalism professor, LaRue W. Gilleland, devised a simple formula for asking effective interview questions. His students named the formula Gilleland's GOSS Formula because the acronym GOSS—from the key words *goal, obstacle, solution,* and *start*—

provides a memory-jogging device. It reminds the interviewer to ask questions similar to the following:

- Goal-revealing questions. What are you trying to accomplish? What's the real purpose of your organization?
- Obstacle-revealing questions. What problems did you face? What stands in your way now?
- Solution-revealing questions. How did you handle the problem? What plan do you have for resolving the conflict?
- Start-revealing questions. When did the program have its beginning? Whose idea was it?

The Lead Paragraphs

> I keep six honest serving men
> (They taught me all I knew)
> Their names are WHAT and WHY and WHEN
> And HOW and WHERE and WHO
> — *The Elephant's Child* by Rudyard Kipling

Call in your "six honest serving men"—the five Ws and, if appropriate, the one H. The most common straight-news lead paragraphs use them. In general, the structure of a news story is the opposite of other literary forms. In a straight-news release, it's what's up top that counts! There is no buildup to a climax; you must boil the story down to its principal facts and lay them all out, right in the lead paragraphs.

Content.   Your summary lead contains answers to questions readers want to know:

- *Who(m)* is the story about?
- *What* happened?
- *Where* did it happen?
- *When* did it happen?
- *Why* did it happen?
- *How* did it happen?

It is sometimes, but not always, necessary to answer the final item—how it happened. Actually, write the answers to these questions from the facts of each specific news story as part of your outline for each release.

Try to work the name of your organization high up in the lead so it cannot easily be cut without destroying the meaning of the story. Set down your facts, one by one, for the first paragraph. If the lead paragraph runs longer than about 50 or 60 words, distribute the five Ws and one H, if used, in two paragraphs.

Story Summarization.   Capture the essence of your story in the lead paragraphs. The art of writing a news story demands that the writer tell something of value to the reader; it insists that this something be told quickly; and it demands that it always be told honestly.

"Whatever you write, have consideration for your reader. He has little time. You have to tempt him. Make it worthwhile," advises Peter Arnett, a Pulitzer Prize-winning Associated Press correspondent.

Remember that your lead paragraphs are a summary of the entire story. The reader should be able to stop immediately after having read your lead and to know that he or she has captured the significance and the nature of the entire story. He or she can read on for the details.

Your lead should convince the editor either to use your story or to send a reporter to cover it. In other words, the lead should hook the reader, particularly if that reader is the editor of the newspaper you are submitting to. (Sample leads are shown as part of the sample news releases in Appendix A.)

News Story Body

After your lead paragraph or paragraphs, flesh out the details of each of the five Ws—what, where, when, why, and who. The *body* of a news release explains in more detail the facts covered in the lead; and each paragraph diminishes in importance to the end of the story.

Inverted Pyramid.   The structure of a news story is an *inverted pyramid*—an upside-down presentation of important information. This inverted pyramid technique is used so that editors can lop off final paragraphs to fit space limitations without cutting important information. (In Chapter 2, both a short news story and a long news story are diagramed in the inverted pyramid style.)

The Pyramid and the Telegraph.   Did you ever wonder how this completely unique foundation of American reporting came about? Technology was the culprit. Early reporting was wordy and disorganized until the advent of the telegraph. Telegraphing news was highly desired, but it was also costly and often unreliable. So editors demanded that the basic facts be sent first, just in case the rest of the story was lost in transmission. And, of course, publishers—those watchdogs of the budget—recognized and welcomed the savings from sending shorter stories.

Use the organization's name several times throughout the body of your release, always in a manner that makes its use relevant to the rest of the story.

The Importance of "Who."   Don't downplay the importance of "who" in a news story. Remember, the editor likes names because people like to read about people and because names sell extra newspapers. So it's well worth all the effort that may be required to submit *all* the names of the members, delegates, officers, guests, or other people involved in your story. Sometimes it isn't fitting to include full lists; but if in doubt, *do it!* Of course, you're not expected to fit all the names into the lead paragraphs, just the most important ones. Lists of names should be used farther into the body of the story. If you doubt that they all belong in the story, use only those names you are sure are appropriate and attach a list of the remainder with the final copy of the release.

If your release will, in any way, elicit a public response or a desire by readers for more information, be sure to include a final line that will preclude calls to the newspaper (e.g., "for further information, please call [give an authorized name and phone number]").

Newspaper Style Sheets.   The glossary tells you that *style* is rules on writing, spelling, and so on. One of the style rules (that all newspapers follow) is, use figures for dates, times, street numbers, and sums of money, except when beginning a sentence. Whenever possible, avoid starting a sentence with a number, but if it is necessary, spell out the numbers that fall first in the sentence, and spell out numbers one through nine and use figures for 10 and up. For other rules of style, refer to the *stylebook* or *style sheet* used by the particular newspaper to which you are releasing. Two stylebooks that are popular with a number of newspapers are published by United Press International and The Associated Press. (Ordering information and descriptions of the two stylebooks are provided in Appendix E.) But if you are in doubt, call the copy desk during off-deadline time. Someone there will give you the name of the stylebook used by the newspaper for which you are writing.

Imitation

With a minimum of effort and training, imitation can help you develop skill in presenting the facts. Follow the style and construction of articles that already have appeared in your newspaper. Keep your sentence structure simple and your information direct. Don't expect the editor to rewrite, although most of the time he or she will assign a rewrite—for his or her purpose, though, not to clean up your writing.

Examples.   It is helpful to cut out examples of various types of stories from the newspaper, paste them in a notebook for easy reference, and follow their patterns when a similar situation arises for which you must prepare a story. As you study these examples, take note that many schoolbook writing rules are broken by practical reporters and editors; and you may want to break the same rules they do. Certain rules are broken because newspeople know that their product—the newspaper—must sell, and to do it, the style and writing must be alive and kicking. If you do it, do it for the same reasons, and the recipients of your releases will love you for it.

Schoolbook Rules.   A classic example of a schoolbook rule regularly broken in newswriting is this: A single paragraph must contain a single idea or thought. In newswriting, one thought may be extended over several paragraphs, or *grafs*. This keeps paragraphs short and easy to read. Another rule often broken is the introduction of a new thought in the last sentence of one paragraph to catch the reader's interest and carry him or her on into the following paragraph.

Completeness

Don't assume the reader (or the editor, for that matter) has any background knowledge of the subject. It is far easier for an editor to cut unneeded details than to dig them up to include in a story. Chances are high the editor won't bother.

You can also submit a fact sheet with your story. (What to include in a fact sheet and how to tailor one to your specific purposes is included in Chapter 10.) Attaching a previously prepared fact sheet that contains information about your organization may be an excellent method for presenting background details. The fact sheet may provide the editor or reporter with a better understanding of a news release.

Editorializing

Don't editorialize the facts in a news release; don't pass off your opinions or
beliefs as facts. However, you can add "meat" to a news release when you
present another person's opinion in quotes. The quote must be word for word,
not your interpretation. It must be relevant, and it must be fully attributed
(the source's name and title or other pertinent information).

Attribution. In regard to attribution, it has become increasingly
important to give the name of an information source, rather than to use a
phrase such as "sources said." David S. Broder, author of *Behind the Front
Page: A Candid Look at How the News Is Made,* assigns blame to the press itself
for the public's loss of faith in the truth of information attributed to unnamed
sources. One of several examples he gives is the famous falsehood presented
by Janet Cooke in *The Washington Post* about an eight-year-old heroin addict.
Broder states that overuse of the phrase "sources said" worsens the credibility
problem. The more the phrase is used, the less readers trust a story. Using an
eye-catching, stimulating quote that is fully attributed, however, can be a
very effective way to begin a news release. Using quotes throughout the story
is good journalism.

Words That Express Your Opinion. To avoid editorializing, watch
the words you use. John L. Dougherty was an editor at the Rochester (NY)
Times-Union at the time he compiled and edited *Learning in the Newsroom.* In
one of Dougherty's earlier news stories, he wrote about the quarterly report of
the old Boston Elevated System, which had a nearly unbroken record of
deficits but was at the moment in the black. In the article, he stated, "*The
Boston Elevated had a remarkable record for January—it showed a profit.*" He
relates his experience concerning the article as follows:

> The old night editor brought my copy back. He knew I was green. In a
> kindly way, he spelled out the trouble. "Remarkable is not a reporting
> word," he said. "We just tell the facts. Tell the story so that the reader
> will say, 'That's remarkable.'"

Editorial "We." In straight-news releases or in reporting, the first-
person pronoun "I" is never used. In a letter to the editor to *The Los Angeles
Times,* recognition of the universal acceptance of the editorial "we" is given:

> The President and the Governor always refer to themselves as "we"
> when they really mean "I." Only two groups of people are entitled to

refer to themselves as "we"—the editors of newspapers and fellows with tapeworms.

There's a theory, purely facetious, about why newspapers use the editorial "we": so the person who doesn't like what's printed will think that there are too many to lick!

Names

Always spell out the name of your organization in the first use, then follow the name with the accepted initials in parentheses—if the organization is well known by its initials [e.g, General Electric (GE), Platt Accountants Service, Inc. (PASI), and The Resource Assistance Center (TRAC).] After the first, spelled-out use of the name, use of the acronym throughout is acceptable.

When using people's names, follow the publication's style when you know it. It is common practice to use each person's full name—for instance, Mary J. Jones (with her title or other identifier)—when the name is first used in the story. Further references then use only the last name (e.g., "Jones will take office at the next . . . ").

There are, however, exceptions. *The Wall Street Journal, The Dallas Morning News,* and a few other newspapers, after the initial use of the name, use the abbreviations *Mr., Mrs.,* or *Ms.* with the last name throughout the remainder of the story. In addition, some papers always use Ms. (instead of Mrs. or Miss) with all women's names. The majority of newspapers, however, after the first use of a full name, will subsequently use only a person's last name in the story, regardless of whether the person is a man or a woman.

Closing

To complete your news release, add a final, standard closing paragraph that succinctly describes the function, purpose, mission, operation, services, or work of your company or group. Expect this last paragraph to be cut, but, occasionally, an editor's need to fill news hole space will permit use of the closing paragraph.

Keep on hand a previously prepared paragraph to save yourself the time required to construct a new one each time. Your model paragraph can be extensive and can contain more information than is appropriate for the release you are currently writing. It is easier, however, to edit a standard paragraph to fit each circumstance rather than to create a new one for each release.

Editing

Look for ways to make the writing more intelligible and brief. Look for words that aren't precisely what you mean. Mark Twain expressed it this way: "The difference between the right word and the almost right word is the difference between lightning and the lightning bug."

Excessive Wordiness.   Good journalistic writing is vivid, clear, concise, and simple. Write tight, and keep it short, are expressions every newspaper reporter hears over and over, meaning that all the flab around the midsection of a story—and particularly in the lead—must be eliminated.

The nth degree of obese flab is demonstrated in a paragraph that appeared in a U.S. Department of Labor publication (as reported by The Associated Press). It surely was not written by a trained newswriter:

> *The occupational incidence of the demand change is unlikely to coincide with the occupational profile of those registered at the employment office. Translation: The jobs may not fit the people.*

Clarity.   Accuracy, simplicity, and objectivity are essential in writing news releases. And perhaps most important of all is *clarity* in your writing. Remember Mark Twain's rule: "Say what you propose to say, don't merely come near it."

An amusing statement familiar to many people (and edited slightly here so that it can be a gentle reminder to write clearly) is as follows: "I know you believe you understand what you think I wrote, but I am not sure you realize what you read is not what I meant."

Even as an extremely busy businessperson with little extra time, you still can take advantage of not being a reporter on deadline who has no time to rewrite. Do write a draft. You may make several drafts before you have copy ready for release. Don't be concerned with the mechanics or the final format at this time. Just get the words down. If you think better in longhand, that's fine. It is only the final copy that must be typed.

Accuracy

Try to make every news release you send to an editor as accurate and impartial as a news story prepared by one of his or her own reporters.

California Publisher listed the following grammar "unrules." Call this list your "chuckle check"!

1. Don't use no double negative.
2. Make each pronoun agree with their antecedent.
3. Join clauses good, like a conjunction should.
4. About them sentence fragments.
5. When dangling, watch your participles.
6. Verbs has to agree with their subjects.
7. Just between you and I, case is important too.
8. Don't write run-on sentences they are hard to read.
9. Don't use commas, which aren't necessary.
10. Try to not ever split infinitives.
11. Its important to use your apostrophe's correctly.
12. Proofread your writing to see if you any words out.
13. Correct spelling is esential.

Final Draft Checklist

Perhaps you've done several drafts. Now the material is as carefully prepared, concisely presented, and clearly written as you can make it. You're ready to commit it to the final, typed release form. But again, wait! You will buy yourself a lot of insurance (that your news release will be used) if you take a few more moments to give it a final test:

- Is it of interest to a large number of people?
- Does it include names of well-known people?
- Does it have a human-interest angle?
- Does it have a local angle of interest to the readers reached by this particular newspaper?
- Are spelling and grammar 100 percent correct?
- Is it an ad?
- Do you have a headline?

News Release Headline

The headline you put at the top of your release is for one purpose only—to tell the editor what the story is about. It is *not* meant to be used by the newspaper, and it won't be. The headline that actually appears in the newspaper over your news story is the newspaper's sole responsibility. Whether it uses your story verbatim or rewrites it totally, the headline will be written by someone at the newspaper. The headline you write for your news release is merely a summary statement.

Special Constrictions for Headline Writers. You may find it interesting to know how real newspaper headlines are written. Headline writers have sharp minds, literally, and sharp pencils, figuratively. They produce under confining rules, each of which is an excellent guideline to help you write your summary-release headline:

- Present the most important facts of the story.
- Attract the reader's attention and pique his or her interest.
- Be accurate and brief.
- Use a verb but do not start with one.
- Use present or future tense.
- Use active voice.

A Headline-Imperatives Game. Headlines that start with verbs are infinitely easier to write, and that is why such a headline occasionally slips by. An editor at a Pennsylvania daily paper liked to play a little game when he found one of these no-noes—the game of answering headlines written in imperative form. Here are some of his gems that appeared in *Editor & Publisher* magazine:

PROPOSE THEORY ON ENIGMA	(You give me the enigma, I'll try it.)
PLAN PARADE ON HALLOWEEN	(I think it would be better if it were planned before Halloween.)
NAB YOUTHS FOR STEALING MOTORCYCLES	(I'm not sure I could catch them.)
FIND MAN GUILTY OF ROBBERY, ASSAULT	(I can't. I wasn't on the jury—and therefore don't know the facts.)
CONFIRM, PROMOTE GENERAL JONES	(This is beyond my province.)
BOMB STRATEGIC BRIDGE	(I did, in that nasty war—let someone else do the dirty work.)

| LAUNCH FIRST OF TV SERIES | (Would that I could, then I might make a lot of money and get out of the newsroom.) |

Completion

Now, at last, your final draft really is completed. You've checked it several times, and you have edited and reedited until it is as clear, concise, and carefully written as you can make it. It is ready to be released. (Chapter 8 presents the basic rules for submitting copy—the mechanics that will put it into an acceptable format. Knowing this format can make a difference in whether the story gets across the editor's desk and into print or whether it is tossed into a very large wastebasket because it looks unprofessional.)

Obituaries

There is one other news release you may need to know how to write—an *obituary*, or *obit*. If someone in your organization dies, you may be the person who sends out the information to business journals and papers or to other special publications.

An obituary is news—straight news. The time factor is important, so you can't procrastinate in sending the information—in a news release or a fact sheet—to appropriate publications. Remember that, because this is straight news, there is no place for editorializing. Often the person who has died is of such importance that editorial comment is warranted, but leave that to the editorial-page writers. Emotional writing has no place here, either. An obituary is a brief, factual news report about what happened and about the accomplishments that the person achieved.

Content

The following list gives the appropriate information about an individual to include in an obituary. (If possible, include all of the first five items in the lead.)

- Full name
- Occupation
- Date of death
- Cause of death (if family approves)

- Age
- Date, time, and place of services
- Noteworthy information about the deceased and his or her family
- Short paragraph about education, if appropriate
- Facts about business affiliations, church, and club memberships
- Survivors' names, with spouse leading the list (if a woman, first, maiden, and married—use "Janet Brown Jones" not "Mrs. John Jones"), followed by children, then parents, siblings, and grand-children
- Details regarding memorials, if relevant

An example of an obituary is included in Appendix A.

## 7

Feature-News Stories

*How to write features
that can build an image
and possibly present only
one side of the story—yours*

If the building your
organization is housed
in burns down, that is a
news story. When,
where, and why is reported.

How people feel about
the burning, is a feature
story.

Newspaper features concern
themselves with
anything and everything
that has emotional appeal
for readers.

A "Dog Bites Man" Story

Every journalism student and newspaper reporter knows the timeworn maxim: No "dog bites man" stories! There also is an old, old story about a go-getter reporter, a newly hired young man, who laid that canon firmly to rest. Upon being told by his city editor that there is little news value in a dog biting a man, but big news in a man biting a dog, the reporter exclaimed, "I can get you that story!"

"What!—A man biting a dog?" asked the editor. "Yes, sir," replied the novice reporter. "He does it often."

The city editor laughed, wondering if he had made a mistake in hiring the young man. However, the reporter brought in a story about an old-fashioned veterinarian who bobbed puppies' tails by biting them off. That young reporter was a born feature-news writer.

Differences between Straight News and Feature News

An old-time reporter describes the differences between straight news and feature news: News stories provide the facts for a person's mind. But feature stories provide the human interest for his heart.

Jules Loh, a renowned reporter, writing in *Reporting/Writing from Front Row Seats* describes the differences this way: "A news story lets the reader know what happened; a feature story tells him what it was like to have been there."

A newspaper *feature story* is at heart a news story. It reports facts—the more the better. It can include opinion, but always remember that personal opinion isn't fact. Newspaper news stories must be printed *now*—today. A news story cannot be held over until it is convenient—or until there is space—to print it. It is immediately used, or it is dead.

Although a feature story may also inform, expand the facts given in a news story, and offer background information, the timeliness of its information is not vital. Usually, it can be be printed a day or two, or even weeks and months, later.

Feature News as Publicity

For the very reason that time is not such a critical factor, feature-news stories are excellent publicity vehicles. If your goal is to keep your organization's name before the public, in addition to sending out occasional releases of special news items you will want to employ the use of feature stories.

Because features are more appealing to readers, publications are depending more and more upon them to attract and hold readers. This means that the market for your publicity is greatly expanded, and chances are considerably higher for the use of your publicity features. Use of features for publicity purposes is fruitful because they can help project to the public a favorable image of your organization and the people in it.

Advantages of Feature News

A feature story that shows your organization as made up of real people will do more to create a favorable image than any number of news stories. The first letters in the term *publicity features—p* and *f*—could stand for the two most important ingredients in a feature story:

P = People—real people
F = Facts—loads of them

Even when your organization's self-interest is your primary concern, it should be a secondary consideration in writing a feature-news release. Think first of what will be of interest to the public and to the newspaper's readers, or your release will never make the paper.

You may have noticed that Sunday editions of large metropolitan newspapers usually consist largely of feature-news material. Because Sunday papers are considerably larger than weekday editions, editors have much earlier deadlines for many of the sections—in some cases a week or two in advance—to get them out in time. So features are used. Only the strictly news sections of Sunday papers must adhere to daily deadline schedules. And even in these sections, features are used to fill in last-minute news holes.

In addition to the accomplishment factor of getting your feature story printed, you may enjoy the added, purely personal satisfaction that rarely happens to publicity practitioners—the pleasure of occasionally seeing your byline in print.

The "What" of a Feature-News Story

Feature-news stories deal with human interest and emotions. They satisfy curiosity or arouse it. They may provide a chuckle. They can give little-known information about famous people or provide news about little-known people who are interesting because of their experiences, jobs, or personalities. Business, management, travel, science, social problems, and practical guidance are a few of the many popular feature-news topics.

Features have a style of their own. A feature story is like a short story, and we read both for the same reasons—to share the experiences and emotions of other people and to reach out from our own world to someone else's.

Feature Syndicates

Some columns in newspapers are *syndicated features*. They may be written by people whose bylines have become known to readers all over the country, distributed by a feature service to many newspapers and thereby cutting each newspaper's cost to only a fraction of the full payment to the columnist. Many of these writers look for and appreciate submissions of feature material or ideas. Keep alert for such columnists, and add them to your media lists.

The Emotional Appeal of Feature Stories

In order to involve a reader's emotions and develop human interest, a feature story appeals to the five senses: touch, taste, smell, sound, and sight.

Ernest Hemingway described the best feature writing when he said the following:

> The good and the bad, the ecstasy, the remorse and sorrow, the people and the places and how the weather was. If you can get that so you can give that to people, then you are a writer. [You are the best of feature writers!]

Events and decisions reported in a feature story are not necessarily important in themselves; what is important is the human appeal it possesses.

The "How" of a Feature-News Story

There are two ways to get your feature story written. The first is to get in touch with a reporter who has covered your organization in the past and try to interest him or her in writing the story. There is high incentive for this option: If the reporter *agrees* to write the story, it means that he or she has cleared it with the editor; odds that the story will run are about as high as they can get. Using this method, however, also means that the story will have limited circulation; it will run only in that reporter's publication and cannot be circulated to other publicity outlets.

Your second option is the do-it-yourself method. You write it and you submit it.

Either way, the biggest part of the work remains for you to do. You must dig out the information for the article and come up with several angles for presenting it.

The Reporter as Writer

If you elect to work with a reporter, try to choose one who knows your organization and who has worked with you previously. Send your ideas, written in outline or descriptive form, along with an attached note stating that you will be in touch by telephone to discuss it with him or her. When you phone, be prepared to emphasize pertinent points or to explore with the reporter other directions in which the story might be directed. Be tactful and courteous, with no hint of demand or insistence. In other words, treat the reporter in a way that will make him or her want to "do business" with you.

You as Writer

If you decide to write the story yourself, be aware that there is no set formula for writing a good feature-news story. There are no rules as there are for writing straight news. Prize-winning Associated Press European correspondent, Hugh Mulligan, described the enigma in *Reporting/Writing from Front Row Seats:*

> When it gets down to actual writing, most of us, even after all these years, still don't know whether to head up the street or down the street. Whether to start with a note or an anecdote; whether to begin with something new and then work into the background or lay down an orderly chronological tale in the manner of a crime story in the British press, which always starts with the constable and his torch going down Grosvenor Road and finding a body.
>
> There are no writing cookbooks that can tell you precisely how many quotes and how many anecdotes one must blend and stir to come up with, say a humorous story, compared with an informative piece.

Tips for the Do-It-Yourself Road

You should know the important differences that set feature newspaper stories apart from straight news stories. Following are some of those differences:

1. Feature news is *not* written in inverted pyramid style. Because a feature plays up the human side of the news, its style is closer to that of a short story than to that of straight news.
2. The five Ws lead gives way to an opening that, in some way, will arrest the reader's attention.
3. A straight-news story is never written in the first-person singular, but sometimes a feature writer does use the word *I*. In using the first person, however, you must still remain as objective as possible.

4. Feature leads follow no set pattern. You may begin your story with any of the following items:

   - An eye-catching quote, as with a news story, to create interest and spirit.
   - An anecdote.
   - An arresting short sentence that makes its point quickly.
   - Two contrasting statements that seem contradictory.
   - A pure description, a word picture.
   - A question, also as in a straight-news story.

5. Feature writing is similar in many ways to fiction writing, with a strong opening that catches the reader's interest and builds to a strong, often surprising, close.

6. The first responsibility of a newspaper feature story is to provide facts. Jam-pack it with facts, but adorn them, dress them up, make them appealing and attractive with very alive, three-dimensional people. Make the facts come to life with the real experiences of real people. Remember your memory joggers—P and F—that stand for *people* and *facts* and also for your ultimate goal, a *publicity feature*.

Reader Attention

Hugh Mulligan says there is no set pattern for beginning a feature story. But there is one "decree": The lead must grab the reader's attention. In other words, good feature writers "bait their hooks" in their leads, then follow up with the facts (the five Ws) later in the story.

As with news stories, remember to work in your organization's name early in the story and wherever and as often as is appropriate, so that you will achieve your publicity objective.

In a straight-news story, you *must* be objective. You may not insert your opinion into such a release. As a newspaper feature writer, you may offer a decided point of view, and you may present only one side of a story. There is no requirement that the feature story must be objective. And you do not have to strive for that lean, concise writing style that marks a straight-news story. A feature story's chief purpose is to entertain or instruct; so, like a short story, it must read smoothly, build in intensity, and carry the reader along right to an end that is a climax.

Tips for Using Adjectives

The late Frederick Othman of United Press International shared his knowledge of newswriting back in 1945. It stands as true today as it did then:

> When you use an adjective, use a concrete one. "Beautiful," "ugly," "very" mean little. If a girl looks like Lana Turner that means plenty and there's no reason why you shouldn't say so. If a gent wears a dark brown coat, say it's chocolate-colored. Not only is that descriptive, but it gets food into the story. Any word connoting food adds interest value.

Saul Pett of APNewsfeatures adds this:

> The reader wants to know more about a man's personality than that he is "mild-mannered," "quiet," or "unassuming." Willie Sutton, the bank robber, was mild-mannered, quiet, unassuming. So was Dr. Albert Schweitzer.
>
> > He was "forceful." How? Who says so?
> > She was "charming." To whom? How?
> > She was "chic." How? Describe.
> > She was "gracious." How, please?

Joseph Pulitzer's Instructions for Writing a Feature

According to Michael and Edwin Emery's The Press and America: An Interpretive History, in the last year of his life, Joseph Pulitzer sent the following guidelines to one of his New York editors:

> Apropos of enclosed clipping from the London Times showing that a feature article is properly worked up. Pick out the most interesting cases. What were these homicides? Who committed them? What was the motive? Give a table of motives, of social rank, of age, of nationality, etc. But print the facts more reliably, more strikingly than would the magazines. But don't print it from the standpoint of mere sensationalism, but rather from the moral point of view. It should be a thoughtful article with a great moral to it. Compare the figure with Paris, and with London, and with other great European cities. Allude also to the administration of justice and the methods of dealing with murder cases in the different countries, with statistics of indictments, convictions, executions and failure to punish or to solve murder mysteries.

Rewrites

You may find that, even with all these tips and techniques about what a feature is and how to write it, the story just isn't coming together (and it happens to the best writers in the business). When this happens, stop and rewrite it. Learn to stop fighting to make it come together early on. Chances are high that, when you begin to write it again, it will jell nicely and quickly.

Accuracy Check

When you've finished your final draft, you will wish to hone your copy to a fine point. Just as with any information you send as a publicity release, be sure of your facts and figures. Take care that names are spelled correctly, and that all quotes are accurate. Be sure that your feature story is neatly typed, using the same mechanical rules for setting up the pages in a straight-news release (Chapter 8), except for one. Because this is a feature, timeliness is not critical. Therefore, don't indicate immediacy in the release timing line. Use "For Release at Your Convenience" rather than "For Immediate Release."

Editor's Standards

The points by which an editor judges and ultimately uses your publicity feature article include the following:

- Interest value. If you are deeply interested in the subject, chances are that your interest will show through and intrigue the reader.
- Exact facts. The more the better, but be sure they are *interesting* facts, or facts presented in an interesting way. Statistics are facts, but seldom are they interesting until you have given them some perspective.
- Strong, moving verbs. Use as many as you can, and cut down on adjectives.
- Adherence to basic newspaper style and writing rules.
- Anecdotes. Use several of those lively little stories, often of an amusing nature, which help to flesh out a fact, an incident, or a personality.

Sources for Feature Material

An alert person with a sense of news value and an understanding of how to write in an interesting manner finds feature stories everywhere. Spotting stories is elementary once you are tuned in to look for them and to know *what* to look for.

Businesses are rich sources for feature stories. Among other things, you can write about their employees, customers, services, or products.

The history of an organization is excellent material. You can trace its growth, but it must read like a story. Use quotes and anecdotes; make it come alive through the people who have been involved with it throughout the years.

Biographical material also is a source. In it you can emphasize a person's character, activities, and achievements with the organization. The subject could be an important officer or manager or a little-known employee or volunteer.

"How-to" information is high on the list of readers' choices. As the name implies, the article gives advice to the reader about how your organization or someone in it overcame an obstacle, achieved a goal, or handled a problem. The information must be factual and accurate. No fiction here.

Background-news features enlarge upon a straight-news event. Suppose, for instance, your group staged an event (a lecture by a prominent speaker, a fund-raiser for a community project, a workshop, or a seminar). You can find great feature material about the background and business life of the speaker; about previous work with a community group and how your people have assisted it in the past; or about an unknown but humorous incident that happened before or during the event.

"Fillers"

There is no need for a feature to be long. The most widely read stories in any newspaper are the one-or two-paragraph human-interest *fillers*. It is safe to say that *all* newspapers use fillers and even safer to state that they never have enough *good* ones.

If yours is a serious, ongoing publicity program looking for additional means to get your organization's name before the public, don't overlook fillers. Some of the most productive publicity comes from fillers. Longer news stories and full-length features are a publicist's dream come true, but with today's hectic life-styles, how many people actually read through those longer articles? Fillers—showing that the people in your organization are real and human—are also priceless because they are so well read.

A filler is a very short, interesting, and perhaps humorous news item that an editor can use to fill space below or between longer articles. Its chances of being used far outnumber straight or longer feature-news stories because there never seem to be enough fillers when an editor puts a page together. If it includes a chuckle, its odds for being used increase even more.

An example of a filler comes from The Associated Press, repeated by Singer Education & Training Products in a sound filmstrip:

> *Operations at the Cat's Paw shoe heel plant were brought to a sudden halt Wednesday night by an alley cat.*
>
> *The feline's nine lives ended in a 13,000-volt flash when it fell from a ledge into the plant's circuit breakers, knocking out power for two work shifts.*

Letters to the Editor

Every person who advises and instructs about garnering publicity warns his or her students to leave editorials alone. Editorials are the province of the newspaper itself to express the paper's own thinking and recommendations. Yet one of the easier forms for getting a name before the public (and of reaping the fruits of publicity) is actually a kind of editorial: a letter to the editor, published on the *op-ed* page (the page opposite the editorial page). Call it a do-it-yourself editorial.

Research shows that letters from readers are widely read and that they are excellent devices for commenting on some item in the news or for making your point. There is higher readership of letters than of guest editorials or guest opinion columns.

Keep your letters short and to the point, and address them to the attention of the editor. They should be clear, concise, and well written. They should not be small-minded personality tirades or recitations of petty issues or opinions.

The most effective letters to the editor are written by respected, well-known local leaders. If you do not wish to sign such a letter, enlist the help of someone who is well known in your organization or someone whose title demands respect.

The Formula

A simple formula for writing one of these do-it-yourself editorials—a letter to the editor—is as follows:

- State your opinion.
- Give facts to support it.
- Suggest some action.

For example, present a fact showing a need for attention. Give two, three, four, or more facts with supporting evidence. Finally, restate your opinion and the action you suggest; or, state the intended conclusion you hope the reader has reached, and suggest some type of action.

Gene Bullard's Rules

After 30 years of writing letters to the editor—and getting a goodly number published—Gene Bullard of Dallas, Texas, knows a thing or two about what gets an editor's attention. He says, in *The Dallas Morning News*, "I learned how *not* to get published by reading the letters for years and years. You write a letter too long, your letter is not well constructed, your letter is not fair— especially if it's mean-spirited in opposition to the publication. Like, 'You've got a dumb, conservative paper.'" Bullard also says he has figured out that it can't hurt to include a clever line or two for the editors to pull out as a headline.

The First Op-Ed Page

In a recent letter to the editor, signed by Charles M. Antin, *The New York Times* was gently chided for giving an impression that it had created the first op-ed page. The writer explained that, "the idea was conceived by Herbert Bayard Swope, an editor at *The World* newspaper in the 1920s, who used the name Op. Ed." The writer then quotes Swope, writing to newspaperman Gene Fowler, from *The World of Swope* by E. J. Kahn, Jr.

> For a long time while I was on the outside, and later when I was the City Editor, I would notice, from time to time, that the opinion stories which had crept in, in spite of our hard and fast principle of having little or no opinion in our news columns, had been dominantly interesting . . . nothing is more interesting than opinion when opinion is interesting, so I devised a method of cleaning off the page opposite the editorial, which became the most important in America . . . and thereupon I decided to print opinions, ignoring facts.

The only difference from op-ed pages then and now, says the letter writer, is that Swope did not print unsolicited letters from the general public; he rounded up big names to write the letters instead.

Rewards for Bad Writing

Now, after all your efforts—and success—in turning out a top-rated feature story, it's fun to know that there is an annual contest that recognizes *bad writing!* It is the Bulwer-Lytton Fiction Contest, founded by Scott Rice, an English professor at San Jose State University. The contest is named for Edward George Earle Bulwer-Lytton, a contemporary of Charles Dickens, who began an 1830 novel with the phrase, "It was a dark and stormy night . . . ."

A recent year's winning entry began, "The notes blatted skyward as the sun rose over the Canada geese, feathered rumps mooning the day, webbed appendages frantically pedaling unseen bicycles in their search for sustenance, driven by cruel Nature's Maxim, 'ya wanna eat, ya gotta work,' and at last I knew Pittsburgh." Another winner, in the Purple Prose category, began, "The sun rose slowly, like a fiery furball coughed up uneasily onto a sky-blue carpet by a giant unseen cat."

Somehow, now we can better understand all those admonitions about cutting down on the use of adjectives, using strong, moving verbs, and loading the piece with facts.

8

Copy Preparation for News Releases

How to accomplish the nuts-and-bolts mechanics of news-release copy

Daily Word Deluge

"If you think the editor sometimes makes a mistake in what he gives you to read, you ought to see the mess of stuff from which he saves you." That remark dates back a few years, to a time before today's multitude of information sources existed.

On the average day, a metropolitan daily newspaper receives about 8 *million* words of copy from wire services, feature syndicates, correspondents, and special and staff writers. Add to that all the press releases—for which there is no known word count—that a newspaper receives. Then consider that there are only a total of 600,000 words in the English language, and the more than 8 million words of copy take on some meaning. Of all that copy, a metropolitan daily can use only about 100,000 words of reading matter a day.

Professional Appearance

The first and major means a news editor uses to quickly reduce the flood is to eliminate as many publicity releases as possible. That first run-by is based on appearance alone—difficult-to-read typeface, sloppy typing, overused typewriter or printer ribbon, handwritten copy, and anything that bespeaks nonprofessionalism can disqualify a news release. The editor simply does not have time to read them all.

Competition for space is intense, and there are an infinite number of other things that can happen to kill your news story, which means that you need everything possible going for you. It is essential, therefore, that news releases give a professional appearance.

Appearance also is important because it affects an editor's reaction to the *content* of your release. The look of your news release is unspoken testimony to the care and concern given in your preparation of the story. Equally harmful, a sloppy, carelessly prepared release tends to create an impression of incompetence for the entire organization. Ultimately, a professional-looking release reflects well on you and on your organization.

The bottom line is that you are expected to be an expert in producing technically and mechanically correct releases, no matter how much or how little experience you have in producing publicity. Because publicity is nine-tenths *written* copy, this chapter takes you step by step through the processes of generating professional *hard copy* news releases. You may not be an old hand at writing news, but if your release is typed, neatly presented, following accepted format, and easy to read, it will stand a far greater chance of being used. In other words, make sure your release is user-friendly!

Appearance Guidelines

Points to remember are listed here:

- Neatness counts. *No typos, misspellings, or cross-outs.* No excuses, please! If your typewriter or computer is in the shop for repairs, that's your problem. Borrow or rent one. The editor doesn't want to hear your apologies any more than you would care to read a line in the newspaper saying, "Sorry, this story in today's paper is handwritten because our equipment is being repaired." If you use a computer or word processor, be sure your printer is set for letter-quality type and has a new ribbon.
- Do not use "exotic" typefaces. Script and italics are harder to read—and to edit—so an editor is more likely to toss such copy when his or her time is critically limited.
- Use business-size, 8½-by-11-inch paper. Do not use onion-skin, colored, or erasable paper.
- Keep handy a current directory or list of officers, board members, executives, and employees. If you represent a club, include members and volunteers. Your directory should include anyone and everyone who is part of your group. Use the directory to check spelling and residence

locality and to have addresses and phone numbers handy if a reporter or editor calls to follow up on an angle of your release.

Tools of the Trade

Items to keep close by for quick reference are as follows:

- A good dictionary, for word spellings and meanings.
- A thesaurus, to give you synonyms for words you repeat too often within a release.
- *The UPI Stylebook, The Associated Press Stylebook and Libel Manual,* or the individual style sheets from the newspapers you service. Use these to check whether to abbreviate or spell out such things as the name of a state, an avenue, or a street; how to present figures; and so on.
- *The Elements of Style.* This will serve as a guide to correct language usage. See Appendix E for ordering information and for a more complete description of each manual.

Preparation of News-Release Copy

The following are guidelines and instructions for preparing your news releases. The format guidelines, listed first, give general information and tips; the format instructions present specific steps in the actual typing of the copy.

Format Guidelines

Your typewriter, word processor, or computer printer must be in first-class shape and your typing must be neat and accurate. Observe the following guidelines for preparing your final copy:

- Type the release on your organization's letterhead. If there is no official stationery, it is not difficult to create your own. Using white bond paper, paste the logo of your organization, with address and phone number, at the top. Some releases include the word *News* or *News Release* printed at or near the top of the page, but that is not a requirement. Take your paper to a quick-print shop and photocopy as many copies as you will need. (A word of caution: Be sure the copy machine has adequate toner to produce top quality reproductions.) You can also use plain, white 8½-by-11-inch paper and type all the necessary information onto it.

- Type on only one side of the paper.
- Leave ample margins. Leave 1½ inches for the side and bottom margins. (If your release is used, copyeditors will use the blank spaces for notations.)
- If possible, give each newspaper in the same geographical area a release with a different lead. Each paper will be more likely to use your copy if there is a local angle in the lead and if local names are used.
- Never end a page so that a part of a sentence or a single word ends a page or heads the next page. These are called *widows* and *orphans*, and allowing one to slip through does not indicate a professional appearance. If possible, do not end a page in the middle of a paragraph. If an entire paragraph will not fit at the end of a page, start it at the beginning of a new page. If this leaves an unattractive amount of space along the bottom margin, drop the entire news story copy (beneath the summary headline) to compensate.
- If the story requires more than two typed pages, read it over carefully and do a little more editing. Writing concisely, in a simple understandable style, takes effort and time. Thoreau is often quoted as having said, "Not that the story need be long, but it will take a long while to make it short." Benjamin Franklin said it a little differently (in a letter to a friend): "If I had more time, I'd write a shorter letter."
- If you are sending more than one copy, run off the copies on your printer or word processor or have a good, clear, sharp original copied commercially.
- Use paper clips to fasten the pages together. Do not staple them.
- Be sure to keep a dated copy in your files.

Format Instructions

The following instructions will help you type your release in the proper format. Use Figures 8.1 and 8.2 as guides. Instructions 1 through 6 pertain only to information that must be included above the actual news release copy. Instructions 7 through 10 apply to the format for the lead and body copy of your release.

1. If you are not using letterhead or "instantly created letterhead," type and center (at the top of the page) the following information about your organization:

- Name
- Address
- Telephone number

2. Type the contact information. Immediately below the letterhead or typed organization heading, at the left margin, skip a line or two and type the contact information. Align it at the left margin, and align each telephone number under the respective names.
   - Type the word "Contacts," then your name, then space down one line.
   - Type your telephone number (if it is different from the one listed in the letterhead logo), then space down two lines.
   - Type the name of an alternate contact: a responsible, knowledgeable board or staff member, then space down one line.
   - Type the alternate contact's telephone number.

3. Summary headline. Space down two lines and insert, flush left under the contact information, a summary headline. If the headline runs to two lines, space down only one line for the second line of the headline. This headline summarizes the story for the editor, with the purpose of enticing him or her to read it.

   Newspaper headlines are no longer written in all caps because that style is more difficult to read. Type your headline in upper and lower case. Don't expect your headline to be used. The editor or copy desk editor will write the newspaper's own headline if the story is used.

4. Type the release timing line. This information will go in the upper-right-hand side of the paper, below the organization's letterhead and opposite the contact information. Be sure the release information is the same for all newspapers or for other media to which this specific release goes. Use whichever release timing line is appropriate:
   - For Immediate Release
   - Release at Your Convenience
   - For Release on (give a specific release date). Whenever possible, try to avoid locking an editor into a specific date.

5. Indicate if the story is an exclusive. An exclusive story should be marked as such at the top of the copy. Any exclusive must be honored. Let the editor know by typing the word "exclusive" in capital letters above the release timing line. Then, don't give the story to any other news source. (This means television and radio, too.)

6. Type the mailing date (optional). There are two schools of thought about whether releases should or should not carry a mailing date. Many professional publicists do not include the mailing date because a slow mail delivery can work against the release being used. (It may appear to be outdated.) If you choose to include the mailing date, it should be at the top, directly beneath the letterhead logo or organization heading. Whether or not you use it on your news release, be sure that you note the mailing date on your file copy, for future reference.

Instructions for News-Release Lead and Body Copy

7. Insert a dateline. Type the dateline flush left (not indented as for all the following paragraphs). The dateline is actually only an identification of the city and state from which the story originates; it usually does not contain a date. There is no need for a dateline on releases that are distributed only to local newspapers.

The word *dateline* comes from past years when transmission of news was slower (particularly from outside the newspaper's immediate coverage area) and when newspapers did list dates along with the city of origin.

The first paragraph (lead) immediately follows the dateline. Indent the following paragraphs of the lead and body copy five spaces.

8. Indicate when the story runs more than a page. If the story runs to more than one page, type the following at the bottom center of each page (except for the last page):

— more —

9. At the top of the second page and on each succeeding page, type a line using a shortened version of your summary headline, and follow it with the page number.

10. Signify the end of the release copy. At the end of the copy, center and type the following:

# # #

or

— 30 —

Figure 8.1 shows placement of the information you must include.

FIGURE 8.1   Sample Format for a Newspaper Release
(When no letterhead is available, use plain white business-size paper.)

PLATT SERVICES, INC. ·

1234 West First Road
Abbotsville, Rhode Island, 85123
123/456-7890

Contacts: Jane Jones
123/666-7878

For Immediate Release

Stephen Sullivan
123/456-7890

**Tax accounting firm adds new service for
nonprofits; can be boon to local economy**

ABBOTSVILLE, R.I. — Platt Services Inc., a company previously known

only for its accounting and tax functions, is introducing an added service

that will search out grants donors and prepare proposals for area nonprofit

organizations.

The service is believed to be a first, says Gerald G. Gannon, owner

of Platt Services. "Now that government grant dollars have been slashed

so drastically, nonprofit groups must compete for private dollars, and many

don't have the expertise and experience required to produce these high-

stakes grants proposals."

— more —

FIGURE 8.1   (*continued*)

Platt offers new service for nonprofits—2-2-2

According to Gannon, Platt's new service covers researching foundation and corporate funding sources that are receptive to individual nonprofit's special services; gathering supporting data and documents; then writing a proposal that is well conceived and well documented and presents the group's special needs in an appealing, attractive and appropriate manner.

"The goal of this new service," states Gannon, "is to increase funding to Abbotsville-area nonprofits, thereby increasing the level of services at a time when needs are dramatically increasing yet funding is being slashed to the bone."

It is not generally recognized, says Gannon, that increased grants monies coming to local nonprofit groups can be a substantial stimulus to the local economy. There is, he says, a three-time turnover of the monies before they leave the area.

Platt Services, Inc. was established in 1977 in Groveton, N.J. and moved to Abbotsville in 1983. It serves clients within a four-county area.

— more —

FIGURE 8.1 (*continued*)

Platt offers new service for nonprofits—3-3-3

    Nonprofit groups interested in this service should contact Ms.

Joanna Johnson, who heads up the function for Platt Services, at

123/456-7890.

\# \# \#

Copy-Preparation Tips

The following items are worth noting:

- Never trust your typist—particularly if the typist is you! (People tend to see what they think they wrote when they try to proof their own work.) *Proofread each page.*

    Typos don't do much for your story in the newspaper, but they often become the laugh of the day in newsrooms around the country. This is one that appeared in the *Fort Worth Star-Telegram:* "At a busy airport terminal, a harried passenger stepped up to the ticket counter and inquired, 'How long a hangover will I have in Chicago?'" Here are some other "slips" from *Reader's Digest:*

  - The pilot apparently lost control moments after ouchdown.
  - An Israeli bus driver suffered minor injuries when his but was hit by a firebomb.
  - We will widow-shop and exercise.

- Never, *never,* play favorites among newspapers, editors, or columnists. Be impartial when there is more than one paper in an area. Mail your releases so that each has an equal time break in using them.
- Never, *never,* **never** double-plant. This means never place the same story with more than one person on the same publication.

- Check that all names are proper, given names. Do not use nicknames, even when writing about children.
- If you include a date, such as Thursday, October 3, check that Thursday *is* October 3. Also check that the exact hour for an event is given.
- Check and recheck spelling of all names in your copy. If the correct spelling is unusual, write "CQ" over the word. People—other than child abusers, drug purveyors, and bad-check writers—nearly always like to see their names in print. The newspaper likes to use names because a person whose name appears in the paper (mentioned in a complimentary way and spelled correctly) will buy several copies.
- Do not break and hyphenate words at the end of a line. It's not a good policy and hyphenation errors can be disastrous, as happened in the following instance, told in *Word Perfect 5.0 Desktop Publishing in Style*, by Daniel Will-Harris:

Throughout his long career, he was known as the-rapist of the stars!!!

"Therapist of the stars" was the original intent of the writer.

- If there is any information in the release that is technical or controversial or that could create a problem for your organization, and if you are an appointee or staffer, get your boss or an officer to initial a file copy of each release. Don't hesitate to check your copy with your sources.
- If you have any question whatsoever about the meaning of a word in your release, look up its meaning and spelling in the dictionary.
- Address your news-release copy to the appropriate editor. Even if you personally deliver it, address it to the proper person so that it can be left if he or she is not available at the time you are there.
- If you include a note, write it on a separate sheet of paper and attach it with a paper clip.
- If you attach a list of names, paste together the pages (if there is more than one) so there is no danger of their getting separated. Then fold the long sheet to match the size of a single sheet and attach it to the release with paper clips.
- Don't expect the editor to rewrite (although he or she probably will).
- Remember the KISS aphorism: Keep it Short, Simple. You soon will perceive that it is a lot more gratifying to see a brief item in print, with all its essential information intact, than to commiserate over a beautiful, long story that found its resting place in a wastebasket.

- Better never than late! (As stated in the second "commandment" in Chapter 5: "Thou shalt not procrastinate.") Use of your release could hang on its timeliness. Routine material should be in editors' hands at least 24 hours prior to the day of publication. If at all possible, get the release into the hands of recipients one to two weeks in advance of an event or specified release date. If the release is for use in a Sunday or weekend edition, it must be sent at least one week, possibly two, in advance.

- Be sure you keep a dated copy of your release in your files so that you can answer questions if you are called or so that you can compare the original with the final, printed version and thereby learn from it.

News Over the Telephone

You won't have anything going for you if you try to phone in your story. One of the worst ways to get along with newspeople is to ask them to do your job for you. Even if they have the time, phoning in copy substantially increases chances for misunderstandings, misspellings, and possibly the miscarriage of your efforts.

If ever, for any reason, you *must* transmit information over the phone, such as to correct an error noted after sending out the release, time the call away from the paper's crucial deadlines. For afternoon or evening papers, call in the afternoon; for morning papers, morning is a better time.

Suppose, however, that all your news releases have been written and sent out. You've followed all the rules; you've mailed or carried in your releases instead of phoning them in. You are proud of the job you've done, but *suddenly*—the event is canceled! (Or, there's a change in speakers or dates.)

What do you do? Very simply, immediately notify the newspaper. This *is* the time to phone.

If there is no crisis situation, however, please don't call to find out when your story was or will be used. (Many an editor has had such calls, with the caller saying, "Oh, I don't read your paper. . . . " Even if you don't say exactly that, the implication is there. That is no way to get along with the press.)

Fact Sheets

If, in the beginning, the writing of a news release baffles and intimidates you, you may wish to use a fact sheet as an alternative. Use a fact sheet only if you wish to count on the editor or a reporter having time and inclination to write the story from it.

Chapter 10 includes information on what should be included in a fact sheet and how to prepare one. A sample fact sheet is included in Appendix A. Note, however, that your odds of achieving a news story from a fact sheet in any given newspaper are substantially reduced, even if for only one reason—the shortage of time and staff to write it.

Clipping Services

The warning has been made several times—*do not* ask an editor or a reporter to send you a copy of the news item you sent to him or her. If all of your releases are local, you will be able to watch for and clip publicity stories as they appear.

However, if your media list is not confined to your immediate locale, your organization may wish to subscribe to a clipping service. If one exists in your area, you will find it listed in the Yellow Pages. (The major national clipping bureaus and their addresses are listed in Appendix E.)

9

Publicity Photos
Why a picture truly is worth hundreds of news-release words

The Power of Visual Images

Pick a subject—a space launch, the exodus of Kurds and other minority groups from northern Iraq, the plight of starving children in Africa, a presidential news conference—and your first response will be a visual one.

Nobody remembers much of what was written or said during student demonstrations in China in 1989, but some of the images are unforgettable: a young man standing against a line of tanks and unarmed students resisting the military. For the 1989 San Francisco earthquake that occurred during a World Series game, people may remember images of a city in mass confusion. Those images, remembered and reprinted, may bring feelings of fear, anger, sadness, helplessness or any number of other reactions to people all over this country.

People use pictures as a necessary reference, and they need that visual reference to many news stories. Kenneth Byerly, in *Community Journalism*, quotes an editor of a weekly newspaper: "If names make news, so do faces. . . . And a news photographer uses a camera just as a reporter or publicity writer uses a typewriter."

Someone once kidded that photography is a snap judgment! Don't laugh. That's what this chapter is all about: how to get your photos past the critical eye and the harried snap judgment of an editor.

Instant Impact

A photo often is more valuable than a story in transmitting your message. The greatest advantage of photographs over the printed word is that they make their point in an instant. They illustrate and clarify a news story and often improve the impact. They can create curiosity or pull the reader to a new view of the familiar. They can and should create readership, and that is a responsibility a newspaper doesn't take lightly.

Advantages of the Publicity Photo

Whether the publicity photo is sent as a stand-alone separate release or as part of your written release, it is important to your publicity efforts for a number of reasons:

- It can graphically describe and show what words cannot.
- It can attract readers' eyes to your news or feature article.
- It cannot be edited, other than by *cropping* (trimming edges to fit space).
- It will seldom be missed by a reader, and your news story can be "read" at a glance.
- It can be run with a publicity "plug" for your organization, when an editor has no space for a printed release but is still short of eye-appealing material with which to dress up pages.

The Photo Editor's Job

A photo editor is primarily interested in a photo with the following qualities:

- Storytelling ability
- Technical quality of the print
- Complete and accurate caption information

Keep in mind that a photo editor of a newspaper receives hundreds of photos every day. On average, he or she can use only one of every 10 photos that crosses his or her desk. Your job is to see that your photo is good enough to compete for that valuable news space. Where do all the others go? Right! In the wastebasket. (Don't expect the photos you send to be returned, and do not ask for them.)

Your Job

You do not need to be a photographer in order to submit photos for a news release. You do not even need to know how cameras work. There are some things, however, that you must know about newspaper photos.

First, and probably most important, you are the one who must *plan* the photo. Even when the publication sends its own photographer, it is your job to contact the editor in advance to "sell" the merit of the photo assignment. If you are using your own photographer, do not expect him or her to plan the picture or to know the purpose for the picture. Plan your photos well. When possible, have a conference with the editor and photographer in advance.

Here are some tips on planning your photos:

- Write outlines of the pictures.
- List the props necessary for each.
- Plan for each photo to tell a story, and make a blueprint.
- Be original.

In addition to the above information, keep newspaper space limitations in mind. Pictures for a *photo spread,* in which several pictures appear, almost always are made by the newspaper's own photographers. However, space is so precious that a photo spread is highly unusual and would have to be of an event of major significance—a highly publicized charity event or a social, business, or celebrity event involving nationally or widely known people. Seldom would a for-profit organization qualify for a photo spread. However, sponsorship of a major event often produces caption credits.

Types of Photos

Most local dailies and weeklies with limited photo staffs will expect you to provide all photos. These could be of a woman selling the major tickets to a charity affair; of a presentation of an award winner; or of any other publicity photo opportunities; or they could be standard head-and-shoulders photos or *mug shots* (head only) of your organization's newly announced executive or newly selected committee chairperson.

The Right Photographer

Maury Falstein, a newspaper photo editor of *The Chicago Sun-Times* for more than 35 years, described at one of his lectures how an excellent shot was turned into a second-rate shot by a photographer who didn't recognize the human-interest factor or understand its value in newspaper photography:

> *I once watched an emotional tear-jerking reunion take place in Union Station while a photographer waited on the sidelines to set up his picture.*

Then he posed the new arrival with relatives kissing her on each cheek. Instead of capturing the realism of their event, he played the role of a director restaging life in a stereotyped pattern.

Technical Aspects

Maury Falstein gave the following advice on the technical aspects of taking pictures.

> *I realize that much thought goes into the planning of a publicity campaign. But when it comes to pictures, too many persons are inclined to let the camera do all the thinking.*
>
> *To get a good news-feature picture, preplanning of the composition and action is more than 75 percent of the job. The technical aspects of photography—the focusing, the exposure, and the lighting—are important, too, but they rate second to the picture message.*

If you don't know a good photographer who is experienced in taking newspaper shots, ask your editor. He or she undoubtedly will know several you can hire. Before you retain anyone, though, do a little research. Study the kinds of photos the paper uses; they vary from paper to paper.

Vertical Format

One thing you undoubtedly will notice as you become more aware of publicity photos is that newspaper photos usually fit a vertical format rather than a horizontal one. Yet most photographers, unless they are trained news photographers, tend to shoot horizontal pictures, particularly if the purpose of the release is to announce the entire new board of directors.

If your picture plans call for any kind of a lineup, you should know that such pictures—of a group of people looking into the camera or of someone signing a contract with a lineup standing behind him or her—have been dead for 20 years (unless it's the president of the United States). This kind of photo is sure to be rejected.

As you make your plans, ask yourself, "Is this picture intended for use in a four-column, two-column, or one-column space? Is there room for cropping vertically or horizontally?

Compact Shots

An editor often can use a small, close-cropped photo when the available space cannot accommodate large ones. Or, the editor might wish to use two small photos in preference to one larger, horizontal one. The more adaptable the size, the better. The best photos are so compact that an editor can run them in a three- or four-column space or crop them to a one- or two-column size, and still maintain the picture's meaning.

When possible, query the editor in advance, particularly if you anticipate a picture story or if you plan to send more than one shot. And be sure to check the newspaper's photo deadlines. Photo deadlines often vary from copy deadlines.

If you have a picture story or if the editor indicates an interest in one, send your photographer to the newspaper and let the editor look at the *contact sheets*.

Composition and Direction

An assigned newspaper photographer is the best judge of composition and direction of a photo—whether a shot is good, where and how the person should be posed, and whether it is worthy of being used. He or she may even resent your attempts to direct a shot and consider your efforts as meddling.

If, however, the photographer has been hired by you, collaborate with that person. He or she will know best about composition and technique, but if you have studied your outlet and the kinds of photos it prefers, your input will be valuable in decisions about picture content. The photographer should know from you if the photo is intended for use in four columns, in two columns, or as a mug shot. And discuss with the photographer whether there will be room for vertical or horizontal cropping.

Backgrounds. The photographer, whether hired by you or sent from the newspaper, should recognize conflict of backgrounds, but it is your job to envision possible problems. Arrange in advance for photo subjects to come dressed according to your background setups. A person in a light outfit should be seen against a dark background; a person in a dark outfit should be seen against a light background. There is little room for anyone dressed in a "busy" print or a large pattern. Large patterns in men's ties do not photograph well either. And "busy" backgrounds are equally difficult for a photographer to work against. Try to choose simple, plain backgrounds.

People being photographed may want to remove eyeglasses so that light from a camera flash won't create a reflection.

To protect against such problems, professional publicists often carry their own props to photo sessions—from the right kinds of neckties, to plants and flowers, to a makeup kit for a last minute touchup. You may wish to do the same.

"Deadly Cliché" Photos.   A former picture editor at a major metropolitan daily moaned over what he called "deadly cliché" photos submitted by many publicists. He said these are the two men and a piece of paper award or proclamation pictures, the deadpan plaque presentations, the routine ground-breaking shots, and the dull luncheon pictures where the rolls and water glasses in the foreground have as much animation as the characters seated behind them.

You will need to be original. Otherwise, why waste the time of the photographer and of the people being photographed, and why waste the funds you have budgeted when the editor will surely discard a "deadly cliché" photo. Picture editors agree on the following suggestions.

- Be as candid as possible when covering an award presentation. Try to catch the expressions at the original ceremony, if possible, rather than attempt to restage it. Look for an offbeat approach. If an award is being presented for traffic safety, for instance, get the winner in a spot where the background will show a busy traffic pattern.
- Try a new angle. Sometimes a low angle or overhead view will help dramatize a situation.

What these suggestions say is that it is necessary to find situations that evoke some kind of emotional response—that precious ingredient called "human interest"—and the picture will sell itself to the newspaper. Don't be a lazy planner and let the camera do all the thinking. Preplan each photo.

Equipment.   When you make the picture assignment, you should give the photographer not only the place and time, but also a description of the area in which he or she will be required to shoot so that the proper equipment can be brought. Is it a confined area? The photographer will need wide-angle lenses. Is there ample light, or are lights needed? Remind the photographer that the photos are to be used in a newspaper and state whether they are to be in black and white or color so that he or she can bring the proper film.

Just in case an overhead angle is necessary or desirable, you may wish to have a ladder handy for the photographer to use.

The Day of the Shoot

If you have planned well, there is very little for you to do at the photo session. When the photographer is a staffer from the newspaper, provide him or her with a typewritten sheet giving background information, correct spelling of names and titles, and any other pertinent information to take back to the editor.

Arrangement of Poses

Have everyone and everything there before the photographer arrives. Try to see that the principals in every photograph are as close together as possible, almost crowded. It is well to remember that the fewer people in a picture, the better the picture and the better each person will look. Also, if possible, unless it is a portrait or mug shot, have the principals doing something, not just looking at the camera or at each other. In other words, use action shots, not group portraits. This isn't always easy, but it can and should be done.

Here are a few more tips. One bit of advice is to try to avoid pictures of people eating or drinking. Few people have good manners when they're eating.

Remember this tip in case your organization wishes to alert the public to some new type of equipment: There is nothing more static than a photo of equipment. Include people in the photo—using the equipment or doing something with it—and then hope for the best.

If you are shooting for more than one newspaper in the same area, arrange different shots for each paper.

Photographic Release Forms

There may be a rare time when you must provide a newspaper with a signed *photo-release form*. Be sure to obtain a release if you have, for instance, hired a model for a shot or included a child in a photo that you hope can be used later in an annual report or in some form other than a straight-news shot. (A standard photo-release form that may be copied is included in Appendix B.) Keep the original, signed form for your files, and attach only a reproduction with the photo. (Also included in Appendix B is a copy of instructions to nonphotographer staff members in an advertising or public relations organization. You can adopt these instructions as the standard photo instructions used by your organization.)

That's it, then. You've done your job. The photographer has taken the pictures and gone. There's nothing more for you to do until he or she has delivered the contact sheets, you have chosen the best shots for your purpose, and he or she has delivered the final prints.

Mechanics for Submitting Photos

Always submit glossy, 8-by-10-inch (or larger), black-and-white or color photos, unless the newspaper you are shooting for has a different size preference. A 5-by-7-inch head-and-shoulders shot is appropriate to accompany the announcement of an individual's election or appointment to a new position. Some smaller papers use an electronic engraving process that calls for photos to be the same size as they will be when they appear in the paper. Find out in advance what size photographs your newspaper's editor prefers, but don't expect to get them back.

A word of caution for when a photographer is assigned from the newspaper. Do *not* request prints for your use unless you know the newspaper has a policy that allows you to *purchase* them.

One of the great problems for editors receiving publicity prints is the prints' poor quality. Newspapers that must reproduce photographs on porous newsprint demand top-quality, high-contrast prints to start with. If a subject's dark clothing blends into a dark background, the picture will look like a smudge when it is printed.

Captions as the Photo's "Story"

Caption information is important and must be accurate and complete. An otherwise usable picture must often be discarded because of inadequate or inaccurate information. Pictures are discarded if, for instance, they show seven heads but list only six names in the caption, or, just as bad, six heads and seven names.

Usually the caption very briefly tells what the picture is about. Here is an example:

> ABC Inc. *senior vice president Jeanne Jones and president Lawrence Smith, in front of the new sculpture at the entrance to corporate headquarters. The carving by well known artist Henri Johanssen symbolizes the vigor and enthusiasm with which the company serves its customers.*

- Study captions in the publications to which you will send your releases, and use their individual form and style.
- Use a summary headline, centered rather than aligned flush left as in your news or feature releases.

- Identify the people as they appear in the photo from left to right. If the subjects can't be identified in a left-to-right manner, draw a diagram of the photograph and number the heads. Then list the names by number.

- Spell out the full name. Initials for first names are not acceptable. It is advisable to ask a married woman how she wishes to be identified—by her husband's first name, by her own given name, or by her maiden name. To be safe, in the case of first names you may prefer to give both names, such as Martha (Mrs. John) Smith.

- Try always to include the name of your organization in the caption, along with as many pertinent points from the accompanying news story as are compatible with caption space. This way, if the news release itself doesn't make it, the picture and caption can stand alone and still be effective as publicity. Remember, however, to keep captions *brief*.

- Do not double-plant within a newspaper. Don't send identical or similar photos to different people or to different sections at the same newspaper. If you send photos to two newspapers in the same area, be sure the photos are not identical.

Final Preparation of Photo and Caption

Neatness counts. A typed caption is essential. Follow these guidelines to prepare your photo and caption:

- Include all the proper identification of your organization: its address, your name (as contact), and your telephone number, all single-spaced. The caption itself must be double-spaced.

- Use letterhead if the identifying logo is small enough that it and the caption information require only about a half-sheet of paper. It is better, however, to use plain, white paper, but be sure that your organization's name, address and phone number and your name (as contact) and phone number head up the typed information on each caption.

- Type the caption, double-spaced, on the *lower half* of a sheet of plain, white paper, or leave enough space at the top of the paper to tape the caption, face up, to the bottom of the print. Do this so that picture and caption may be studied by the editor simultaneously. (Place the tape on the back of the print.)

- When the caption is ready to be mailed, fold it up over the photo to protect it and to fit it into a mailing envelope. (This is why letterhead

usually is not as useful as plain paper: Seldom is there room above a
letterhead to provide space for taping the sheet to the photo.)

Photo Safeguards

Do *not* attach anything to the print with paper clips or staples, and do *not* type
directly onto the back of a photo or write on it with pen or pencil. These
practices damage the print for reproduction purposes. As insurance, you may
wish to attach a pretyped, gummed label—with your name, your organization's name, and a telephone number—to the back of the print, just in case
the caption becomes separated from the photo.

Most editors prefer to receive photos by mail. Enclose them, along with
your release or your fact sheet, in a large, strong envelope with sheets of
cardboard protecting the front and back of photos. On the envelope, in large
letters, write plainly for the post office, "Photo. Do not bend."

Finally—and this is very important—avoid phoning a busy photo desk.
It won't be noticed that you didn't phone, but it surely will be noted,
negatively, if you do.

Photo Syndicates

There are outlets that can distribute your photos nationally for you, *if* the
quality is outstanding and *if* the content has widespread appeal. The outlets
are called *photo syndicates*. (*Editor & Publisher International Year Book* lists
photo syndicates.) These syndicates will make no compromise in quality or
content, and they are probably the most demanding and exacting among any
in the news business. Amateurism is not tolerated.

Suppose, however, your photos can meet the impeccable standards and
a syndicate does distribute it. The gains will be greater than those achieved by
any other means of distributing publicity material, because so many publications use syndicated photos.

Whereas newspapers don't appreciate receiving the identical photos
that have been given to their competition, syndicates do not object. You can,
therefore, supply identical photos to all syndicates on your customized media
list.

Most photo syndicates have offices in major cities throughout the
country. If you believe your publicity photos can qualify, contact the office
nearest you, and request information about the specific requirements of each.
It will be worth the extra effort, and, because demand is so great for the
syndicate's pictures, they are always receptive to any that can qualify.

New Technology

Now there is camera technology that produces newspaper photos from a camera that needs no film. It is called *still video*. This camera records up to 50 images on a computer disk small enough to fit in the palm of a child's hand, and it requires no developing before the image can be seen on a video screen.

The process was only introduced in mid-1990 for newspapers, and it is being tested at *The Dallas Morning News*. It undoubtedly will quickly gain wide acceptance among large newspapers because of the benefits it offers.

According to *The News*, images are transmitted almost instantly to Dallas from other cities by placing a tiny disk from the camera into a video deck connected to a telephone line. A similar video deck receives the photo in Dallas, then passes it to a Macintosh computer for selection of size and shape. From there the image travels into a high-quality color system, which produces the color negatives used to print the page containing the photograph. The paper is then printed on state-of-the-art color offset presses owned by *The News*.

The News states that the camera appears to be a normal camera, is hand held, and uses lenses regularly used by the photographers with their other cameras. That, however, ends the similarities to a normal camera.

Inside the new camera are two "chips" that capture color and light separately, then combine them into a color image known as *high-band still video*. The photo image has higher resolution than ordinary video seen on a videocassette recorder. The camera is called the Sony Pro Mavica 5000.

10

Press-Kit Preparation

*How to help reporters
so they can help you*

The Press Kit as a Publicity "Tool"

A press kit can be a powerful instrument in an organization's publicity "tool kit." One press kit, with an enclosed plastic trash bag and other informative data, produced 19 column inches of publicity in one of the country's largest metropolitan daily newspapers for a local chapter of Keep America Beautiful Today.

Nineteen column inches! That's the amount of space that extends from top to bottom of a standard-size newspaper. And this particular paper divides each page into five columns instead of the usual six or eight columns, which increases the number of words in each column inch. That is a lot of publicity space, probably achieved only because a press kit was enclosed with the press release that gave additional information the reporter could use to lengthen the newspaper story. Few publicity releases without supporting material ever produce such a publicity windfall.

Another press kit, sent to newspapers all around the country by the City of Atlanta in mid-1988, weighed "roughly 27 pounds," according to one reporter who received it. But the reporter, Dave Barry, said, "A big factor in Atlanta's recovery has been its booming economy, which is apparently based on the manufacturing of Official Media Information Kits, which are everywhere." Perhaps Atlanta's motto is, If it works, work it to death!

Although it is unlikely that the press kit really weighed 27 pounds, the contents were obviously considerable and garnered 15 column inches of image-building, friendly publicity for Atlanta in just one newspaper, *The Dallas Morning News.* The total publicity achieved in newspapers all across the nation undoubtedly was extensive.

The Press Kit Defined

It used to be called a *press kit*. Newspaper people and many publicists still call it that. But nowadays some may call it a *media kit,* or a *media information kit,* in acknowledgment of electronic-news media. Whatever you choose to call it, if you hold a press conference or any activity to which newspeople are invited, you should have press kits on hand to give them.

A *press kit* is a special package of news releases and other information related to an event or to the purpose of a press conference. It can serve a more prolonged publicity purpose if it is constructed so that recipients find it valuable enough to keep as a reference tool. The kit can contain comprehensive information about your organization and its products or services.

Simply stated, a press kit is merely a collection of materials that can help reporters do a better job reporting *your* story.

Purpose of a Press Kit

The primary purpose of a press kit is to help newspeople report your story more thoroughly and equitably. It can be an excellent means for saving a reporter's, and your, time at a press conference or event. Instead of giving a lengthy verbal presentation that requires extensive note-taking by reporters, you can briefly summarize your project and then hand each reporter a kit. Tell them that you believe all the information required is inside. The savings in time will be appreciated by busy press people.

Reporter Perspective.   Not everything in a press kit will be used by the newspeople reporting your story because reporters prefer to develop their own stories. However, something in *your* kit may be the item or tidbit that allows them to add interesting information or to present slightly different perspectives or approaches than other newspapers' stories on the same topic.

Reporters almost always are pressed for time. They seldom have the luxury to research or explore additional sources of information that will flesh out a story to make it a more interesting, more comprehensive report. A press kit gives reporters the extra information they don't have time to dig for, and provides insight—from *your* point of view—that might not otherwise be available.

Presentation of Positives.   A press kit gives reporters—or others who may receive the press kit—the *positives* you wish to present the public. Some call this slanting a viewpoint, but as the person responsible for your organization's image, you need the public to lean favorably in your direction.

Herb Baus, the late nationally known journalist, public relations practitioner, and author of several publicity and public relations books, said, "What people believe is to them the important thing, because it is to them the truth . . . [and] the job of public relations is to make people believe the truth."

When the end result—the printed article in the newspaper—provides not only immediate particulars of your announcement, but also substantial added information about your organization, that is indeed highly profitable publicity and excellent public relations.

Press Kit Format

A press kit can be an elaborate, custom-designed folder with your organization's name imprinted or embossed on the front cover. It can also be a very simple, inexpensive pocket folder that is identified by typed stickers.

Any format is acceptable, if it is capable of containing the contents you decide are essential. The most favored formats are folders with inside pockets, loose-leaf notebooks (sometimes with divider tabs), spiral-bound booklets, and even large envelopes. Your publicity budget may dictate which format you will use.

If your firm or group has a special, distinctive logo, you may wish to include that on the exterior or cover. It is not the cover that matters, though; it's the contents.

Cover

How often have you heard, You can't judge a book by its cover? But many people do, particularly when it comes to *press kit covers.*

If your press kit is issued by a business whose income is generated by its own initiative, such as through sales of products or services, then the cover and its contents—or just about anything else, for that matter—can be more elaborate than for an organization that is funded by public monies. Anticipate any criticism of your group's fiduciary judgment that might come as a result of too ostentatious an offering. If yours is a charitable organization funded by grants or donations, modesty may be your best approach so that no one questions how the public monies you receive and are seeking are being used.

A press kit cover often can be used for several additional needs by merely changing the contents according to the circumstances. You can use press kit covers at seminars or workshops for employees; send them to potential donors; give them in advance to visitors on a plant tour; mail them in a promotional campaign; and file them as material reference for speakers, sponsors, or another, later, press conference. Your executives and employees undoubtedly will think of many, many uses for such a cover. So consider what uses it may be put to, before you make a final decision about yours. Design it accordingly. Also, if you anticipate other uses for the same cover, producing a larger number of them can substantially reduce per-unit printing costs.

Contents

Your press kit should contain as much information *as will be useful* to the recipient. Make sure that you don't forget to include information that will be crucial to the success of your package. The following list contains some examples:

- The most important pieces of information in a press kit are: name of your organization, its address and phone number, and your name (as contact) and phone number (if different from that of the organization). It is amazing how many press kits have been issued without this essential data. Someone just wasn't thinking! Some kits attach the contact's business card to the inside pocket, where it is easily seen and not easily misplaced. Others make the organization name, address, and phone number a permanent part of the cover information. The latter method requires that the contact's name be prominently displayed inside the kit so that recipients can easily locate it if there is a question of any kind.
- For a news conference, always include a "stand-alone" news release. A stand-alone release provides all the essential, principal facts or purpose of the news conference, and can stand alone to be used by recipient newspapers as presented. This news release should tell the complete story without causing the reader to want additional information, and it should be written in the inverted pyramid, five Ws news style.
- A publicity calendar of upcoming events can be a worthwhile enclosure, particularly for nonprofit organizations with a schedule of ongoing community events.
- A fact sheet may be included. A fact sheet can substitute for a news release and may be used by a writer who is unsure about how to write a

release. However, the chances that a busy editor will assign a reporter to write your story from a fact sheet are considerably less than that the editor will pass a news release to the copy desk for editing or rewrite. (Constructing a fact sheet is addressed later in this chapter.)

- A *backgrounder* contains all the information the recipient could possibly want about your organization. Or it can provide additional information about the product, service, or event that is the subject of your principal release.

    For example, if you are announcing a new product or service, you might include a separate sheet that outlines the product or service's development since inception, and the reasons for that development. The backgrounder can provide information about the field as a whole including when, where, and by whom it was introduced; what its impact over the years has been, and what its previous successes or failures have been. You might even include a backgrounder sheet outlining the research-and-development efforts that went into your product or service.

    As another example, a backgrounder for a nonprofit organization might very well summarize goals and objectives, list some significant accomplishments, describe when, how, and by whom it was founded, detail its area of influence within the community, and so on.

    A Los Angeles nonprofit orphanage headed its backgrounder, The Who, the What, and the Why? of its fund raising drive, and followed with subheads that asked—and, more importantly, *answered* the following questions:

    —Who is asking for this money?

    —What sort of children do they care for?

    —What does (the organization) do for these children?

    —What do they need this money for now?

    —Didn't I give to this last year?

    —Am I allowed tax exemption on my gift?

    —Why should I give?

    Each answer was a powerful pitch on behalf of the group and its work.

- Include a history of the organization. Essentially, this also is a backgrounder. It provides additional information for reporters to draw upon in describing the group responsible for the announcement. Keep it a concise compilation of key highlights about your organization that can help establish reputation and standing in the industry or community.

If the announcement involves another entity, as in the case of an acquisition or a merger, the kit should also include a separate history of the other organization.

- A *quotes sheet* is an excellent means of providing interesting information that will expand a news story written by a reporter. Quotes dress up a news story; they can turn an otherwise dull recitation of information into an interesting, readable news piece. Also, names make news and sell extra newspapers, so be sure to attribute each quote to a company official or outside person and always identify the person by title and function. Attribution provides insurance as to the accuracy of the quotes used, rather than dependence upon the reporter's memory or scribbled notes.

  Here is where you can logically provide the information about the organization's past efforts to achieve the result that now is being announced or to give testimony for a product, for a service, or for your group.

- Include biographies (*bios*) of organization officials or leaders who are important to the announcement or the event. The bios should be brief and should give only pertinent information.

  If the announcement is about an event that includes a speaker or speakers, the kit should include bios of each person and text of each speech, if available in advance. Arrangements to acquire copies of speech texts must be made in advance by you.

  A 5-by-7-inch, head-and-shoulders photo can accompany each bio. Each photo should carry an identifying caption in the event the photo becomes separated from the bio.

- Previously printed news or feature stories about the organization can provide insight for reporters. Reproductions should *prominently display* the date the article appeared and the name of the publication in which it appeared.

- Brochures may be included if they contain data germane to the announcement. For instance, an annual report often is an excellent provider of information and data you wish the publication to use and, possibly, to keep on file for future reference. An operating manual for the product is another helpful piece of information for a reporter writing a story about a complex product.

- Photos of a product with descriptive captions usually are included. You may also include photos of the exterior, or pertinent parts of the organization's interior may be included.

Other than mug shots, all photos distributed to print media should be 8-by-10 inches and have a glossy finish, and they may be either black and white or color. Each should carry an attached caption.

Organization of the Press Kit

The most popular press kit is a folder with interior pockets. Information can be divided between the pockets in an organized way. For instance, the left pocket can contain background information such as history, bios, and so on; and the right pocket can hold current data about the event, product, or service being presented. Place the news release on top in the right pocket so that it is the first thing seen by the user.

If all the information is contained in a large envelope, you should probably cut down on the contents and use some method for coding them, such as various colors of pastel paper for different types of information. No dark or neon colors, please—not even for emphasis!

An index of contents is a possibility, but that calls for a three-ring binder with dividers so that the contents remain in the order in which they are listed in the index.

Another popular method of organization is to present various types of information on varying lengths of paper in a two-pocket folder. All papers are the standard 8½ inches wide, but each set of information is a different length so that, when the sets are placed in the folder, headlines on each can be seen easily. This type of kit is probably the most easily read by reporters, but it is not readily adaptable to other uses, inasmuch as each section must be specially sized and printed.

Long-Term Use

Newspeople often will keep a well-constructed press kit on file. That's a plus you should aim for. If your kit is well organized and contains valuable information, there is more likehood that it will be kept by anyone receiving it. Make it a point to design your kit and its contents so that it will be a valuable addition, not only for filing in the publication's *morgue,* or library, but by any others who receive it.

The Press Kit as a "Blueprint"

There are added uses for press kits, such as to provide other executives or committee members in your organization who are responsible for publicity, with the organization's official, authorized history, facts, and details (especially if yours is an organization with branches, chapters, or affiliated memberships). In this case (but only when used for other than press purposes), the kit should be expanded to include the following:

- A basic model news release about the organization.
- Copies of logos, stationery, or other organization identification graphics.
- Photos of and background information about other organization products, services, or functions, and copies of previously distributed releases about them.
- Photos of equipment, people using the equipment or performing tasks relevant to the organization's purpose, or appropriate interior and/or exterior shots.
- A history of the organization, written so that each division or committee can extract and use the portion that pertains to it.
- Appropriate bios and mug shots.
- An instruction sheet with precise details and examples of the rules and mechanics of publicity.
- Fillers. (See Chapter 7 for more about fillers.)
- Suggestions for local participation in organizationwide events, anniversaries, contests, and so on.
- Reprints of previously published news or feature stories.
- The standard closing paragraph you wrote earlier, which succinctly states the purpose of your organization and pertinent information and data about it. Describe its uses and explain how it can be edited and tagged onto each future release.

Other Uses

Well-prepared press kits might also be used for business meetings, as a tool for salespeople, and for seminars or workshops.

It should be obvious that not everything listed must or should be included in each press kit. The nature of a kit's use dictates its contents. But if you have doubts about an item, it probably is better to err on the side of including it and risk its not being used, than to exclude it when reporters might use the information. For the City of Atlanta, it definitely paid off to include all the extras—even if the newspaper humorously reported the kit weighed 27 pounds!

Fact Sheets

A fact sheet can substitute for a news release if you are reluctant to try your hand at writing a release. As mentioned previously, however, a fact sheet may be a poor substitute for a release; an editor with strict time constraints may not assign a reporter to write a story from a fact sheet. It is far easier and much quicker for an editor to edit an already-written release. A fact sheet can also serve to provide additional information when you do not wish to send a press kit. Attach the fact sheet to the news release with a paper clip; do not use staples.

There are no hard and fast rules about a format for fact sheets. There are strict dictates, however, about including certain information, and about typing on only one side of the paper. Every fact sheet must include the following:

- Your organization's name, full address, and telephone number with area code. As for your news releases, this information may be typed at the top of plain sheets of paper, or you can use regular or "instantly created" letterhead.
- Type the words *Fact Sheet* in a prominent position near the top of the page.
- Also in a prominent place near the top of the page and above the body of facts, type Contact: then your name and your telephone number if it is different from the one listed for the organization. (As for your news releases, it is wise to also give a knowledgeable alternate contact name, along with his or her telephone number if it is different from the number listed for the organization.)
- Include the date on which the information is distributed—not as a release date—so that the age of the information in this particular fact sheet can be easily recognized as outdated, and discarded, if you issue a new one at a later time. It also is helpful when you update and produce new fact sheets that the new fact sheets have a different appearance

from those previously distributed. A change in paper color, if the color is subdued, is one method of changing the appearance.

- If you have a FAX number, it too should be included for the convenience of those who wish to reach you by this means.

This is the information that is required on every fact sheet. The body of information can be presented in any way you consider to be easily read and understood.

If the fact sheet is to substitute for a news release, it should present the information you would set down in your preliminary outline for the news story. It should give answers to the five Ws: who, what, where, when and why. If how—the H—is appropriate, also include that information.

If the fact sheet is to accompany a news release rather than substitute for one, it should provide important information about your organization. Or it can give additional data about a new product, new service, or about the industry in which your organization operates.

Two sample fact sheets are included in Appendix A. They are presented as possible examples. The amount and kind of information you wish to present may dictate using another style, such as in an outline form. Just be sure that the user is able to easily understand and extract the facts listed.

11

Press Conferences

How to offer something in person that you can't offer in a press release

"Doonesbury" on Press Conferences

"Doonesbury" cartoonist, Garry Trudeau, in four comic-strip panels picturing the White House (each with a few lines of dialog) presents his pithy view of press conferences and subtly gives us a rule about when *not* to call one:

> *"I'm telling you, Dan, I've had it! If Ziegler doesn't give us a decent briefing today, then I'm quitting the White House press corps for good!"*
> *"Sshh . . . Keep it down! . . . Here he comes . . . ."*
> *"Good afternoon, Gentlemen! Today the President had lunch at 12:30. Later, he made many important phone calls! Thank you."*
> *"THAT DOES IT!!"*

"Doonesbury" doesn't need translation. The message is clear, and it is as true today as when the strip appeared in 1973 and Dan Rather was Chief White House Correspondent for CBS: Even the President's publicity representative shouldn't call in the media without good reason.

Advice on When to Call a Press Conference

Public relations specialist John T. Gillan tells us that the typical financial editor of a major newspaper gets an average of 20 invitations a week to attend press conferences. That's more than a thousand press conferences a year!

There is general agreement among editors, Gillan says, that there are far too many press conferences called on subjects not worthy of a meeting. The editors say that a press conference just isn't necessary unless a product requires demonstration. "If a product can be adequately described in words, a news release can do the job—and the story will receive just as much consideration in this form as if presented at a full-blown dog and pony show," Gillan states.

Gillan's advice is sound. An extension of that advice is that you will not make media friends if you call a press conference that reporters feel is a waste of their time. The feeling will extend to a reluctance to accept future invitations.

Prime-time presidential press conferences have given most people a familiarity with the basic concept of press conferences, but they may have misled many too: Press conferences do not have to be of the size and splendor of those prime-time choreographed "specials." In the real world, the smallest organization can and should hold a press conference *if* a situation warrants it.

Perhaps a few words of explanation are needed here about the seemingly random interspersal throughout this book of the terms "press conference" and "news conference." Print journalists and long-time publicists tend to use the term "press conference." Those who deal extensively with both print and electronic news media try to call them "news conferences." Because this book is focused to the interests of small businesses and nonprofit organizations that rarely have news of sufficient magnitude to attract television news representatives (most radio stations obtain their news reports from national services), the term "press conference" is used. It is preferred by newspaper people, but you should use the term with which you and your organization are most comfortable.

Reasons for Holding a Press Conference

A press conference should be called for the following reasons:

- To provide personal presentations, explanations, descriptions, and opportunities for the media to direct their questions to responsible organization people and thereby benefit more than they would from a press release.
- To provide an opportunity to personally view and experience the way a product or service works to encourage media interest and, ultimately, public interest.
- To introduce a newly appointed or elected executive whose association

with the organization will have impact on the organization's direction, employees, members, consumers, customers, or constituents.

- To declare an extensive expansion program.
- To announce procurement of important new financing such as new funding for a business, or a grant or a donation for a nonprofit organization.
- To announce, describe, and pictorialize acquisition of a property.
- To give a progress report that is better presented with visual aids and opportunities for specific questioning.
- To review a crucial situation such as a labor difficulty; an actual or rumored financial difficulty; an allegation of misconduct by organization persons; and so on.

Questions to Help You Decide

The most important questions you should answer before scheduling a press conference are as follows:

- Can your organization offer something in person that can't be offered in a release?
- Do you have a *real* news story?
- Will the empathy and understanding of newspeople in fact be heightened (by holding a press conference)?
- Will this opportunity for the press to personally meet and question your people establish a friendlier relationship and boost esteem and respect for your organization and its individuals?
- Is the news value sufficient to warrant the time to attend required by busy reporters?
- Is the time and effort required to organize and conduct a worthwhile conference warranted?

Press Conference Preparation

Unless the reason for a press conference is a crisis of some kind that requires the conference to be called immediately, sufficient time, thought, and effort should go into its preparation so as to produce a productive, well-organized event. The guidelines for generating a successful press conference are as follows: Your list of guests should be as carefully drawn up for each conference situation as your media lists are adapted to fit each news release. For instance, if the news is of interest only to business publications and business page editors, eliminate all others.

Invite all reporters who regularly cover your organization or the general industry in which your organization is included. This may mean financial editors or specialists in certain business or nonprofit categories. If yours is a specialty field or a business of special interest to specific groups, locate and include those special-interest publications.

If you don't know which individual person to invite from any specific news outlet, send the invitation to the newspaper's city editor or to the managing editor of a specific publication. This then puts the responsibility on these executives to assign whomever they consider best suited to cover the story. [Information about broadcast media is in Chapter 14.]

Invitation

The format of the invitation can be in any of several businesslike printed forms. A letter on your organization's letterhead, however, is the most common style of invitation, and it should describe the purpose of the conference. It should be signed by the person best known to those invited, preferably that of the owner, chief executive officer, president, or chairman of the board.

Never telephone an invitation.

Include date, time, and place and name and phone number of one or two individuals who can provide additional information about the purpose of the conference. If directions are required or would be helpful, include a carefully drawn map.

The invitation can be put into press-release form, but there is a distinct possibility that recipients will not recognize it as an invitation, and it could be processed as a release or even mislaid or thrown away.

Time the arrival of the invitation so that it isn't received so far in advance of the date that it is misplaced or so close to the date as to prevent or make difficult the assignment of staff to attend.

Schedules and Media Convenience

This is a press conference, therefore it should be timed for the convenience of newspeople and for widest coverage, rather than for the convenience of your own people. If your locale has both morning and evening papers, to avoid showing preference you may wish to alternate times and hold a midmorning

conference for the evening newspapers and a mid- or late-afternoon conference for the morning newspapers.

If you include television reporters, a morning conference is suitable, and
a midafternoon conference will accommodate both dinner-time and late-
evening newscasts.

Conference times for Sunday editions of daily newspapers and for weekly
newspapers should be set according to a specific day rather than hour.
Scheduling the conference for a Monday will allow the greatest majority of
weekly newspapers to meet their deadlines and will also accommodate Sunday edition staffers who usually work on midweek deadlines.

You may wish to schedule a separate, special press conference for
monthly publications such as trade magazines and business journals. They
have far greater lead-time requirements, often up to four months. Established, respected publications can be expected to honor your release dates.

Principal Representative

In almost every case, your organization's owner, chairman of the board, or
chief executive officer (CEO) should be the principal representative of your
organization at the conference. He or she should lay the groundwork and then
turn the conference over to a specialist in engineering, research, finance or
whomever is best suited to offer the particular information called for and to
field questions about it.

For instance, if the news is about a new product, your principal representative should present introductory information, then turn the conference
over to a vice president or engineer in charge of development of the product.
When the subject deals with finances or economics, the chief financial officer
(CFO) should be present and called upon.

When the conference has been called to introduce an organization's
new president, executive director, CEO, CFO, or comparable high-ranking
executive, be sure that there is sufficient interest—in the individual, in his or
her responsibilities, or in the group he or she represents—to warrant calling a
conference.

The decision about who should be on hand for the meeting is contin-
gent on the reason for the meeting, but only *one person* should be in charge.

Press-Conference Coordinator

Chapter 12 outlines the necessity to have a coordinator for a staged event. A
press conference, after all, is an event staged to create news, and, here also, a

coordinator is essential. The choice of coordinator depends not only on who within the organization has the ability, but also on who can give the amount of time necessary to do the job.

Seating Arrangements

Here is a word about the physical arrangement of tables and chairs for the seating of press people. Under no circumstances should you place your people behind tables or separate them from the audience as though by an invisible partition. A good seating plan helps to build rapport between reporters and your people. The principal representative can be seated in front of a table or desk or leaning comfortably against it, and other executives can be seated casually among the press representatives. In this type of arrangement, there can be no perception of "us and them" thinking on your part.

You may wish to do a little advance research on the effects of your people's body language on those listening and questioning them. Excellent information has been written on the subject, and a consciousness of how to use body language as a PR "tool" is well worth the time and effort in reviewing it.

Prepared News Releases

In certain situations, you should prepare a news release and in other situations a fact sheet will be sufficient. In a few cases, however, you should definitely *not* prepare a news release.

When the reason for the press conference is to present, demonstrate, or describe a new product or service, a press release is mandatory. In these situations, the release should give basic details, and it should be accompanied by added explanatory material such as an operations manual (to give details and data that some reporters may wish to add to their stories).

When company policy is part of the reason for the meeting, there should be no release or statement for handout or as part of the press kit.

Photos

By all means encourage the media to bring their own photographers. If television people are included, you will expect them to have cameras with them, so provide for special seating arrangements. Set up the room to enable the reporters to sit close and the television cameras to shoot over their heads.

When a press conference includes television cameras, it probably will be necessary to seat all of your scheduled speakers at the front of the room. But, please, do not sit them behind a table barrier that in effect says, We need protection from you reporters; you intimidate us.

It is expedient to have a still photographer on hand, not only to provide file photos for your own records, but to provide photos to accompany press kits to reporters, who are unable to attend. The photographer can also be enlisted for shots for a reporter who does not have his own photographer present.

Press Kits

A press conference is one of the most widely existing reasons for constructing press kits. The special package is designed to give reporters the added information that allows them to make their stories different from those of their competitors. The press kit includes a release, if one is called for, or a fact sheet related to the purpose of the conference; it also includes appropriate photos of individuals, products, physical structures, or other pertinent visual depictions; background and historical data; and whatever else is considered appropriate. (If you do not yet have press kits, see Chapter 10 for the ground rules on designing one.)

Location

Choose a place that is comfortable for everyone, that can accommodate sound and lighting equipment (if electronic-news media are included), and that is as convenient as possible to all invited media.

Room size is important. Pick a room to fit the numbers expected to attend; it is better, however to choose a place that is a trifle too small. If your room is too big, it might create the false impression that your conference is not well attended. As you watch the next presidential press conference on television, notice that the room always appears to be filled to absolute capacity. This transmits a feeling of high importance for the conference.

If your organization has a conference room that is adequate in size, this probably is your best choice because staff can be included or made readily available.

The location for your conference should be easily accessible to the press. If your building is located in a suburban or rural area not handy for your guests, transportation to and from the conference should be offered.

Nonprofit organizations often have the advantage of being able to borrow—at no cost—well-located, nicely appointed rooms from other organizations or from corporations. For-profit organizations seldom have this privilege, and must rent outside accommodations if their own facilities are inadequate or not conveniently located.

Drinks and Food

The question of whether to serve food and drinks is a difficult one to answer. Keep in mind that a press conference is a strictly business affair. Press parties and receptions are sometimes inaccurately thought of as press conferences because they often include, in a more social setting, a special announcement, a product showing, or the introduction of a notable figure. Press breakfasts and luncheons also often are held to make special announcements, but they are more businesslike than receptions or press parties. Press conferences, however, are no-nonsense business affairs.

A rather general rule of thumb is this: For a straight press conference, it is usually not necessary to serve food or drinks; for press breakfasts, luncheons, or parties held to generate a somewhat social atmosphere and to create some business-social relationships, food is expected.

Coffee and tea always are appropriate, even for straight press conferences, unless the conference is called for an "emergency" and time does not permit arrangements to be made. Soft drinks or juice can be added, if the weather is warm and cool drinks would be appreciated. A bar for liquor or wine is wholly dependent on the attitude of the press in your area and on your organization's position in this regard.

Decisions about serving food can be calculated on the basis of timing: A 4:00 P.M. meeting is probably too close to the dinner hour even for snacks, but at 9:00 A.M., breakfast rolls may be appreciated. The part of the country in which you are located, the local customs, and the size of your budget dictate these decisions.

If you opt to include food, a refreshment table with sandwiches or finger food may be sufficient. If the food is to be catered, in your own or in a borrowed facility, check in advance that equipment such as refrigerator and microwave or stove are available and operating.

Dress Rehearsal

If this is a first-time experience for the principals involved, a run-through may be an excellent idea. It also may be a good idea to prepare a written statement for your organization's participants, on the essentials of the announcement to be made, especially if it is complicated. You can expect plenty of questions from the press, so, together with your own people, try to anticipate as many of these questions as possible and figure out the best answers. Be better prepared than the person who once said that she could always come up with the perfect answer—an hour too late.

When the subject matter is controversial, it helps those who will be on the "hot seat" to be alerted for what to expect. These people then can be more at ease with their questioners, and they can reply in an informal, convincing, assured manner, which will create a much more favorable impression.

The Day of the Conference

The following guidelines will help ensure that your conference runs smoothly:

- Prepare an agenda ahead of time, assigning each topic to a specific individual, and setting time allotments in advance. This is a requirement for a smooth-running, professional meeting. Remember the constrictions of time on newspeople, and keep the meeting moving right along.
- Have your people in place a few minutes before the announced starting time. Then open the conference *on time* out of respect for those who arrive on time and for their often close-cut schedules.
- Provide name identification badges (with titles listed) for each of your people in attendance. Make sure the badges are large enough to be read by reporters who will be sitting some distance from the speakers. This courtesy will be appreciated.
- Open the conference with a statement about the purpose of the meeting and a brief summary of the agenda. Then introduce the principal participants, the persons who are most closely identified with the subject of the conference.
- Open the meeting for questions after all preliminary statements have been made.
- Do your best to arrange exclusive interviews, if there are requests for them, but do this only *after* the conference, so that there is no hint of preferential treatment for any one reporter or medium. Give everyone the same opportunities.
- Announce the availability of a photographer for reporters' use—if you have one—during opening statements. Introduce the photographer so that those who wish to use the service can locate him or her. You may wish to give the photographer a preliminary assignment to make photos for your own records.

- Do not bar, under any circumstances, any media representative from attending your press conference because he or she or the medium he or she represents has committed some real or supposed slight against your organization or one of its members.

Follow-Ups

During the conference, listen for and make note of any questions that were not answered or that were inadequately answered; note the name of the reporter requesting the information; get back to that reporter as quickly as possible with answers. You may wish to assign this task in advance to someone who has fewer responsibilities than you.

It can be helpful to tape the entire session in order to recall the questions that weren't adequately answered. A playback during the more relaxed hours following the conference also might help to improve on the ways that information is handled in future meetings.

If the press conference was called in response to a crisis situation, you may need to schedule follow-up meetings. If the crisis extends over days or over a longer time period, a responsible official who can speak with complete authority should be available to the media throughout the entire period. Let the media know who the person is and how to contact him or her.

"Private" Press Conferences— a General Electric Innovation

John Gillan, who was with General Electric's (G.E.) Chicago News Bureau, tells of an innovative way that G.E. handled the conflicts of time and pressure on editors in that highly competitive news area. G.E. held "private" press conferences in the offices of each editor without a single G.E. representative being present!

Gillan says that the reaction of the press was nothing short of fantastic. The challenge was to use only a limited budget, to get maximum exposure in the trade press for a new miniature battery-powered DC motor. The key media were headquartered in 10 cities around the country and represented such diverse areas as product design, appliance manufacturing, electronics, hobbies, toys, and automotive engineering.

At a previously arranged time, a messenger arrived at each editor's office with three packages and a cover letter. The introductory letter welcomed the editor to his or her own private press conference and directed the editor to open, in order, three plainly wrapped packages, marked "A," "B," and "C."

Package A contained a new product release, six product photos, a short "talk" by the marketing manager, a product bulletin, and a bulletin release on the motor.

Package B contained a G.E. electric toothbrush and a ¹/₂₄-inch-scale slot car (each with the new miniature motor installed), plus a separate motor, all of which the editor could use for photographs, testing, or otherwise. A cover note explained the significance of the package.

Package C included a closing letter advising the editor that he or she could secure additional information by calling collect that afternoon to the product department in Morrison, Illinois, where personnel involved in the motor's development were standing by to accept calls. The conference closing included an American Express "Be My Guest" certificate for lunch, bearing the greeting "Have lunch without us."

Shortly after the private press conferences, a letter was sent to each participating editor, asking how he or she liked receiving news of important products in this manner. The response was exceptional. Letters were received from all 28 editors involved, and phone calls for specialized information numbered over 20.

Thus, the four basic steps of any campaign—research, planning, communication, and evaluation—were honored and bore fruit in the private press conference, says Gillan.

A Final Personal Word

A volunteer, whose name and whose organization's name are now forgotten, gave some excellent advice: *"Be professional. Only you should know it is your first press conference. It's okay to panic as long as no one, particularly the press, knows it."* Tuck it into your memory, for future use.

12

Staged Events

How to stage an event to create news

Early-Day Staged Events

The Romans regularly staged events—chariot races, public debates, and luncheons for lions, where the entrees for the lions were malefactors and offenders. The Romans are believed to be the first to introduce staged events; although newspapers, radio, and television did not exist at that time, there is little doubt that many of the events were staged to mold public opinion. These events did attract the public, and they also provided entertainment. They may even have been financially successful for their promoters. Certainly they provided word-of-mouth publicity.

This book produces no earth-shattering news in recalling early-day history or in revealing that nonprofit organizations have turned for years to staged events to attract public interest, create publicity, and make money. Giant corporations also have become known for "the big event." What may be news to some readers, however, is the degree to which *small businesses* have come to depend on staged events for very similar reasons to those of nonprofit organizations: to create publicity, build name recognition, project a specific image, and attract attention that ultimately translates into profits and raises public support.

Differences between Press Events and Staged Events

Someone once said that media are the tools by which an organization tells its story to the public. And the event you stage gives you access to those tools. Therefore, the differences between the previously described press conferences, parties, and receptions and the staged events that will be described in this chapter should be made distinct.

Whereas a press conference (Chapter 11) is strictly a business affair, press parties and receptions usually are held to display and demonstrate something that cannot be as graphically presented with a news release. All of these are media events meant to create news, but each is held strictly for media. The majority of staged events, however, and particularly those presented in this chapter, include the public as well as media.

Outline and Checklist

One of the all-time great publicists, Herb Baus, wrote the *Public Relations Handbook,* which is now long out of print. In this book, he uses the bedrock foundation of straight-news reporting (the five Ws and the H) to set forth the basic elements of a staged event. These rules are just as applicable now as when Baus wrote the book.

Baus's list provides a working outline, which can later be used as a checklist for devising, planning, and producing an event that creates news and attracts the press.

What? Name of event, its scope, necessary buildup, budget, elements of program.

Why? Purpose and objective.

When? Full schedule of timing, with deadlines for each preliminary, all worked out as to dates and hours.

Where? Geographic locale, facilities, including ample facilities for every detail necessary to complete functioning.

Who? Who will engineer, star, be invited, attend, follow up?

How? How will all these things be done? Advance planning for full coverage. Announcements by press, [television], radio, magazines, direct mail, outdoor advertising, and other media. Stockpile of stories, pictures, features. Mechanical arrangements for coverage—pressroom, typewriters [word processors], telephones, accommodations for press, provisions for photography, wiring for radio [and television]. Information arrangements—advance copies of speeches and reports, programs, interviews, press conferences. Checking coverage—stenographer to check details, photographer to get pictures for distribution afterward to publications not taking own pictures. Follow Up—thank you notes, scrapbook, final report.

Created News and Controlled Publicity

As mentioned in Chapter 2, there are two kinds of news—spot news and created news. Spot news is spontaneous and beyond your control, and, sometimes, it contains information you'd rather leave unpublicized. Created news most often comes from a staged event that produces controlled publicity. Dick Hitt, reporter for *The Dallas Times-Herald,* calls them "the patter of little feats!"

It's the little feats creating the news that keep a small business's or all-volunteer organization's name before the public—through the media. However, leave the big "fetes" to the giant corporations!

To keep your organization's name before the public, you almost have to rely on staged events to create news. When do you ever have enough news to announce—in publicity releases—a new product or service, the appointment or election of a new executive, a new project, an award, or a recognition of or by affiliates? There's only so much ready-made straight news that can come out of an organization. (Feature news is another means of creating news that results in controlled publicity. Producing news features is covered in Chapter 7.)

Herb Baus defined special events as "acts of news engineering." The single, most important point to remember, however, is this: Although news may be created, even engineered, *it must be news.*

Types of Staged Events

Media event, public event, publicity stunt—a staged event can be any one of these:

- Press conferences and press parties are strictly *media events.*
- Banquets, luncheons, bike-a-thons, seminars or workshops, auctions, lectures, or performances are all happenings used by charitable groups, and sometimes businesses, to increase awareness and/or to raise money. They are *public events* that can be media events.
- Open houses, plant tours, and building dedications are also public events and media events.
- Macy's Thanksgiving Day Parade is a public event and a media event

that brings millions of dollars to the City of New York at the same time
that it creates megapublicity for the department store.

- A rock concert in which celebrity performers speak up—and act up—for
  a cause, can be a *publicity stunt* as well as a media event and a public
  event.

- A barrel ride over Niagara Falls is a *cliché-type publicity stunt*, but it also is
  a media event that creates media attention for both the individual and a
  commercial or nonprofit sponsor, if there is one.

All of the above are media events designed primarily to grab and hold
the attention of the media. This is because the media are the key to reaching
greater numbers of people than any individual event is capable of attracting
on its own, no matter how large it is.

Publicity Stunts

Never refer to your event as a publicity stunt, even if it basically qualifies as
such. Today's media is truly gun shy about both the word and the type of event
that it represents. The publicity stunt achieved its bad reputation from early
Hollywood publicity events—stunts that were staged by motion picture studio
flaks. Flaks is an unflattering name that was given to press agents who devised
outlandish things for actors to do or to take part in to achieve great amounts of
publicity. The term flak is obsolete except when used in the most derogatory
manner by old time journalists.

Today, professional publicity practitioners work hard to achieve and
maintain credibility and respect and to live down that earlier reputation.
Seldom, if ever, are the events they now stage to create news referred to as
stunts.

Leona Helmsley versus the Media

The media know the term *publicity stunt* well, and they still use it when they
believe it is warranted. Media stories branded billionaire, hotel-magnate
Leona Helmsley, "the queen of mean," when she attempted to overcome a
bad public image. The following excerpts are from a news story that appeared
in *The Dallas Morning News:*

> [Helmsley] suddenly became so enthusiastic about America that she recently
> decorated the outside of the Empire State Building (which she owns with her
> husband) a patriotic red, white, and blue. . . .
>   She says she's just furious that Mr. [Saddam] Hussein calls the hostages
> "his guests." . . .

"I know something about how one is supposed to treat guests, Mr. Hussein," she says in an ad. "I have been inviting guests from around the world into my hotels for 18 years. . . . "

But poor Leona, the news media completely misunderstood her intentions. They actually implied that maybe this was a *publicity stunt*. And it gets worse. They even hinted that she might want to use this to get her four-year-prison term overturned on appeal.

"Outrageous," Leona keeps saying to the media. She says she only got bad press because her attorneys told her she couldn't speak to reporters during the trial. But now she's ready to clear things up.

For the press, the term *publicity stunt* immediately calls forth just such dubious images. Avoid the S word completely. It has nothing but negative implications that serious organizations want to avoid.

Choice of Event

Your choices of staged events are only limited by the confines of your imagination and by your budget. The kind of event you choose should be conceived to fulfill three fundamental ends:

1. To tell a publicity story.
2. To influence public opinion.
3. To carry out the long-range goals, objectives, and plans you set forth in Chapter 3.

If your staged events are creatively designed and produced to fulfill these ends, they can not only give you excellent publicity, but they can help to favorably *enhance or change* your group's image. Further, a worthwhile event that is well thought of by the media and the public, can win prestige, dignity, approval, and credibility for your organization. Credibility is the *key* ingredient in attracting support: financial support, media support, and, ultimately, public support through the media.

Advantages and Disadvantages of News-Media Coverage

Consider some of the advantages and disadvantages of having the news media cover your staged event:

- As careful as you may be, a reporter may put his or her own interpretation or slant on your story—and that slant may not necessarily be to your liking.

- You cannot always count on the news media to go along with your "great idea." On the other hand, if the media are cool to your idea, that well may be an indication of the public's acceptance!
- To get the press to attend, you must set the time and place well in advance. Unfortunately, your carefully planned date may just happen to fall on a day on which the biggest news of the year breaks—a day such as August 2, 1990, when Iraq invaded Kuwait. That story may fill every inch of available news space and knock your story right out of the ballpark.
- On the other hand, the date of your staged event could easily turn out to be the slowest news day of the year, and your event might be given undreamed of space and treatment for the simple reason that newspapers have too much space to fill that particular day.
- Created news can be customized to suit your needs *and* your budget.

Purpose for an Event

Before a decision to stage an event is made, full evaluation should be made of *why* the group will have the event. Image—building it or changing it—can be all the grounds needed to justify the decision. A specially created event can be designed to foster and mold a favorable public image for an organization that may be thought of as remote and cold. Any organization *can* change its image. Perhaps this is the time to consider it, take action, and make the change.

Advantages of the Staged Event

Although this book's focus is on publicity, you may be considering other kinds of promotion. You should be aware that a staged event, which gets you both promotion and publicity, often is far more cost-effective than, for example, the cost of airtime for commercials or broadcast production or the cost of a direct-mail campaign. For a company with a product or service to promote, a staged event can initiate more media and public notice than other types of publicity, public relations, or advertising.

Never lose sight, however, of a basic fact: If you stage an event that is overtly commercial, the media will not attend, nor will they report it. If it is lackluster, commonplace, or poorly conceived and managed and they *do* report it, the coverage may not give the positive image you hope for.

An event that is enthusiastically received can become a regular, perhaps annual, event that, over time, builds and strengthens the public's—and the news media's—perceptions of your organization.

Event Timing

Timing is an important element in planning an event. If you are considering an event that can be held only on a specific day or date, check local calendars to be sure yours will not run head-on into another well-established event scheduled for the same date. The chambers of commerce in most cities have community calendars that list events for a full year in advance.

Newspaper Listings

Local newspapers usually include listings of events and activities, and some radio and television stations also have calendars of events. These informational calendars are not set far enough in advance to provide solid information about possible date conflicts, but they do provide something else—another publicity outlet for your upcoming event.

Community Calendars

As another means of getting your message to the public, send the information about your event to each outlet that has a community calendar. It will pay to check each station and newspaper for its specific calendar requirements. Most outlets require the same information that you would normally include as the lead of your announcement release—in the form of the five Ws.

Begin sending your calendar notices about six weeks in advance, and continue to send them weekly until the event.

Brainstorming an Event

Brainstorming can help you decide on what kind of event you wish to stage. Consider the following points when you prepare for your brainstorming session.

- Know the event's purpose and objectives.
- Choose an event that is right for your organization and complies with your organization's purposes and objectives.

When these points are indelibly etched into the concrete tablet on which you will set forth strategies, call in the best brains in your organization and hold a brainstorming session.

Because brainstorming is such a productive means for arriving at solutions to numerous kinds of problems, Appendix D is devoted to it. Refer to this section whenever you need to produce results. Brainstorming is a creative problem-solving technique, an excellent description of which is included in *The Path of Least Resistance* by Robert Fritz (A Fawcett Columbine Book, published by Ballantine Books). Fritz describes brainstorming as a process "in which you attempt to blitzkrieg through your preconceived 'mind-set' by fanciful free association. The idea is to generate alternative solutions by overcoming your usual manner of thinking." Fritz recommends that, while brainstorming, you "suspend your critical judgment so that you can be more inventive."

Imagination, creativeness, and inventiveness are the fundamentals for designing a successful event. If it's "old hat," or dull and overdone, no one— media or public—will want to attend.

The Enjoyment Factor

The enjoyment factor is an important one to consider in your brainstorming session. For an event to be successful, it must also be entertaining. Yet making entertainment a major purpose would seem to give an almost unprofessional or unseemly luster to something as earnest as an effort to attract publicity that will build integrity, image, and recognition for an organization. Without a substantial enjoyment factor, however, for even the most serious seminar or training session, neither media nor public will be pleased. For truly serious events such as seminars or training sessions enjoyment for participants can come from productive learning; an event needn't be thought of as "showtime" in order to be enjoyable.

If your staged event is perceived by media and public as pleasurable, different, unique, and worthwhile, it will successfully fulfill all your requirements and it could very well become a regular event that attracts a following for your organization. With such success will come the certainty that others will copy your brainchild. For you, that merely means it's back to the brainstorming sessions. You must continue to innovate and update to stay ahead of the pack.

Unused Brainstorms for Later Events

A by-product of your initial brainstorming session can pay off later: Ideas that were generated but not pursued can be reconsidered, updated, and, perhaps, "piggybacked" on to renew or revise the successful event or to create an entirely new event at a later time. Here is a suggestion: Tape and transcribe all brainstorming sessions, and retain them in your files for future reference.

Something to consider when you are finally choosing your event is whether it is interesting enough and newsworthy enough to get into the competition arena against all the syndicated material—features and such—available to all media without any expenditure of time or effort on their part.

If you are looking for television coverage, be sure that the event provides *visual* elements that will satisfy television's demand for movement.

Ideas to Get Your Brainstorm Session Moving

There are too many possibilities of feasible events to try and present a list here. What follows are a few well-known kinds of happenings. Some may be a bit overdone, but they still can get the ideas rolling:

- All manner of shows, from product and business to home shows.
- Ethnic galas that celebrate with foods and cultural exhibits.
- Exhibits such as art, crafts, or manufacturing.
- Concerts for serious music lovers, teenagers, or families.
- Tie-ins with local events (a particularly effective type of event) such as special days, holidays, or weeks.
- Plant or company tours. (Caution: Unless the public or the media is otherwise banned from these facilities, a truly interesting aspect of the tour exists, an exciting new product is being manufactured, or the manufacturing process itself is exciting, plant and company tours can be *deadly dull*. Beware of just opening the doors and expecting all to rush in. If you do decide on such an event, be sure to have tour guides who are completely informed and enthusiastic about your product.)
- Unveiling or previewing an *important* new product, a product breakthrough or disclosure, or a landmark achievement.
- Social events such as fashion shows, dances, teas, or formal dinners.
- All manner of sports events.

Market Assessment

It would seem to take only common sense to assess in advance the market you wish to attract. Sometimes, however, the desires for a certain kind of event by those developing the plans overcome this common sense.

Some people are avid golfers; others live for tennis or biking; and there are those who believe that anything of an artistic or crafts nature will provide enjoyment for everyone. Heed the old Indian admonition (in this slightly edited version) to "walk a mile in the moccasins of those you want to attend your event." It is excellent advice. To ignore the desires and interests of those you want to attract is to risk choosing an unappealing event that offers all the work and expense and few of the rewards.

The people you wish to attract may have specific interests. To establish what those special interests are, talk to people who are potential patrons. There is no need for a full-fledged survey or analysis, although either can be vastly productive. Merely talking with people who make up your potential market can give you excellent insight into reactions—both positive and negative—and assure a more accepted response to your event.

Benefit Events and Profits

There are some very good reasons to arrange for your event to benefit a local charity. This can result in substantial publicity and even in financial assistance. Of course, if you *are* a charity, you already know about these benefits.

First, the fact that proceeds will go to an established, popular charitable cause almost assures that publicity about and for the event will be used by the press. However, Federal Communications Commission (FCC) regulations prevent all mention (in the form of public service announcements on television) of a commercial sponsor of an event that benefits a nonprofit organization. There is a little more leniency by radio. (Additional information about PSAs is presented in Chapter 14.)

Second, a tie-in with a nonprofit organization can possibly mean that space in a centrally located, large corporation's building can be obtained for free, or that rental charges for a larger facility may be reduced and subsequently deducted by the grantor as a charitable contribution. If explored, there can be additional "in-kind" contributions that can cut costs considerably.

Third, a portion of the receipts from a ticket charge can be used to offset event costs with the remainder going to the charity. For the sake of media and public approval, make the percentage given to charity substantial enough that no criticism will deflect on your organization.

Considerations for Staged Events

Careful thought must be given to plans for events. The following are some of the considerations you should be aware of:

Newsworthiness

When is an event news? Herb Baus spells it out in *Tested Public Relations and Publicity Procedure,* a manual that he edited for The National Research Bureau, Inc.:

- When it is new
- When it is novel
- When it relates to famous persons
- When it is directly important to great numbers of people
- When it involves conflict
- When it involves mystery
- When it is considered confidential
- When it pertains to the future
- When it is funny
- When it is romantic or sexy

Cost Estimates

How much your staged event will cost may be the first question you must ask—and answer. After several successful events, you may be able to estimate costs based on previous experience. However, there is only one way to project a monetary figure for your first media event: Get valid estimates.

First, figure the numbers of people who will attend, including the news media, the public, and your own people. The numbers are much easier to gauge if the event is invitational as compared to a public-invited event. After you have listed every item that will be used, get solid per-person cost estimates for each item, and multiply these figures by the numbers of attendees.

Your total cost estimate will provide you with enough information so that you can decide whether or not the event is financially manageable.

Items to Budget For

There are several items to consider when you budget for your staged event:

- Location. Will the event be held in a "no-cost" organization meeting room or boardroom or in local rented space? You must consider not only size of the space but also whether the location provides easy access for the media you have invited. If your own location is a distance from town or a distance across town from newspaper and broadcast facilities, you may have to rent a room closer to them. If you do not wish to do this, then you must add in cost estimates for transporting the media to and from your event.
- Food and drinks. If the event is to be held on your organization's property, there undoubtedly will be catering costs. If it is held in a public facility, can the facility provide the food or must it be catered? Shop for caterers and check restaurant prices if you do plan to serve food. If there is to be a drink bar, costs of soft drinks and/or liquor or wine must be estimated. Costs for service people often are a forgotten expense.
- Invitations. You must decide whether invitations are to be printed and also whether they are simple or elaborate. Postage or more elaborate hand-delivery costs must also be figured.
- Press kits. Every member of the news media who is invited should receive a press kit. Some people may request more than one, so plan to have plenty on hand. If you have not yet prepared a press kit for your event, check Chapter 10 to get an idea of what the press-kit contents should be. From this information, you can estimate the cost of producing yours.

Evaluation Questions

Before you make final decisions, ask questions of yourself and of those concerned with producing the successful event. Insist on honest answers even when the answers may not be what you and they hope to hear.

- Is this event appropriate for your community? Will the community like and respond to it?
- Will the news media respond positively to it?
- Will it produce the returns you have set as goals?
- What will your returns be?

- Do you have the resources and capabilities to carry out the event successfully? Do you have the budget, staff, enthusiasm, and organizational ability?
- Are the estimated costs manageable?
- Do plans include the "sizzle" that will sell this event to those you wish to attract?
- Finally, and perhaps most importantly, to achieve real success, do your own executives, line staff, and members, like it? Will they support it wholeheartedly?

Staff Members

Reverend Frank Pounders, minister of a small church in Texas, was attempting to enlist volunteers for a project that is a major fund-raiser for the congregation. It requires many people to organize it, staff it, and mop it up afterwards. He used his pulpit as one means of making the appeal and included the following as part of his invocation.

> This is the Tale of Four People named Everybody, Somebody, Anybody, and Nobody. There was an important job to be done and Everybody was asked to do it. Everybody was sure that Somebody would do it. Anybody could have done it, but Nobody did it.
>
> Somebody got angry about that because it was Everybody's job. Everybody thought Anybody could do it but Nobody would do it.
>
> It ended up that Everybody blamed Somebody when Nobody did what Everybody could have done. At least, now Everybody understands that Nobody cares.
>
> And the moral to this Tale may very well be that, in this life, you can only depend on Nobody and Yourself.

The lesson from the "Tale of Four Persons" should probably be put into question form: Do you have adequate people to organize and staff the event and to mop it up afterward? Or do you have only the infamous "Four People" to assist you?

Event Coordinator

If you are the head of an organization, you probably do not have time to arrange a successful staged event. You must find someone whose assignment with regard to the event is very much the same as yours as entrepreneur: organizing, operating, and assuming the risk.

There's an excellent definition of a coordinator: someone who brings organized chaos out of regimented confusion. Actually, it is the coordinator's job to plan, organize, *and* coordinate the plans and the event staff. If the event is small enough, perhaps only one person is needed. If the event is complex or of any size above small, it probably will require assistants. A full-scale event requires an extraordinary amount of advance planning and preparation. The numbers of people needed are directly related to the complexity and size of the event. Don't underestimate the work involved or the numbers of people required.

Press Contact

In addition to the coordinator, one person should be designated to be in charge of the press at the event; the best person for the job is the person whose name is listed as contact on press releases. If you are the head of your organization, you may be able to afford time for this special assignment, and that can be an excellent decision for two reasons:

- You know the answers to questions that reporters may ask.
- You can get to know the press, and they can get to know you.

There is also another assignment that is better served by the entrepreneur or principal executive than by the event's coordinator: spokesperson at the event.

Event Publicity

The information that follows is best directed to the event coordinator, whether that person is the executive in charge of the organization, or a specially appointed person.

Inasmuch as the primary motivation and justification for holding this little bash is to attract media attention, it is time to zero in on how to assure worthwhile results. What do you do to get their attention?

There are three stages in an event's publicity plan:

1. Advance publicity

2. Day-of-the-event coverage
3. Follow-up coverage, roundup of results, and evaluations

Advance Publicity

Yes, it is publicity for the event itself that should be dominating your thinking up to this point. But why pass up the opportunity for additional coverage? Actually, you must have advance publicity to assure satisfactory attendance and success for your main event.

Advance publicity can come merely through sending out advance news releases. Or, it can come through special advance events with their subsequent press coverage. These decisions depend on the size and kind of main event you are planning.

A number of events precede the Pasadena Rose Parade, and they range in size: small luncheons to a preparade ball to the Rose Queen's coronation, and her attendants' presentation. The smaller events begin months in advance, and each produces publicity for the main event. You undoubtedly are not thinking of an event of such size!

A small event, such as a training seminar that brings in a well-known person to conduct it, may profitably be preceded by a publicity-producing advance event, such as a press luncheon or a cocktail party, to introduce the personality to the press.

The point here is that advance events can be as simple or as elaborate as you wish. Some events don't call for any kind of an advance happening. But every event calls for advance publicity.

Advance press releases should go out to attract an audience to the event. Details can be distributed over several releases to announce time, place, purpose, celebrity participation, and other relevant details; or all the information can be included in one release.

Memos as Reminders

In addition to advance publicity releases, there is a certain amount of insurance in sending reminder memos to all local media on your media list. Give time, place, purpose, speaker and celebrity names, event features, and provisions that will be made for reporters. Also state whether a photographer will be in attendance for the reporters' convenience, and give the names of the persons who will be there to assist them, along with telephone numbers where those persons can be reached prior to the event. A reminder phone call a couple of days before the event can help, too.

Day-of-the-Event Coverage

One unknown author gave the following advice: "How many of you have been bitten by an elephant? By a lion or a tiger? By a dog or cat? By a mosquito? The moral here is, It's the little things that'll get you!"

In the same vein, some people will cite Murphy's Law: Anything that can go wrong, will.

So, now that you've been warned by the above profound advice, be prepared for something to go wrong on the day of your staged event, no matter how fully you and your staff have planned for it. Whatever does go wrong probably will be a seemingly inconsequential "little thing" that was overlooked in your preparations.

Now, with that negative thought behind you, look to your plans.

A Room for the Press.   Events of less than two or three days' duration do not require elaborate setups, such as a pressroom with all the accoutrements that reporters need to report their stories (such as banks of telephones, electric typewriters and word processors, and informed and knowledgeable staffers on hand). It may be helpful, however, if the public attends and if there is a special speaker or celebrity whom reporters will want to interview, to provide a separate room for such interviews.

Press Kits.   Have plenty of press kits on hand. (Chapter 10 guides you in preparing them.) Each kit should contain the following:

- News release giving the event's major points for reporters to flesh out and use or to draw on for their own stories.
- Fact sheet for those reporters who wish to write their stories from scratch.
- Backgrounder about your organization (and of the sponsoring organization and the beneficiary, if the event is sponsored by a for-profit organization to benefit a nonprofit).
- Concise history of your organization (or include two: of the sponsoring organization and the beneficiary).
- Bios of celebrity speakers or special personalities as well as of organization executives in whom the media would be interested.

- Quotes sheet of quotable remarks by event participants.
- Operating manual, if the event's purpose is to introduce a product.
- Photos of the product and people using it, the speakers or participating personalities, and any other appropriate subjects.
- Attractive, well-prepared brochure, such as an annual report, that gives additional background information (optional).

Support Staff. Remember to provide for adequate support staff for day-of-event coverage:

- Assign a sufficient number of *informed, knowledgeable* representatives from your group to meet, greet, and assist the press.
- Assign a sufficient number of "gofers" to run errands, so that you will not have to abandon your post and your responsibilities.
- Assign a special assistant to meet and greet the celebrity who will speak and to assist that person in any way that is requested.
- Plan ahead for traffic and crowd control (if the event is large). If police are required, check that they are on hand.

Follow-Up Coverage

When the event is over, you may be surprised if you think you are finished! No, there is more; and it too must be coordinated.

Mop-up. Your plans should include provisions for returning the facility to its original state, particularly if the place is on free loan or in a company room that will be used again shortly after the event.

Publicity. A more important task than mop-up is that of follow-up on publicity. Use the following guidelines to ensure that your publicity efforts will be successful.

- Offer additional information or extra pictures to reporters. Send these items in plenty of time to make the reporters' deadlines.
- Send a press release, a press kit, and a cover letter to each media representative who did not attend. Mention to each that he or she was missed.
- Write and distribute a "following-the-event" news release to those who attended and those who didn't. Include in it a round-up of information

about the event and its success, the amount raised (if for charity), a few quotes from the speaker or notable persons present, a quotable remark or two of your own, and any other appropriate *new* news about the event.

- Send thank-you letters to all media representatives who attended.
- Send thank-you letters to all who assisted, from those who made contributions of space to those who contributed time.

Final Evaluation

Another essential follow-up assignment entails looking back on the event to assess it fully, before sharp recollections fade. Whether or not you believe you will repeat the event, it is important to make a comprehensive evaluation of it and to keep a complete file of that evaluation for future reference. Keep *everything!* Chances are high that you will have another event of some kind; records from this event can provide valuable information for a future event, even if they are totally different in nature.

Follow-Up Meeting

Call a meeting of all who assisted in the event, and, together with your assistants, assess the event's successful aspects and decide which of these can be repeated another time, in part or in whole. An appraisal also should be made of any weaknesses and of any places where improvements can or should be made in the future.

Make a rating of the quality of the program and of the speaker or celebrity. Request, from anyone and everyone who participated, individual, candid feelings and reactions about the event; be sure to include your own. This includes feelings of disappointment, boredom, or other less-than-positive reactions and feelings of satisfaction related to portions that were well done.

Written Evaluation

When you have completed your follow-up meeting, get its results down *in writing,* so you will have records for reference. Do this while the project is still fresh in your mind and in the minds of your assistants.

Include the following in your written report:

- Evaluation of whether and how the project met your group's goals and objectives.

- Evaluation of whether attendance—by public and by news media—matched prior estimates.
- Comments on how press coverage stacked up against expectations.
- Narrative report of both media reaction and public reaction, gathered from everyone who had any contact with either group.

Keep file copies of the following items:

- Media list(s) used.
- Invitation list(s) with addresses and individual identifications or titles.
- Program and schedule.
- *All* releases—advance through follow-up.
- Invitations, letters of invitation, and all correspondence related to the event.
- Projected budget(s) and final costs with comparisons.
- Press clippings or a scrapbook of press clippings.
- Set of photos or negatives or slides from which the photos were made.
- Anything and everything that was used in planning or carrying out the event.

Later, when memory has blurred, you or someone else with the responsibility of coordinator will have a full and valuable reference file. You can use the file and its supporting documentation to follow the same path to an identical event or to shift in another direction.

13

Wire Services and Syndicates

How they can help you reach readers you couldn't otherwise contact

Communication Links to the World

In few businesses is a fraction of a minute so mighty and does infallible communication mean so much. Wire services provide the primary communication links that enable the daily press to keep its constant "watch on the world." They can provide significant publicity bonuses that should not be overlooked by organizations.

Wire Services and Your Publicity Efforts

Aside from local and area news, wire services provide the bulk of the stories in daily newspapers across the country. Therefore, if a news release has broad interest beyond that of the local newspapers, wire services can be a boon to your publicity efforts.

These services provide broader distribution than can be managed by mail servicing and there are no mail distribution costs; they welcome news from publicity people. They often pick up such news from newspapers and other media. Be forewarned, however, that the content and writing of a news release must be especially good to be accepted by a wire service.

Syndication

Trains and airplanes put the Pony Express out of business. Wire services have been for newspapers what trains and planes were for mail service. Even with the advent of satellite transmissions, wire services are still performing essential services. There are, however, significant improvements in the way these services are currently transmitted. Transmission by teletype is pretty much a memory.

Wire services are in fact *syndicates*—news syndicates. There are straight-news and feature-news syndicates, and photo syndicates; there are also specialty syndicates that distribute articles on travel, entertainment, human interest, business, personal finance, life-style, health, and legal issues and just about anything else that interests the reading public.

Not only do newspapers subscribe to wire services, magazines, radio, trade journals, business newspapers, and tabloids also subscribe.

International Communication Networks. Because speed is as important as thoroughness and accuracy, wire services have efficient communications facilities for sending news and photographs just about anywhere. Each wire service has an office in every major news center in the world, from which reporters can be sent to cover news of an area or a country.

The main office of a wire service is primarily a dispatching office, gathering the news sent in from staff offices and then sending it on to the appropriate office for redistribution. For example, a news event might take place in Edinburgh, Scotland, and be covered for United Press International (UPI) by the *wire reporter* in nearby Glasgow. The story would then be sent to the central office in London for dispatching to the United States. When it is received in the central office in Washington, D.C., the story from Scotland would then be sent over a nationwide network to all members or subscribing newspapers in the United States.

In the United States alone, The Associated Press (AP) lists 48 major domestic bureaus, UPI lists 15, and Reuters Information Services, Inc., lists 8. These bureaus are all in addition to their main offices.

A Story's End Destination. At recipient small newspapers the process may work much as it did when teletype was the means of transmission. The city editor, news editor, or wire editor (who is solely responsible for incoming wire material) evaluates the story, decides if it should be used in that day's edition, and designates it for a particular page and position. The story is then sent to the copy desk, where it is edited, trimmed for size, and headlined.

At the majority of newspapers, however, transmission within the newspapers is through computers. John Davenport, whose title is Special Assistant to Management, describes how the process works at *The Dallas Morning News*:

> No longer is there the clickity click and the clackity clack of hard copy coming in. Now we write and edit all of our stories on computer screens, and that is the same way we receive wire copy. Every terminal has access to the computers, and each news person has a set of commands that call up whichever wire is needed. In other words, if I want what's running on the state wire, I type in "DS fifty forty." The computer then accesses that wire right to my desk. I can do this from any desk that has a computer terminal.
>
> In answer to the question, are there wire editors anymore? Basically the answer is yes, although that isn't a title at our newspaper. In effect there are individual wire editors: the assistant national editor scrolls the national wire, the assistant international editor scrolls the international wire, the features people scroll the features wires. Editors in various departments are responsible for the news on their wires, and each is virtually a wire editor. There is, however, one person who performs some of the functions of the old wire editor. Although she is primarily responsible for international news, and her title is assistant international editor, she is also responsible for seeing that all departments are made aware of news that is germane to their work. She is the gatekeeper, and if she sees something that is of interest to a specific department she alerts that person. Unlike the earlier wire editor, however, she doesn't print out hard copy and carry it to those she alerts, she flags them by computer. For them, it's like having incoming baskets on top of their desks.

Benefits of Wire Services

Without assistance from wire services it would be impossible for newspapers to provide the amounts of information that readers receive each day.

Staff Extension

For newspapers, wire services (that provide news) and syndicates (that provide other kinds of information) are projections of the newspapers' staffs. Not even the largest newspapers can have reporters and photographers everywhere in the world where news is breaking.

The size of a newspaper largely determines the methods it uses to cover news happenings beyond the field that its newsroom reporters can physically reach. Large newspapers often have news staffs or bureaus in their state capital, in Washington, D.C., and perhaps, even in other cities in their state and other states. Small newspapers usually rely on the wire services for news both from Washington, D.C. and from within their state. Newspapers of medium size, if unable to afford a full-time reporter in the state capital, will try to have one of their staff present for important events such as legislative meetings. These papers rely on wire services for broader coverage, including news from the nation's capital.

Financial Advantages

Savings for Newspapers. At very small cost, each newspaper can print the writings, photos, and drawings of the most talented men and women of America, because the cost is spread across many subscribers.

In an article in *Saturday Review,* Boyd Lewis, former president of one of the largest basic newspaper feature services, described the advantages of syndication:

> [Each subscriber newspaper] can present articles by the foremost authorities on medicine, psychology, child care, nutrition, cooking, and other specialties. It can expose the thinking of the finest thinkers in the land. It can use countless comic strips, panels, and colored pages. And it can get all of these for a tiny fraction of what the originators are paid.

Contributor Earnings

Syndicates work to the advantage of the contract contributors, too. It has been estimated that Charles Schulz, who draws "Peanuts" for United Features Syndicate, an affiliate of Scripps-Howard Newspapers, grosses more than $20 million a year. It also is estimated that more than 250 million people around the world follow the daily doings and sayings of Snoopy and his pals.

Although you are in a sense a "contributor" when you submit your news story to a wire service, you will not receive payment for it (any more than you would from the newspapers to which you send your releases). As a matter of convention, it is considered unethical to receive compensation from both the media and the organization you represent.

Style Differences

If you believe your news-stories or photo releases merit wire service or syndicate distribution, it will be a wise move on your part to contact the nearest office for each service and to request information about how to conform to its standards and requirements. There *are* differences in preferences between wire services and newspapers and even among wire services.

For instance, one difference is that photo syndicates usually prefer negatives rather than prints. They usually do not mind, however, if other photo syndicates receive identical pictures.

If you believe that your news story or feature has broader appeal and interest than a straight-news release provides, and if national or worldwide publicity is a paramount objective, you will want to make personal contact with the nearest wire-service office; these services frequently will work with you to develop a story you have in mind.

If a wire service has expressed potential interest in your news release, a copy should be sent to each service at the same time you distribute it to local news media.

Types of News Wire Services

The principal news wire services (or *news wires*, or *news services*) are UPI, AP, and Reuters Information Services, Inc. (for world news distribution). Along with independent news-gathering agencies some cities have *city news services* that provide only local news, and there are several other categories of news services.

Business-News Services

Specialized business-news services such as Dow-Jones News Services, Business Wire, and Business News Features handle only news of interest to business publications and to the business pages of newspapers.

One business-news service focuses specifically on news for small-business service owners and independent retailers, and others have broader business-news interests integrated with other types of news and features.

Feature-News Services

Syndicated newspaper features cover many fields, from advice to the lovelorn, to cartoons and comic panels, to analysis of the weightiest issues.

You probably recognize the names of the popular feature-news services that supply newspapers; you've doubtless seen their names as bylines or in credit lines on articles that have caught your eye. *Los Angeles Times* Syndicate, King Features Syndicate, Inc., and *The New York Times* Syndication Sales Corp. are among the best known.

Information on Wire Services

If you decide to try for publicity through wire services, you probably can locate information about them in your library. Look for the following resources:

- *Editor and Publisher Syndicate Directory* is an invaluable resource.
- *Writer's Market* not only lists names, addresses, phone numbers, and editor's names, it also describes the kinds of news and articles and the specialty interests of each service it lists.
- *Bacon's Publicity Checker/Newspapers* is another directory that gives wire services' names, addresses, and phone numbers, editor's or bureau chief's names, and in some cases, the names of special-section editors.

Achieving acceptance of your news and features isn't easy, and after several seemingly unsuccessful attempts you may feel as Reggie Jackson, one of baseball's great players, described it: "It's like trying to eat coffee with a fork." Don't give up, though. The results can provide your greatest publicity "coups."

The Future of UPI

As this book goes to press, there are important developments regarding UPI. It is anticipated that the sale of UPI to a corsortium of news media companies will be finalized before the end of 1991. The consortium will consist of between four and seven internationally known news media organizations from North America, Europe, and Asia.

UPI's senior vice president for corporate affairs, Milt Capps, sees the development as giving UPI "a stronger international presence. In addition to continuance of the basic reports we offer today such as the national report, the international report, news photos, sports, et cetera, I think we will see new products and new editorial services coming out of UPI."

The mid-1991 approval of a second wage cut by UPI union employees strengthened the prospect of new ownership in UPI's future, according to the news service's chief executive officer, Pieter VanBennekom.

Capps says he cannot anticipate exactly what adaptations UPI will make but, he says, "we will continue to evolve and continue to adapt to the marketplace for news and information products."

14

Broadcast Publicity

*Why and how radio is different
from TV; how radio and
television are different
from newspapers*

Excellence in Broadcast Material

Comedian Fred Allen once said that television is called a medium because
nothing on it is well done! There are those who would agree with him about
some of today's television programming, but Allen's statement is not valid for
television commercial time. Some of the most compelling and visually
stimulating broadcast material is seen in television commercials today; and
your public service announcement (PSA), news item, or commercial spot
will be in direct competition for viewers' attention. Radio news also requires
high quality production. You truly need to know what you are doing in both
mediums.

Disadvantages of Broadcast Publicity

This book focuses primarily on newspaper publicity for very elementary
reasons:

- Electronic-news media have little time available for positive, image-
  building news. Television news is inclined to focus on crises. In a
  cartoon strip by Tom Wilson, "Ziggy" tells it like it is. Sitting in front of
  his television set, Ziggy hears the lineup of the nightly news: "Welcome
  to the six o'clock news . . . I'll be reporting on the Middle East

crisis. . . . Barb will report on the budget crisis, . . . and Bob Thur-
man and Skip Ramsey will be here later with the weather crisis and
sports crisis!"

- Newspapers not only have space for business news, they welcome it.
  They also solicit news about nonprofit, charity, and volunteer activities.

- Print publicity is scrapbook material that can be reproduced or quoted as
  often as desired for promotion and marketing purposes.

- Considerable costs are almost always involved in producing anything for
  television or radio. Many small businesses and charity groups do not
  have the resources for this type of publicity.

Occasions do arise, however, that call for publicity releases on radio or
television. When a message doesn't qualify as news, a commercial might be
used; and often public service announcements (PSAs) are a possibility for
nonprofit organizations. This chapter provides the "how-to" of radio and
television publicity and PSAs. It also gives information that you should be
aware of about broadcast commercials whether you write and produce them or
hire professionals to do it for you. When publicity is called for, many of the
same rules given for newspaper publicity apply, but the formula for presentation may be very different.

Choice of Medium

Should you include radio, television, or both in your publicity or advertising
schedule? What would be most effective? Radio and television reach larger
audiences than do newspapers. Radios are everywhere—in kitchens, bed-
rooms, and cars and also wherever kids are. Television is not yet basic
equipment in every car, but the amount of time most people spend watching
television outside of their cars is mind-boggling.

Television and radio can do some things that newspapers cannot: They
can put you right on the scene as it happens, of a fire, at your favorite team's
football game, or on the sands of Saudi Arabia.

On the other hand, the listener or viewer (at least a viewer with a
regular set) cannot hear competing programs simultaneously, nor can he or
she go back and review a program for better understanding or for study unless
he or she has taped it. And the viewer or listener can't clip an item and tuck it
into wallet or purse for reference, something that can be done with newspapers.

Advantages of Using Both Television and Radio

When your desire is to reach as many people as possible, and when you have sufficient budget and time, the best approach is to use both radio and television in addition to your newspaper campaign.

Television does what no other communication medium can: It adds visual motion, and thereby is more effective than radio or print in some instances. It is, however, more costly and difficult to produce. Television production, when combined with the cost of airtime, can be a budget buster.

If you use only radio, then you are employing only the spoken word, and your production task is simplified significantly. Radio also has the advantages of short lead times and limited production costs. A radio commercial can be written, given to a station announcer in script format, and prerecorded or read live on the air—all within a matter of hours.

Audience Selection

Now is the time to draw from your earlier research and evaluations and decide precisely who you wish your audience to be.

Radio, more than television, gives you the flexibility to target specific groups: teens, home workers, retirees, young children, ethnic groups, and so on. Each radio station may attract a completely different audience, and each audience may be a highly vertical group. There are rock stations, classical stations, news stations, "talk" stations, religious stations, foreign-language stations, and many others. Each aims its programming to specific listeners.

Most television stations, like newspapers, are aimed to the general public. (Public television stations, however, claim that they attract a more educated audience.) But, as with newspapers, you can direct your message to a particular audience by your choice of visuals, sound, and copy.

The above information pertains more to the purchase of commercial airtime. There are considerations also with regard to news released to television and radio. Large numbers of television stations maintain news operations; the majority of radio stations do not. Radio stations that include substantial news segments or those that have all-news formats also maintain news departments.

News versus Advertising

Like newspapers, most radio and television stations accept both news and advertising. And, like newspapers, advertising time can be purchased; an actual news announcement cannot. Advertising within news programs *can* be purchased, just as advertising can be placed alongside news in newspapers.

The same basic yardstick measures acceptability and value of straight and feature news in both print media and broadcast media. The principal difference is that broadcast news is abbreviated because of time restrictions. No less a news figure than Walter Cronkite called it a headline service. Print news has space to give details.

Broadcast-News Operations

The methods of operation for television and radio news are considerably different from those of newspapers, and many operational methods between television and radio are different from each other. Some elements, however, are the same or similar for radio and television.

Similarities between Radio and Television

Formula for Electronic News

Your news items should follow exactly the qualifications for every good print news story: Give briefly and concisely the who, what, when, where, and why of your newsworthy event.

Unlike print news, however, with both television and radio every word counts because there is such a premium on time. Eliminate any word that does not contribute to better understanding of the message.

Four Major Categories of Programming

For both television and radio, the kinds of programming vary widely from station to station, but the categories basically fall into the following types:

1. *Special Programs:* Interviews, panel or group discussions, demonstrations, and so on either in a series or in a one-time-only presentation.
2. *Program Segments:* Similar but shorter presentations inserted as "participating" features of other programs.

3. *Spots:* Brief announcements lasting one minute or less, made at various times during a broadcast day.

4. *Personality Spots:* Announcements by on-the-air personalities such as news anchors, disc jockeys, farm directors, weather forecasters, directors of women's or family features, and so on.

Just as you should be familiar with newspapers' special sections, columns, and styles, you should also know your local broadcast media, their programs, and their forms for presentation of those programs. The time spent learning these things can pay in enormous dividends in terms of airtime.

Broadcast Editors' Titles and Functions

Broadcasting's counterpart to the newspaper's city editor is the assignment editor, who dispatches crews and field reporters. The news editor, or news director, is the person who puts the newscast together. He or she is the person you want to talk to or to whom you should address your release. Usually the assignment editor is responsible only for breaking news (news in developing stages), although sometimes one person handles both jobs.

As is true in any news operation, print or electronic, these are busy people. Before trying to sell the merit of your organization's news, listen to the station to find out its system. Make your call well away from the station's deadline (or deadlines, since some stations are on constant news cycles).

Suitable News

What are you going to give to the radio or television news director? Your story must be something that's happening soon and that's dealing with an interesting issue.

Examples of suitable news might be your organization's march for abused children, or a company-sponsored debate between teenagers and senior citizens or kids and parents. Do not send the story of yesterday's board meeting—unless something of real news value came out of that meeting. And, if it did, yesterday's news should have been reported by you *yesterday!*

Formulas for Timing Your Copy

Because copy for both radio and television is written to be heard (whereas print copy is written to be read), the timing formula is the same for all broadcast copy. And while newspapers deal in column inches as their form of measurement, radio and television deal in seconds.

It is important for you to precisely time your copy for broadcast spots whether they are purchased commercials or free public service announcements. The following table will help you estimate the length of your copy by number of words per second.

Seconds	Number of Words
10	20
20	50
30	75
60	150

Most people use a stopwatch to time spots. But because some people read faster than others, KNBC-TV in Los Angeles devised a more accurate method for timing spots: five syllables equal one second.

Time is so controlled by today's state-of-the-art electronics that a poorly timed spot that runs too long will be automatically cut off the air at the point it overruns its allotted time slot. Be as precise as possible.

Differences between Radio and Television

Radio News

Radio news operations in many ways are unlike those of television. But, the less understood differences are those among different radio stations' news operations; they vary considerably. Some stations have all-news operations with large staffs; others may be strictly "rip-and-read" operations, with disc jockeys or station announcers who read wire service bulletins at specific times. In many cases, the news coming to radio stations is prerecorded by a news company that sells its services to the station, where it is played rather than read. There is so much variety among radio stations in the sources from which they receive their news that methods must be checked to ensure greater acceptance of your publicity releases.

You must know whether you should supply copy directly to the station or to the services that furnish the station's news. A telephone call to the station should give you that information.

The form for a radio news release should be the same as for newspapers. There is no need to put it into a special format, because the station's news department prefers to rewrite the copy to conform to its individual requirements.

News Services for Radio

Like newspapers, radio stations get the bulk of their material from news services. Most news received from wire services by broadcast stations has been especially written in a conversational style "for the ear;" it is then transmitted over a circuit different than that provided to print media.

If you provide news releases to news services for radio use or directly to stations' news departments, supply them with the same news release you wrote for newspapers. There is no need to rewrite them "for the ear" because as stated above, news service staffers prefer to rewrite them if they find the news sufficiently interesting.

Television News

Television news is the glamorous branch of the news business. Dan Rather, Peter Jennings, and Tom Brokaw are no less celebrities than the biggest motion picture and rock stars. And who doesn't know who Walter Cronkite is, even after all of his years away from the news-anchor desk? Even news anchors in relatively small markets are considered stars and are invited to host various business functions, lend their names to sports tournaments, or head charity drives.

For some people, television news is the main source of information. Television can do something that newspapers cannot: show action. The news is concise and not too complicated; and television news editors think in terms of visual impact, therefore stories are selected for that reason.

Television News Time

Maury Green was for many years a newsman for a CBS-owned television station in Los Angeles. Green offered advice about placement of news with television news departments in his book *Television News—Anatomy and Process* (Wadsworth Publishing Company). His counsel is directed to professional public relations representatives, but it holds up well for anyone representing a commercial enterprise.

> In general, PR [representatives] do not "score" as well with television as with newspapers, for two reasons: (1) because of its time limitations television cannot cover as many stories as the newspaper, and many PR releases are

therefore rejected as too trivial or too limited in interest, and (2) many PR releases are so promotional in nature that to incorporate them into a news show would constitute a "plug" [free advertising] for the PR client.

However, Green also concedes that public relations representatives "of business firms, governmental offices and agencies, political parties and candidates, foundations, civic and community organizations, and numerous other groups provide a large amount of news which appears on television in one form or another."

In other words, if the news is big, involves big names and big issues, and had broad interest value, television news departments are interested in your release. There is little time or place, however, for the average small organization's news dispatch.

Television Stations and Free Tapes

Maury Green stresses that achieving television publicity is difficult. There is, however, a means that may be productive: free tapes.

Can you supply a film or tape of the happening, or at the very least, color slides? If television news has a high priority in your publicity plan, be aware that supplying free film clips or videotapes—called handouts—can provide excellent publicity returns, particularly from smaller, independent television stations. These stations are especially interested in news presented in this form because it provides visual reports of activities that the stations are unable to cover, and it means savings for them in time and cost. If you do supply film or tape, be sure it is something that is visually animated. (Just as in still photos, be sure there is life and action in your clip; someone making an announcement with a lineup of standing executives or with the chairman passing a gavel will never qualify.)

Broadcast Commercials

The preceding information has been primarily about radio and television *news*. The following information pertains to *purchased* spots.

Do-It-Yourself Commercials

This is a book about generating publicity, but there may be times when the only way to get your message out is to buy advertising. If you buy broadcast advertising, you must follow different methods of writing than those used for newspaper advertising.

Before you sit down to design and write either a radio or television commercial, remember the statement at the beginning of this chapter: Some of the most compelling and visually stimulating broadcast material is seen in television commercials; and many radio commercials are produced with the same high quality. If at all possible, arrange for a professional to do your radio or television spot. But even with that assistance, you should be knowledgeable about various aspects of television commercials.

The following sections give rules and hints about *commercial* broadcast spots.

Rates by Time Slots. Broadcast advertising is somewhat harder to plan than print media advertising. The pattern of locations in newspapers (special days, special pages or sections such as business, food, travel, real estate and so forth) on which rates are based is fairly well standardized.

In broadcast advertising, however, there can be a confusion of terms for time slots. For instance, Class A time indicates prime time or drive time, on most radio stations. Some radio stations also have Class AA time strictly for *morning drive time.* Class B time may be *home-worker time;* Class C time may be *evening time;* and Class D time is *time after midnight.* The exact hours these classifications cover are not always the same. You should become familiar with rates so that you understand definitions of the terms used by the stations from which you buy time. The individual station's sales representative can explain the differences, and together you can be sure the terms used mean the same thing to both of you.

Television stations may divide broadcast time similarly, or, more likely, classify their time slots as daytime, early fringe time, prime time, late fringe time, and weekend time.

Time-Slot Planning. Time-slot planning can present your biggest problem in preparing a broadcast commercial. In print media, space is expandable. Pages can be added to take care of almost any number of advertisers. Broadcasting time, however, is limited. There are only so many hours in a day, and some stations are licensed to be on the air for only a limited number of those hours.

Getting the time slots and the programs that will work best for your message probably will be your biggest problem. Often the best time periods are claimed by other advertisers who intend to keep them, which means you must choose between taking a less desirable time or turning to other media.

Successful Selling

If you *purchase* airtime you undoubtedly have something to *sell:* an image, a product, a service, an event, a community program, a plea for funds or volunteers. Whatever it is you wish to sell probably requires that you inform the public of its existence in order to accomplish your goal.

Any good salesperson knows, there are five steps in making a successful sale:

1. Introducing
2. Gaining attention
3. Arousing interest
4. Creating desire
5. Closing

Those five steps give you a measuring stick you can use with any copy that has as its goal to "sell" something.

The steps are not always used in many radio and television commercials. Instead, these commercials often are "sound-pretty" or "look-pretty" spots that fail to *sell.* The sounds and sights are beautiful, and the words "roll like butter off an announcer's tongue," as one copywriter puts it, but they fail to perform the single, most important function of commercial copy: selling.

Radio and Television Guidelines

The following guidelines apply to both television and radio commercials. There are individual guidelines elsewhere in this chapter presenting information applicable only to radio. The section about TV public service announcements (PSAs) gives information that, in many instances, is also applicable to television commercials.

Sound Effects and Music

Sound effects are used to catch attention. However, sound is so much a part of every commercial that you should plan appropriate music or background sounds for your spots even if you don't use sound effects.

Almost every radio and television station has a library of music and sound effects. Some of the music available is in public domain, which means there are no restrictions on copyright. Some stations have both the technical facilities and the talented personnel to produce some of their own sound effects and singing jingles. Salespeople can help you with these aspects of your spot.

The salesperson cannot, however, or perhaps won't care to, advise you about what sounds are best for grabbing attention. Some copywriters call for every spot to start off with a loud, spectacular noise of some kind—to wake up the listener's ear. That's not always the best idea.

Sound effects should be used sparingly or listeners will not just turn off their attention, they may even turn off the station. Sounds should be used only if they have a logical, appropriate tie-in with what the announcer says. They should be interesting enough so that the listener can concentrate on what follows, but they should not be disturbing or just noisy.

Sounds of a baby crying will catch the ear of a new parent, but is your message related to babies or to the parents of babies? The ringing of a telephone can be so realistic that a listener may think for a second or so that it is his or her own phone. It will catch the ear, but does it have anything to do with the information that follows? A catchy musical lead-in is another good way to catch a listener's ear. But again, be sure that the music relates directly to the message that follows.

The most sensational attention-arrester ever used on the air was the one Orson Welles used on October 30, 1938. It sent thousands of people into hysterics and wild panic: "Attention! Attention, everyone! The first Martian spaceships have just landed on earth!" These words are from "The War of the Worlds," a drama about a Martian invasion of Earth, which featured fictional news reports that panicked some listeners who thought that the events being portrayed were real.

An attention-arrester need not be sensational, noisy, or electrifying. It need only be interesting enough to cause the listener to mentally tune in to your spot, because he or she is curious to know what you have to say.

When your spot uses a suitable sound effect or an appropriate piece of music, it will be a production and must be recorded. It will entertain as well as inform. The listener will enjoy it and will *listen to the message*, thus producing the results you desire.

Focused Message

When you've chosen your opening attention-arrester and are reasonably sure you can attract the listener's notice, start at once to arouse direct interest in and desire for what you have to sell. Don't stall with throw-away phrases such as, "Good evening," or "Ladies and gentlemen." Don't waste a second of that precious—and expensive—time you have purchased.

Also remember that the old mass salutations went out with earphones and crystal sets. Be sure that your message is directed to one person, in his or her own living room, kitchen, office, or car. Your announcer isn't up on a stage addressing a mass audience. Your copy must *immediately* grab the listener's attention—or another music station, news show, or talk show will. You have heavy competition for every listener's attention.

Headlines

In Chapter 5, you learned how to write headlines for your newspaper publicity copy and in Chapter 15 you will learn about writing headlines in print ads. Beginning a radio or television commercial with a summary that contains the most important information in your spot and that reads and sounds like a headline probably will be the antithesis of an interesting attention-arrester.

Copy Rules for Both Television and Radio

A few of the following rules apply to print copy, but most are exclusive to radio and television copy.

Conversational Tone

If you are the writer of your radio or television copy, remember that you are not writing it to be read in a book, a magazine, or a newspaper. You are writing words to be spoken by an announcer and to be listened to by individuals.

Use everyday, conversational language, for both radio and television. Maury Green, in his book *Television News: Anatomy and Process*, advises that the language must be casually conversational even to the point of sounding "slangy." He says, "It is spoken language, not literary language," so write the way you speak.

The copywriter's task is to put everyday spoken words down on paper, so that the announcer will sound like he or she is talking, not reading. The copywriter should use the vocabulary and expressions of ordinary speech, not of written language. There is a big difference. If you are the copywriter:

- If you normally use the contraction *don't* when you speak, use it when you write.

- Use the contraction *let's* instead of the words let us.
- Say, "Get your free pen and pencil soon!" and not, "Obtain your free pen and pencil at your earliest opportunity."

Action Verbs

A successful salesperson uses lots of action verbs in a sales pitch. He or she knows that verbs are the most action-compelling words in any language. For example read the following lines:

- *Listen* to *this!*
- *Order* your tickets *today!*
- *Try* it, and *see!*
- *Pick* up the phone, *now!*

Positive versus Negative

Accentuate the positive! Eliminate the negative. The words of this old song should be your motto. Keep it handy to check your commercial copy and remind yourself: Never use a negative if you can possibly avoid it. This may sound a trifle extreme, but why plant a negative thought in a listener's mind when a positive thought will get a better result?

If the point seems small and unimportant, don't forget that any and every small device you can employ to increase the effectiveness of your copy is certainly worth considering. Examine the following two statements:

Positive: Oaks Doctors Referral Service is the best there is.

Negative: You won't find a better way to locate a doctor than through Oaks Doctors Referral Service.

Questions

It is amazing how many times you can edit a piece of copy and still find that the words in it stick the announcer's neck out by having him or her ask a leading question (e.g., "Are you worrying about a safe place to invest your money?").

A listener can think of enough reasons for not responding positively to your message without helping him or her think of more. Eliminate questions.

Almost always a question can be rewritten into an imperative, such as in the following example:

Question: Why not get your copy soon?

Imperative: Get *your* copy . . . *today!*

Plural Predicates with Singular Organization Names

Avoid plural pronouns and verbs with singular organization names! This is one of the most common errors in copywriting. It shouts, amateur writer!

> *Right:* The Resource Assistance Center is generous. It *has* free tax counseling for senior citizens.
>
> *Wrong:* The Resource Assistance Center is generous. *They have* free tax counseling for senior citizens.

The Resource Assistance Center is the singular name of the organization. "It has" is correct, not "they have"!

Especially watch for singular possessives (e.g., "TRAC is holding its (not *their*) annual 10K run."

Clichés

If you were given the opportunity to read an average piece of copy that comes in to a radio or television station, you would find hackneyed, battle-scarred words such as amazing, terrific, sensational, and gigantic. From retailers you might find phrases such as "tremendous assortment," "large variety," "vast array," or "prices that will astonish you."

Copywriters tell you they continue to use these "sacred cow" marvels because they've always been used! Well, sacred cows make great hamburger meat! But even if you are selling hamburgers, sell the sizzle instead.

Crisp and Graphic Copy

A 60-second commercial has only about 150 words and a 30-second spot has about 75 words. You can't afford to waste a word or to write lengthy sentences that are difficult for the listener to follow and understand.

But copy can't be completely composed of short, jerky sentences, either. Variety is the answer. Begin with a longer (but not too long), carefully balanced, well-developed sentence; then use a short one. Eliminate throwaway words such as *the* and *and* whenever and wherever they are not essential.

Summarize

If the attention-arrester at the start of your commercial doesn't in fact, arrest your listener's attention, he or she may not begin to concentrate on your message until it is halfway finished.

To avoid this, repeat enough of the message at the end of your commercial to assure the listener's understanding. In other words, summarize. At the very end of your message, as briefly as possible, abstract the *one* thing you wish the listener to remember, then again mention your organization's name.

Phone Numbers and Addresses

In newspaper advertising, you are urged, literally prodded, to always include your organization's address and phone number. This is not the case in radio and television spots.

If, for some specific reason, listeners are asked to call a number immediately, that is different. Even then, they probably will have to look up the number in the phone book because they've forgotten it by the time they get to the phone. Listeners do not retain telephone numbers, nor do they remember street numbers. Give the listener something he or she can remember, such as "Call Sam's Pool Maintenance. It's in the phone book under S . . . S as in service. Sam's Pool Service."

The listener might be likely to remember this, too: "Sam's Pool Service . . . at 234 West Fourteenth Street, right across from the post office." The landmark helps him or her picture the location in mind and retain it in memory.

Sound Check

The absolute first check you must make is how your copy will sound to listeners. Even for television commercials, sound is extremely important because some of the audience may be listening but not watching as they do other things within listening range of their TV sets.

Read the copy aloud. How does it sound? Is it natural, or does it sound stilted? Is it believable? Does it sound like someone talking or like someone reading? If you can, read the copy into a tape recorder and play it back. You then can hear it as the audience will.

Pitfalls

There have been some disastrous, sometimes humorous, results from copy read by an announcer that had not been *listened* to in advance:

- Ladies, stop in and drop your clothes off.
- Do you have an old bag around the house? XYZ Luggage will take your old bag in trade on a new one.

Children have taught us over the years that spoken words can sound much different from the written word. Many children hear the first line of the Pledge of Allegiance as "I led the pigeons to the flag," according to William Safire, writing in *The New York Times.*

In a spot advertising the merits of a new housing development, the writer, who usually wrote copy for print ads, several times called the development "the land of ahhhs"—a catchy phrase to read. The spot was a total bust because the audience heard the phrase as "the Land of Oz," and couldn't understand the meaning of the commercial.

There are words and phrases better left to your imagination than used here, that have different *sounding* meanings from their spelled meanings. These words and phrases can send your organization down in flames! Listen carefully to your written words.

Checklist

Portions of the following checklist are adapted from information provided by Southern California Broadcasters Association. Use the questions to check your own copy, or to check copy that has been written for you.

- Do the words grab the listener's attention in the first few seconds? Does your spot start out by gaining attention, go on to arouse interest, then create desire, and, finally, come to a close that arouses the listener to some action?
- Does the announcement deliver the main idea quickly? Clearly? Completely? Often enough to stick in the listener's mind?
- Does it strongly register the key facts about your project or your organization? Is the information specific enough to get the idea across?
- Has the copy turned the spotlight on your organization's name? Does it mention the organization's name at least three times in a 60-second spot—in the beginning, middle, and end—and at least twice in shorter spots? Is your organization's name the very last word in the copy so that it is the last thing planted in the listener's mind?
- Is the copy written in simple, clear, and easy-to-understand language?
- Does your announcement maintain interest from beginning to end?

If the copy misses anything covered in the checklist, make the necessary changes. You may find that a rewrite is called for, but accept this as positive. As Maury Green says in his book, "The best writing is almost always rewriting." Rewriting usually shortens and tightens copy so that its meaning stands out sharply and clearly.

General Guidelines for Preparation of Copy

When your copy is fine tuned and ready to be typed, the following guidelines will assist you.

Pauses and "Emphasizers"

Punctuate to help the announcer read your copy.

Words in all capital letters and dots between phrases mean specific things to radio and television announcers.

Words and phrases typed in all-capital letters tell the announcer to emphasize that word or phrase. Dots between phrases tell him or her where to place pauses. Here is some sample copy:

You can make a difference! There's a child who NEEDS you . . . who has a learning problem YOU can help her overcome. Call COMMUNITY CENTER FOR KIDS . . . It's in your phone book . . . That's COMMUNITY CENTER FOR KIDS. Call now . . . or stop by . . . at Community Center Mall . . . on I-62 . . . near Bledsoes.

Pronunciation Clarification

Commercial copy announcers and newscasters should never have to worry about how to pronounce names. The correct pronunciation should be given right in the news copy or commercial copy. Give the announcer who reads your commercial the same break.

If your organization's name, a street address, or any word within the copy, has an unusual pronunciation, spell it out, as in the following examples:

The yo toon HAY man (Jotunheimen)
Center on an goo LEEM (Angouleme) Street

If your organization is best known by its acronym, spoken as a word, write the acronym in capital letters. If the letters are spoken separately, type them separated by hyphens (e.g., U-S-A, G-E, or P-A-S-I). Hyphens (or dashes) are used to instantly alert the announcer that it is not a word, but an abbreviation, in which each letter is to be spoken individually.

Special Guidelines for Radio Commercials

Because radio time generally is less expensive to purchase and radio spots are far less expensive to produce, this medium may be the path to take if you opt for broadcast commercials. (But remember, this is copy written to be heard! There are great differences between hearing and reading.)

Just as with print advertising, there are salespeople at each radio station who can assist you in preparing your commercial radio copy. Call on them so that your radio commercials conform to the station's copy format. Radio reaches only the ear, and words written for radio therefore should form pictures. They should add measure and color. Your assignment is to help the listener form a picture—to see, feel, smell, and taste.

The major challenge in a radio spot is to interest the listener. If it doesn't, it is extremely easy for him or her to switch stations, or make a run to the refrigerator. You have big competition for the listener's attention! There are statistics, however, to show that radio listeners—particularly those in cars—switch stations far less because of disinterest in or dislike of announcements or commercials than do television viewers.

Selective Information

This is one of the first things to be aware of and to remember each time you change your newspaper-ad-copy-writing hat for the one you wear while writing or evaluating commercial broadcast copy: A newspaper ad can list a number of items and present more than one idea, but too many ideas or items in one radio spot are confusing to a listener.

If your organization has never used radio before, you undoubtedly will be inclined to put more than one item or thought in a single spot. Newspaper advertisers often run lists of bargain buys that give both regular price and sale price. In a newspaper ad this is okay. Don't defeat your purpose, however, by doing this in a radio spot. Too many items and too many prices are confusing to a listener and so is more than a single piece of information about your organization.

But what if a legitimate need exists for presenting several bargains or for letting the public know that your organization performs more than one service or sells more than one product? Then write two or more pieces of copy, and put no more than two items in each spot.

Third-Person Address

In a newspaper ad, it is fine to address the reader as follows: "Join us in helping to make this event a success," or "We invite you to . . . ". In a print ad, the reader recognizes that the use of we or us is tied directly to the organization presenting the message because the organization's name and logo are prominently displayed within the advertising space.

Remember, however, not to write it that way for a radio announcer to read. The listener knows that the announcer at your local station is not your partner in business. And the announcer may strongly oppose being put in the position of speaking as if he or she is a member of your organization.

This kind of "personalization" is often presented on television by actors playing the part of an organization's executive or employee. On television a well-known person may be affiliated with and actually speak for a nonprofit group. The easily recognized voice of a celebrity may be used in a radio commercial, but unless you supply special prerecorded audio tapes, radio announcements are read by station announcers, and the listener may have just heard him or her read another commercial for a different organization.

Use third person in all commercial copy. Say, "Go in . . . " not "Come in . . . ," with absolutely no exceptions.

Public Service Announcements (PSAs)

The following sections focus on information about PSAs and how to produce them. The information in these sections is of greatest interest to nonprofit organizations. However, businesses undoubtedly can pick up additional tips for producing commercial spots, particularly with the current trend emerging in which commercials are developed to give an impression of being PSAs.

PSA Defined

First, it helps to understand exactly what a PSA is and specifically who it benefits. There are major—and obvious—differences between print and broadcast. One of the critical differences lies with free airtime, called public service time. PSAs fall within the constraints of public service time.

The definition of a PSA, according to the Federal Communications Commission (FCC), is as follows:

> [A PSA is] an announcement for which no charge is made and which promotes programs, activities, or services of Federal, State or Local Gov-

ernments [e.g., sales of bonds, recruiting, etc.] or the programs, activities
or services of non-profit organizations [e.g., Red Cross] and other announcements regarded as serving community interests.

A business working with, sponsoring, or otherwise allied with nonprofits in supporting charitable efforts finds no limits or no penalties in
receiving publicity in newspapers. But there is absolutely no commercial
name credit permitted in like situations in PSAs on television. Radio appears
to have some leeway in this regard. For television, the restriction extends even
to mentions of places at which an event is held, such as hotel names,
restaurant names, and such. Public service time is an excellent option for
nonprofits.

"Commercial" PSAs

Aetna Life & Casualty is the trendsetter in this category, with a campaign
"that delivers what most insurance advertising tried to avoid—straight talk
about some of the thornier problems facing the public and insurance companies, issues like AIDS, drunken driving and long term care for the elderly,"
according to *The New York Times.*

"We want to be seen as a leader on the important issues of today," said
Christine Farley, assistant vice president of advertising at Aetna, as quoted in
The Times article. The commercials are meant to look and sound like public
service spots.

The drastic stylistic departure from other commercials is likely to catch
viewers' attention.

Free Airtime versus Purchased Airtime

Broadcasting, like print media, is under no obligation to grant free airtime to
any *specific* organization. Unlike print media, however, you can count on the
fact that FCC regulations require broadcast stations to make a certain amount
of free airtime available for public, or community, service.

Generally speaking, stations will give about one-fourth of their commercial time to public service. The station chooses the form its public service
will take, and the station decides who will receive the free airtime.

Format.   The format for public service airtime may be through hosted,
regularly scheduled programs with segments devoted to projects by nonprofit
organizations. Or television stations and radio stations may opt for PSAs.
PSAs are similar to broadcast commercials in their format.

Control.   While receiving free airtime has a definite monetary advantage, purchasing airtime also has its advantages. Purchasing airtime gives you control over the exact time in which your message will be seen and/or heard, so that you can reach certain types of listeners or viewers. You can vary the number of purchased spots for different degrees of intensity and impact. Of course, cost is a factor that may add up to a serious disadvantage if your budget is extremely tight or nonexistent.

On the other hand, PSAs are scheduled at the radio and television stations' discretion—to play at *their* chosen time, which may be 2:00 A.M. And the message you had hoped would be aired many times may receive only a couple of exposures before it is shelved.

If a station gives you free PSA airtime for your message, don't cancel out the possibility of future PSAs by buying newspaper space or airtime elsewhere. Broadcast people not only read newspapers, but check out other stations (called monitoring). They will find out about your purchases elsewhere and close their medium to you for anything other than the purchase of commercial time.

Questions for a Better PSA

If your public service appeal is to be effective, you should have the answers to these key questions even before you contact your local station:

- What is your message? Are you sure of the basic idea you want to get across?
- Who should receive your message? Is it of general interest to a large segment of the listening and/or viewing audience? Can it be tailored to those you want most to reach?
- How can you best put your message across? Does it have enough general interest for a special program? Would a brief announcement serve just as well?

Your answers to those questions, particularly to the What of your message, will largely determine your success in getting free airtime.

Points for an Effective PSA

Writing for broadcast, whether using purchased time or public service time, takes salesmanship, and you can't sell something unless you are completely informed about your "product," whether it is an event, a special service, or a plea for volunteers. You job is to overcome the listener's or viewer's apathy, to create interest in your story, to motivate the listener to do something.

- Determine the objective of the total campaign—the specific goal for the radio and television announcements or spots.
- List all the pertinent facts to be included in the order of their importance.
- Decide on the single, most important thing you want to say.
- Think how you would say it if you were talking face-to-face to one person. Then write it that way, in a conversational manner.

Preparation of Copy for Radio PSAs

Following are guidelines and instructions that apply to radio public service announcements. (Specific information about television PSAs are in a separate section of this chapter.)

PSA Radio Guidelines. Just as for print media, your typewriter, word processor, or computer printer must be in first-class shape and your typing must be neat and accurate.

- Use one announcement per page.
- Type on only one side of the paper.
- Double- or triple-space announcement copy on 8½-inch by 11-inch white paper.
- Use a clean typewriter or a new printer ribbon.
- Use upper- and lower-case letters for regular copy and upper-case letters for emphasis. For instance, use upper-case letters to emphasize your organization's name.

PSA Radio Instructions. For greater understanding of the following instructions, refer to Figure 14.1.

1. If you are not using letterhead or "instantly created letterhead," type and center (at the top of the page) the following information about your organization:
   Name
   Address
   Telephone number

2. Space down two to four lines and type the contact information at the left margin. As in a press release, try to provide two contact names.
   - Type the word Contact: then your name, then space down one line.
   - Type your telephone number if it is different from the one listed in the letterhead. (In the example in Figure 14.1, the person listed first can be reached at the organization so no telephone number is listed.) Space down one line.
   - Type the words "Alternate Contact:" then the name of a knowledge-able staff member or volunteer, then space down one line and type his or her telephone number if different from the number given for the organization.
3. Alongside the right-hand margin and opposite the contact information:
   - Type the words "Start Date:" and space down one line.
   - Type the date on which the PSA is scheduled to start playing, and space down a line.
   - Type the words "End Date:" and space down another line.
   - Type the date on which the PSA is scheduled to stop running.

FIGURE 14.1 **Format example for radio PSA copy**
(When no letterhead is available, use plain white business-size paper.)

THE RESOURCE ASSISTANCE CENTER
1234 South Sixteenth Street
Dumont, Kansas 85123
111/456-7890

Contact:	Mark Whitmore	Start Date:	
Alternate Contact:	Deb Wilson		February 2
	111/222-3333	End Date:	
			February 8

Time: 20 seconds
Words: 47

This is HELP A SENIOR CITIZEN WEEK. This week join THE RESOURCE ASSISTANCE CENTER to help Dumont area seniors prepare their tax returns. Over the years TRAC has helped people of all ages. Now TRAC needs your help. Call today . . . Trac's number is in your phone book.

---

4. Space down two lines and, aligned with the left-hand margin, type the word "Time:" followed by the number of seconds the PSA is set to run.

5. Space down two more lines and type: Words: followed by the number of words in the PSA announcement.

6. Space down four or so lines and type the announcement copy, double spaced.

Television PSAs

When you watch television, the PSAs look easy and sound easy, but they are not. Perhaps you have in mind just running down to the nearest television station so it can videotape you while you read or recite your message. Forget this! You will be courting disaster, unless you are a professional television actor or announcer. Holding the attention of viewers is most difficult.

Try to remember the last political campaign period on television. Remind yourself of how many times you switched away from an announcer merely reciting copy—and those people are highly paid professionals. If they have difficulty competing for viewers' attention, think of how difficult it is for nonprofessionals.

Station Requirements and Policies

Find out individual station requirements and policies, and keep an updated list. The specifications definitely may be different in other geographical areas, or markets, as broadcast people say. Community Affairs Director Mary Alan Bonnick at the CBS affiliate, KDFW-TV, in Dallas, has prepared a brochure that she circulates to organizations that are granted PSA time. The following excerpts are adapted to present information that is more or less universal. To be safe, however, check to verify that the following guidelines and instructions meet your station's requirements.

- The sponsoring organization must be tax exempt and able to so prove.
- No shared commercial message (visual, aural, or both) may be included in any [PSA] for television, and any hint of commercialism such as "charges to cover expenses" of a product or service being offered is strictly unacceptable.
- Names of commercial ventures such as sponsors of events cannot be mentioned even if all proceeds benefit a nonprofit organization.
- Names of hotels cannot be mentioned as that constitutes commercialism.

- Names of ticket agencies cannot be mentioned as that constitutes commercialism.
- Names of individual stores cannot be mentioned as that constitutes commercialism. However, names of shopping malls can be used.
- No event will be publicized that is not open to the public or that does not have broad-based audience appeal.
- PSAs will not be aired using personalities or members of the broadcast media of a station other than [KDFW-TV's], or personalities from another network other than [CBS].
- PSAs will not be aired for membership drives for clubs, civic or social. [Nor will it air messages] for colleges/universities promoting registration days and holidays; [nor] for political organizations or special interest groups; [nor] for individual churches.

Artistic, Creative, and Technical Standards

PSAs must be of acceptable artistic, creative, and technical quality as perceived by station management (generally the public service director).

In its brochure about PSAs, KDFW-TV issues a warning in this regard: "If you produce a PSA at a cable television facility, do not automatically expect it to be aired on commercial stations. Most cable equipment is not broadcast quality because it does not have to be. The horizontal blanking does not meet FCC standards when using cable equipment."

Some stations make studio time available to nonprofits that have little or no advertising budget, but this courtesy differs from station to station.

Video and Audio Format Requirements

Video and audio formats may be completely different from one station to another, depending on each station's equipment. Be sure to check your local station's requirements. KDFW-TV accepts the following:

- VIDEO
  2-inch videotape
  1-inch videotape
  3/4-inch videocassette (not 1/2-inch used in home recorders)
  16-mm film
  35-mm color slides

Super card or artwork

8-by-10 prints (color or black and white)

- AUDIO

1/4-inch audiotape (reel to reel)

Sound on tape (2-inch, 1-inch, 3/4-inch)

Sound on film (16-mm)

Record album (no cassettes or eight-tracks)

PSA Script Guidelines

KDFW-TV's Community Affairs Director, Mary Bonnick, has definite and specific instructions for writing PSA copy. It is presented here, with permission. Some of it echoes the instructions for writing commercial broadcast copy, but it is included here to keep this section on PSAs intact and to make it easier to use.

Scripts

1. What do you want to promote?

   A. A generic PSA for the organization

   B. A specific event benefiting the organization

   C. A program offered by the organization

   D. A campaign

2. The copy must fit the video. Think visually as the script is written.

3. Keep it simple. Stay away from difficult medical terms and tongue twisters.

4. The name of the organization should be mentioned at least twice in the copy. However, if some information has to be edited for time, the name, address, and phone number of the organization can be superimposed on the screen during the last five seconds of the PSA.

5. Don't omit essential information. Check the copy to be sure it tells who, what, where, when, and why.

6. Don't get carried away by trivialities, superlatives and overenthusiasm. Omit adjectives and avoid nicknames. Think economy; your PSA time is a valuable commodity, use it wisely.

7. Do not write scripts up to the 10-second, 20-second, 30-second, and 60-second limit. Leave 2 or 3 seconds to spare.

Visuals

1. Studio Camera
   A. The studio is confining, so keep it simple.
   B. Normally no more than two cameras can be used.
   C. Often live talent is used: talking, singing, acting, or simple dancing.
   D. There are several factors to consider when choosing talent:
      (1) In how many other PSAs or commercials is the talent already appearing?
      (2) Is the person at ease on camera?
      (3) Will the talent be a good spokesperson for the organization?
      (4) Will the message be convincing to the public not only by the talent's image, but how well the lines are delivered?
   E. Props are provided by the organization (plants, director's chair, etc.).
   F. A background can be created by using creative lighting (black limbo, blue or green, star filter) or a process called chromakeying where a picture is inserted behind the talent. A blue or green backdrop is replaced with a video source (camera, tape, film, slide).
   G. Costumes can be worn. If chromakeying, no blue or green can be worn. If talent is Black, bright white and black should not be worn. Actually bright white should not be worn by anyone. Avoid plaids and checks.
   H. A teleprompter is used for the talent so they can look directly into the camera lens and say their lines.
   I. Other video can be shot in the studio to be used as cutaways from the studio talent. These visuals match the script and keep the talent from a straight "talking head" PSA. Existing video or slides can also be used for cutaways.

2. Slides
   A. 35 mm
   B. Color
   C. Horizontal format (action from side to side rather than top to bottom).
   D. TV system will crop edges on all four sides so titles and action must be within the center ³/₄ inches high and 1 inch wide.
   E. Only top quality slides will be used (e.g., tells a story, in focus, good

color contrast because light color will wash out on television, correct exposure).

F. One slide with 10 seconds of copy is not acceptable. Minimum number of slides:

(1) Per 10 seconds—2

(2) Per 20 seconds—4

(3) Per 30 seconds—6

(4) Per 60 seconds—12

3. Prints

A. Minimum size 8 by 10

B. If the subject calls for it, black and white photographs can be used.

C. Use same quality standards and numbers as for slides.

4. Taping on Location

A. The studio is confining so in certain instances location shooting is preferred.

B. Pick a location keeping these factors in mind:

(1) Find a visually pleasing background.

(2) Secure permission from the appropriate person.

(3) If taping inside, check the lighting and electrical outlets of the locations.

(4) If taping outside, check the lighting as well as the noise level of the location.

C. Location shooting often involves talent. Use the same guidelines for choosing talent for location tapings as for studio tapings.

D. Cue cards are often used on location. The cards are clumsy because the talent does not look directly into the camera and often the talent has a problem reading the cards. If possible, request the talent to memorize the script. Also, visuals of the talent in action or in special surroundings can be shot with no natural sound. A voice-over is used in place of talent talking on camera.

E. Visuals of the surroundings or the talent can also be shot to be used as visual cutaways to avoid the talent talking on camera for the entire PSA.

5. Existing Footage

Footage that has been shot previously can be used to create an entire PSA or to create visual cutaways to add to a PSA.

6. Artwork
   A. Artwork (black and white or color) is usually provided by the organization.
   B. White lettering on black camera card is used to superimpose information on the screen.
7. Tagging
   A. It is an FCC regulation that the name of the nonprofit sponsor be mentioned in the script or superimposed on the screen. Normally the name and phone number of the sponsoring organization is supered [superimposed] the last five seconds of the PSA.
   B. Tools used for tagging
      (1) Camera card (white lettering on black) used for supering or full screen.
      (2) Electronic Character Generator at the station (super of full screen).
      (3) Slide (white lettering on black background slide or color slide for supering or full screen).
   C. It is an FCC regulation that if a nonprofit organization buys commercial time, "Paid for by . . . " has to be superimposed somewhere during the commercial. This is to distinguish between commercials and PSAs.

   Audio
1. Talent talking on camera
2. Voice-over using a celebrity (be careful choosing talent. Does the person have a pleasing professional voice?) or the professional voice who records for the station.
3. Natural sounds from footage shot on location.
4. Sound effects (usually taken from record albums).
5. Music
   A. Music enhances a PSA.
   B. Copyright laws are not strictly enforced with PSAs. The stations pay BMI and ASCAP a large sum of money for use of the music. Most classics are public domain, and there is also library music which is not copyrighted.
6. Combination of any of these.

Post-Production Hints

1. Copies of the PSA, for the other stations [in the area] are made at no charge to the organization. Extra copies are made for the organization to distribute as it chooses. However, after seven copies, the organization will be charged a fee to be determined by the station. The station producing the PSA usually keeps the master tape.

2. When picking up PSAs from the producing station, be sure to also pick up any slides, artwork, props, or music used in producing the PSA.

3. Personal delivery of the PSA to Public Service Directors is highly recommended.

4. There is no guarantee for public service time. Do not beg, plead, threaten, or demand public service time. Be brief, courteous, and friendly.

5. If the PSA is to be returned to the organization after airing, tell the Public Service Director. (Generic PSAs are usually aired for six to nine months.)

6. Most Public Service Directors can give the number of times the PSA was aired in a week or a month, but not the times of day it was aired.

Airtime Scheduling

1. PSAs are scheduled [at most stations] by the Public Service Director about a day in advance, except for weekend PSAs, which usually are scheduled on Thursday and Friday.

2. There is no guaranteed Public Service time. Public Service availabilities change daily depending upon the amount of commercial sales and station promotional announcements. After commercials and promos are scheduled, the remaining time is filled with public service:

3. Public Service availabilities are seasonal.

   A. Heavy commercial sales mean less Public Service time.

      (1) September starts the new TV season.

      (2) October, November, through December 21 are ratings months and Christmas sales are heavy.

      (3) November, February, and May are national and local rating sweeps months (blockbuster programming and specials).

   B. Lighter commercial sales mean more Public Service time.

      (1) December 22 through January 1 is heavy Public Service [time]

because advertisers traditionally do not buy as much time between the two holidays.

(2) January—advertising slacks off slightly after Christmas.

(3) June, July, August sales slack off because there are not as many viewers. Repeat programming, vacations and good weather keep the viewer level down during the summer.

The "SMASH" List

Dallas's Public Service Director at WFAA-TV, Alva Goodall, offers the following memory jogger for writers of PSAs. It is used with permission.

- Study each Station. Watch how they handle PSAs and public affairs programming.
- Meet personally with the Public Service Director. Introduce yourself and acquaint him or her with your organization.
- Ask questions. Don't be shy, the PSA Director is there to help you. Find out the requirements for submission of material.
- Submit your material as required by the station. Be on time for deadlines; make appointments.
- Help the Public Service Director help you. Mark your material clearly, including any start and end dates that are necessary.

If you are professional, prepared, patient, and polite, you will be a SMASH!

Tips for More "Insurance"

The following sections add a few tips to those shared by Mary Bonnick and Alva Goodall, to provide greater assurance that your PSA will be used effectively.

Slides

Use slides that are visually stimulating, that show your organization at work, or that picture a social problem with its possible solution relating directly to your spoken message.

If you are doing your own photo work, get in there tight with what television people call a *CU* (close up), or *ECU* (extreme close up). Avoid medium or long shots. Showing action makes your slides more compelling.

For a 30-second PSA, use from 5 to 15 slides. Using several slides puts a feeling of action and movement into the spot. Nothing is more deadly to watch than less than a minimum number of slides. Research shows that the viewer's eye will wander after 7 seconds, no matter how compelling the audio portion of the message.

Calling for cuts from slide to slide produces an animated, lively feeling. Using *dissolves* (the overlapping fade-out of one slide and fade-in of another) produces a slower visual change and a more relaxed effect.

Professional Announcers.   The voice-over narration can be done by someone in your organization who is capable of reading copy in a professional manner. But it is far better to have it done by a real professional. Sometimes the station will assign one of its announcers to read the copy without charge to you, but if there is a talent fee and it is within your budget, you are better off using this service.

Minority Representation.   FCC regulations require broadcast stations to provide a certain amount of minority programming. So include pictures of minorities in your slides if possible. Don't force it, and don't use exploitation. But if it is appropriate, stress this in your message. It may help your PSA to get better play, because it can help the station when relicensing applications come due.

Filmed Productions

No one disputes that moving pictures move viewers. They are the preference of most large advertisers because they are the most effective visual method of presenting a sales message. But film production, even of very short PSAs, is expensive.

There is a way you may be able to have your PSA filmed and afford it, too. If there is a film school or a university or college with a film department in your area, sometimes a student will work free to acquire the experience he or she needs and to provide a sample for a portfolio. *Be sure* to check out the student's ability and have a firm agreement in advance for film and other costs, ownership, delivery dates, and contingency plans for unacceptable end results. Also be sure that the correct film—or videotape—as dictated by the television station's requirements, is used.

If you are able to arrange for a handsome, well-produced film spot, you undoubtedly are assuring that the spot will receive an exceptional amount of airtime.

The NAB Booklet

The National Association of Broadcasters (NAB) publishes a booklet that should be on every beginning or volunteer publicist's desk: *If You Want Air Time.* (See Appendix E for ordering information.) This booklet walks you through the preparation of both news copy and PSAs, includes many of the most important "do's" and "don'ts" for radio and television, gives checklists and rules, and includes samples of PSAs and news releases for both mediums.

Often your local station will have its own guide for achieving free airtime, as do the Dallas stations which shared their information in preceding sections.

Some television stations go so far as to include a cardboard mask in which you can check your slides to be sure all information will be visible when reproduced on a television screen.

Local stations' instructions will provide specific requirements. As an example, the following are three conditions essential to one Los Angeles television station's using PSAs.

- Provide at least 25 printed copies of each announcement of 10-and 20-second copy. Submit both 10 and 20 second copy
- Provide two copies of each 2-by-2-inch slide to be shown. They must be mounted in glass, and the images must be composed horizontally.
- Allow at least three to four weeks before the first contemplated airing, to permit the station's evaluation, processing, and schedule procedures.

A telephone request to each local station's Public Service Coordinator will provide you with such material, if it is available, and save you much effort and time in defining each station's individual requirements.

Television Appearances

If you or someone from your organization is scheduled to appear on television, the most important thing to remember is to be yourself—and to be prepared. Here are some additional tips:

- Wear clothing that has contrasts: A dark suit with a white shirt and dark tie is best for a man. (The guidelines in Chapter 9 give direction for women's dress and hold true for television: no "busy" prints, bold plaids, or such.)
- Accept makeup, if it is offered to you. The station's people are trained to make each person look his or her best.

- Be at the studio early to give yourself time to become comfortable with the surroundings. A television studio is very different from the "framed" set you see on your home screen.

- Review questions in advance (if possible), or at least become familiar with the line of questioning that will be used. Know your subject *intimately*, and don't talk about the subject with the interviewer, while off camera during breaks, or introduce any surprises, on or off camera.

- Avoid gestures; they distract. And talk to the camera rather than to the interviewer. In other words, talk to the television audience.

- Use this politicians' trick: If you are being interviewed and recorded, talk in 20- or 30-second cuts that can be edited and used in newscasts if the content warrants. This often increases airtime.

Thank-You Letters

Even though FCC regulations require stations to donate certain amounts of time for public service, and the stations are always looking for *good* PSAs, the stations will appreciate thank-you letters from you. Not only will it be appreciated, but it also may help them keep in good standing with the FCC when the letters are attached to a relicensing petition. Such letters also go far toward getting more positive responses when your group again requests free public service time.

Community Access Television

In some areas where cable companies operate, community access television is available. (This service provides broadcast access to a cable television network that is available to nonprofit organizations and individual citizens. You can use community access television as an opportunity to communicate needs, interests, concerns, and views on specific issues to the subscribers of the cable network.

Often these community access utilities can provide television production facilities, equipment, and channels to develop and cable-cast noncommercial programs that might include information, politics, education, art, or entertainment.

In some cases, announcements of events and certain kinds of messages can be placed on video bulletin boards. It may be well worth the effort to seek out and explore these possibilities.

News Ethics and Home Video Cameras

Something new has been introduced on the broadcast scene, and it is bringing into question new ethics for broadcasting. Some of the most dramatic moments on television these days are coming from amateurs with camcorders, or home video cameras. These amateur shooters are, on occasion, producing spectacular footage, such as that captured by tourists driving across the Bay Bridge from Oakland to San Francisco when the big earthquake of October 1989 hit and the 1991 Rodney King beating by police in Los Angeles.

It is believed by some observers, however, that television's acceptance of such footage—and now invitations to amateurs to become extensions of news staffs—is also inviting opportunities for manipulation, distortion, camera trickery, and lies.

Fakery already has reared its ugly head. NBC and ABC believed they were showing audiences the first footage of the Soviet Union's nuclear disaster at Chernobyl. It turned out to be misrepresented amateur footage of a fire in an Italian cement plant. The networks were deceived, and their viewers were tricked, according to a story in *The Dallas Morning News*. Matt York, editor and publisher of *Videomaker*, a magazine for home camera enthusiasts, expressed his concern. "The line between amateurs and professionals is becoming blurred, and soon it may be erased." Everette Dennis, executive director of the Gannett Center for Media Studies at Columbia University, believes that when a news organization turns over its responsibility to another party—particularly when it is to untrained newspersons—it is forfeiting its professional control to ensure objectivity in the ensuing report.

Newspapers do not permit self-serving representatives to cover events. Yet, more and more television news services are accepting footage without asking who made it or what point of view is being championed. Activists representing narrow, specific viewpoints, even religious congregations, are gearing up to present biased news footage showing only one point of view.

There is little question in many observers' minds that publicity and public relations professionals will use this means for promoting their clients. The blurring of advertising messages as news undoubtedly will not be allowed because of the infringement upon revenues. But this obscuring of impartiality in news reporting can mean viewers will lose what has been the first tenet of journalism—unbiased, objective reports.

This new development bears watching. It may open new avenues, through which organization publicity may travel.

## 15

Do-It-Yourself Advertising

*What to do when your message
doesn't qualify for news space*

News of the Marketplace

Humorous definitions of advertising provide material for business-luncheon speakers. The following definitions come from *Esar's Comic Dictionary* by Evan Esar, a recognized humor source for luncheon speakers: "Advertising is the art of making people think they've always wanted something they've never even heard of before;" it is also "the picture of a pretty girl eating, wearing, or holding something that someone wants to sell."

Giving a different cast to the subject, Mark Twain said, "Many a small thing has been made large by the right kind of advertising."

Advertising really is news of the *marketplace*. It is not *news* news! Or, as experienced newspaper advertising people agree, "The newspaper sells [advertising] space—but what really is bought is advertising response."

This chapter will give you some findings that confirm that, indeed, it is advertising response that drives profitability and growth.

The Differences between Publicity and Advertising

Throughout this book, you have been warned not to present advertising as publicity news. Businesspeople often are much more familiar with advertising than with publicity. Sometimes there is confusion about the two. Publicity has even been called "free advertising." It is important to know the difference and to respect it, because if a newspaper editor believes that your publicity story is advertising, you can be sure it will end up in his or her "round file," that supersized wastebasket alongside the desk. What's worse, you will make no newsroom friends if you try to sneak an advertising message through in a news release.

There is no free advertising, for reasons that every for-profit organization person understands. Advertising is the lifeblood of commercial, private-enterprise newspapers. Sales of the product itself return only about one-third of a newspaper's revenue. Advertising pays the rest of the cost and provides a profit for ownership.

Separation of News Departments and Business Office

There is an important separation in any newspaper that is as jealously guarded as the separation of church and state. It is the separation of the news departments and the business operation.

The business operation includes the advertising, circulation, accounting, and promotion departments, and none of them attempts to dictate how news is handled or presented. Advertising and circulation departments provide revenue for a newspaper, and they, too, strenuously object to any request by an advertiser to pass off a commercial message as news. Such a crossover would cut into revenue. Some critics of newspapers have charged that big advertisers dictate the handling of news. There is no basis for such a charge against today's ethical, honest, and honorable newspapers.

As a matter of fact, there is substantial evidence against such accusations. A newspaper serving hundreds of advertisers and thousands of readers cannot run the risk of antagonizing other advertisers by submitting to the untenable demands of one or a few. And there is the readily accepted fact that an advertiser needs the commercial reach of the newspaper more than the newspaper needs any individual advertiser.

Further grounds for such separation lie in the fact that no newspaper is dependent upon any one customer or any one group that might be inclined to exert improper pressure. To ensure the protectively guarded separation between news and business, a newspaper must be financially independent.

The Right Form for Your Message

If you are unsure whether your message is news or advertising, test it against the criteria in Chapter 2. If you determine that the information does not qualify for news space, then don't hesitate to get the message out in an ad.

This chapter will assist you in meeting the challenges of buying newspaper advertising space and preparing advertising copy. Also in this chapter are data that establish why newspaper advertising is often a better choice than any other medium, and that your advertising message, as with your publicity message, will reach more readers in newspapers than in any other medium. First, however, you must put your message into ad form.

Do-It-Yourself Ad Writing

When you've tucked this newest accomplishment under your belt, not only can you reap the benefits and feelings of accomplishment, you can sit at dinner in a fancy restaurant—as the characters in a William Hamilton cartoon "The Now Society" do—and ask your companion, "As a writer, which do you find more challenging—frozen orange juice or steel-belted radial tires?"

It certainly is recommended, if your budget permits, that advertising be left to professionals. However, if you decide to go it alone, there is plenty of help available. The people in the advertising department of the newspaper in which you wish to advertise will be glad to assist. They are professionals who will help you in planning the layouts, writing your ads, and preparing your illustrations. They also have clip-art services with such a variety of ready-made illustrations that you are almost sure to find one that is appropriate for your message. On some publications some of these services are free.

The following sections will assist you in writing your own ad.

Focus and Clarity

Every ad demands four decisions:

1. What to tell in your advertising message
2. To whom you should tell it
3. How to tell it
4. Where to tell it

Just as with each publicity release, an ad must be planned. If you don't know what to tell, you won't be able to write the copy. Decide exactly what is the *single, specific objective* of this one ad. Only you and your people know this. The publication's advertising staff can't help you here.

Target Audience

Then you must decide to whom you want to direct the message. What audience do you need to reach—men, women, young people, mature people, retired people with time on their hands, parents with children? They all read the newspaper. Who are the people who can use and benefit from your product or service? Or, who are the people you wish to influence about your organization?

Identify your desired audience as precisely as possible because, when you are able to direct your message to a particular group, you will catch their interest far more readily. A rifle is better than a shotgun when you are out for big game.

Hard Sell versus Soft Sell

How should you tell your message? Decide whether a hard-sell approach is the best way to reach your special audience. Do you prefer to appeal to the emotions of the reader to solicit aid or approval? Do you plan to soft-sell the message strictly as an image builder?

Last, but by no means unimportant, is your decision as to which publications best reach the audience you want to touch. This takes a little study, but each publication should have figures that classify groups by age, gender, income, and other factors that may be important to you in targeting a specific group. Ask the newspaper's advertising people for these data.

Six Elements of a Newspaper Ad

It is important to know the primary elements in a newspaper advertisement that attract readers to a message that is easily understood. The six most important elements are as follows:

1. Theme. The sales message in the ad is best stated in a simple, declarative sentence.
2. Headline. A good headline normally includes the organization's name and a reader benefit. It also should be selective so the reader knows whether or not the ad is directed to him or her. And, of course, the headline should be simple enough to be clearly understood.
3. Illustration. The illustration should attract readers and help tell the

story or reinforce the main sales point of the ad. If possible, it should show the product in use.

4. Text, or body copy. The text, or body copy, should follow the headline. Its purpose is to amplify user benefits, explain, and offer proof that the product or service being advertised is a good one. The text should also end with an action close, which should tell the reader what to do next and how to do it easily.

5. Signature. The ad should end with the organization name or logo clear and visible. Organization address (complete with ZIP code), phone number, and business hours should be included.

6. Ad layout. The ad layout is nothing more than the arrangement of the items in numbers two, three, four, and five above. The layout should be planned to draw readers into the ad, guide them through it, and visually present the image you want to present.

Outline

Most ads are conceived in isolation on a doodle pad, so start roughly designing the space you have to work with and the illustration, headline, and copy elements to go in it.

Be prepared to write leaner and cleaner than in any other communication medium except perhaps broadcast. Every word counts in advertising.

As you did with your first news release, make an outline of what the ad will contain. To begin, don't write any copy other than doodle notes, until you know what you are writing about and what you want the ad to achieve. Then write your first draft. Don't be concerned with word perfection yet. Just get the idea down in rough-draft form.

Headline

It's true: The headline is vital. It must grab the reader and bounce him or her into the copy and make him or her want to read the body copy. If writing this critical part of an ad intimidates you, write the body copy first. Your headline will come more easily when you've trimmed and tailored the body copy into its final form.

As you write the first draft and each revision, strive for conciseness and vividness. Avoid useless words. Advertising space is expensive, but equally important, readers don't want to be bothered with reading wordy copy.

Text

Your first paragraph should be short, and it should tie in with the head. (You may want to hold off on writing the first paragraph and the headline until after you've written the rest of the copy.)

Start with the strongest possible appeal—the point that will be of greatest interest to the reader! You and your organization may have a stronger interest, but a reader doesn't care about that. He or she will respond only to appeals that relate to his or her own interests and concerns.

Include other appeals in diminishing importance, but don't use so many that you will water down the reader's interest. Use no glittering generalities. Be specific. As you write your copy, it is helpful to visualize one person and write as you would talk to him or her. Try to answer his or her arguments, questions, and needs.

Use action verbs and few adjectives. Be persuasive.

The "Do-Something" Appeal

The last paragraph of your body copy should be a "do-something" appeal. Unless the purpose of the ad is merely to build an image or to boost recognition of the organization's name, its chief objective is to stimulate action of some kind. You may want the reader to write for a brochure, place an order by phone, send in a coupon, volunteer time or expertise, or make a contribution of some sort. Whatever it is you want the reader to do, come right out and ask him or her to do it in the last paragraph, then tell how to do it.

Nine Ad-Writing Points

It's how the blank, white space you've purchased is used that spells the difference between being successful and being ignored. The following nine points are adapted from the Bureau of Advertising, ANPA booklet *How to check your ads for more sell,* and used with permission:

1. Be sure your ad has a theme. State the sales message in your ad with a simple declarative sentence.
2. Make your ads easily recognizable. Studies show that ads that are distinctive in their use of art, layout techniques, and typefaces usually enjoy a higher readership than run-of-the-mill advertising. Try to make your ads distinctively different in appearance from those of your com-

petitors, then keep your ad's appearance consistent. This way readers will recognize your ads even before they read them. If you've built a good image, the recognition will create a feeling of wanting to hear from a friend.

3. Use a simple layout. Ads should not be crossword puzzles. The ad layout is nothing more than the arrangement of (*a*) headline; (*b*) illustration; (*c*) text, or body copy; and (*d*) signature.

   The layout should carry the reader's eye through the message easily and in proper sequence, from headline to illustration, to explanatory copy, to price (if applicable), to your organization's name with address and phone number. Don't forget to include business hours! (Make it as easy as possible for the reader to do business with you. Give the reader all the information he or she may want. If a person has to phone to ask your business hours, he or she may pass you by.)

   Avoid the use of too many different typefaces, overly decorative borders, and reverse plates (white on black). All of these devices are distracting and will reduce the number of readers who receive your entire message.

4. Use a dominant element. Use a large picture or headline to ensure quick visibility. Photographs and realistic drawings have about equal attention-getting value, but photographs of real people win more readership. So do action pictures. Photos of local people or places also have high attention value. Use good artwork; it will pay off in extra readership.

5. Use a prominent benefit headline. The first thing a reader wants to know about your ad is: What's in it for me? A good headline states a reader benefit and should try to include the advertiser's name. It also should be selective—addressed to a specific audience—so the reader knows whether or not the ad is directed to him or her.

   Select the main benefit that your service or product offers and feature it in a compelling headline. Amplify the message in subheads. Remember that label headlines do little selling (whether of a product, a service, or an image).

   Always try to appeal to one or more of the basic desires of your readers: safety, beauty, fun, thrift, leisure, popularity, and health.

   "How-to" headlines encourage full copy readership, as do headlines that include specific information or helpful suggestions.

   Avoid generalized quality claims.

   Your headline will be easier to read if it is black-on-white and is not superimposed or overprinted on part of the illustration. And, of course, the headline should be simple enough to be clearly understood.

6. Let your white space work for you.

   Don't overcrowd your ad. White space is an important layout element in newspaper advertising because the average news page is so heavy with small type. White space focuses the reader's attention on your ad and will make your headline and illustration stand out.

7. Make your copy complete. Know all there is to know about the product, service, or image you sell, and select the benefits most appealing to the audience you wish to reach.

   Your copy should be enthusiastic and sincere. A block of copy written in complete sentences is easier to read than one composed of phrases and random words.

   In designing the layout of a copy block, use a boldface lead-in. Small pictures in sequence will often help readership.

8. Urge your readers to act now. The closing text should urge the reader to act *now*. Chances are, if the reader sets the paper or the ad aside, he or she will forget your ad.

   If mail-in coupons are included in your ads, provide spaces large enough for customers to fill them in easily. As part of each coupon, include the name and address to which it is to be mailed.

   If a check is to be enclosed, tell the reader to whom the check should be written. In other words, don't make your reader search through the ad for information. Make it easy for him or her to act now, while his or her enthusiasm is high and before he or she forgets.

9. End with the signature. Readers expect to find the signature at the bottom of an ad because that is where most advertisers place it. You can also try to work it into the headline, and wherever else it is appropriate, but when you sign off the ad, be sure the name stands out loud and clear, complete with address (and ZIP code), phone number, and business hours.

Points to Improve Readability

The following points cover design mechanics for producing your ad:

- The typeface (font) should be simple and unencumbered but not stylized or drastically different from most of the copy in the newspaper. Sans-serif faces tend to be easier to read. (The advertising representative from the newspaper will have a typeface book from which you may pick the type size and style you prefer. He or she also should know which ones are preferable.)

- Headlines in all-capital letters are harder to read than those with an initial capital letter followed by lower case letters.
- *Flush-left* type (*justified,* or aligned, against the left margin) is easiest to read. There is little difference in readability between blocks of copy that have both margins justified and copy that has a *ragged right* margin. In most cases, justified copy uses more space than unjustified copy.
- Related illustrations help pull the reader's attention to the copy or fix the text content in the reader's mind more clearly.
- The length of the lines of type should be between one-and-one-half to two "alphabets" long, or between 39 to 52 characters long, for ease in reading. If you've chosen a large ad space, break your copy into column-width blocks that are no wider than two "alphabets" (52 characters).
- A moderate amount of space between lines of body copy may make it easier for the reader's eye to keep its place as it skips across the page.
- Put lots of white space around your copy. Here's why:

Copy is much harder to read whenwordsarealljammedtogether. It is also hard to read big blocks of type that are jammed together, with the lines of type on one side set flush right instead of flush left.

Five "Don'ts"

As you write your advertising copy, remember the following tips:

1. Don't forget your organization name, address, and phone number. Check every ad to be certain you have included your organization name, address, telephone number, and business hours.

   Even if yours is a long-established name, this is important. According to U.S. government statistics, 1 or more of every 10 families in your town probably moves each year, so you can count on a large number of readers who do not know where you are located. Make it easy for them to find you or to call you.

2. Don't be too clever. Many people distrust cleverness in advertising, just as they distrust salesmen who are too glib. Headlines and copy generally are far more effective when they are straightforward than when they are tricky. Clever or tricky headlines and copy often are misunderstood.

3. Don't use unusual or difficult words. Many of your potential customers may not understand words that are familiar to you. Trade and technical terms or jargon may be confusing and easily misunderstood. Everybody understands simple language and nobody resents it. Use it.

4. Don't generalize. Be specific at all times. Facts convince.

5. Don't make excessive claims. The surest way to lose customers (or supporters if your ad is for a nonprofit organization) is to make claims in your advertising that you can't back up. Go easy with superlatives and unbelievable values. Remember, if you claim that your prices (or achievements)—or anything, for that matter—are unbelievable, your readers are likely to agree.

Spot-Check Questions

With the foregoing input plus the help from the newspaper's advertising representative and its creative staff, your ad should be highly effective. After you have written, rewritten, and edited, and reedited your copy, try testing it on your imaginary reader. If *you* were the reader you had in mind as you wrote the copy, how would you respond to the following questions?

- Would you clip the ad?
- Would you get up, go to the telephone, and call?
- Does the copy hold your interest all the way?
- Is the ad clear and understandable?
- Is the purpose direct?
- Are the statements honest?
- Are there any throw-away words that aren't useful or necessary?
- Are there words that could use a little strengthening, a little more action and impact?
- Is the message interesting and enthusiastic?

Was each answer a positive? If not, work on the element until your ad can successfully pass the spot-check.

Eye-Catching Ads

Just to be sure that your horse is before your cart and that you have a good handle on what makes for the highest readership of your ad, here are additional data that should be helpful. These data were developed over more than 25 years of newspaper-readership research—by the Bureau of Advertising, the Advertising Research Foundation, Daniel Starch and Staff, and many other organizations—through ongoing programs that conduct and analyze research projects.

Eye-camera research shows that, not only do people note more ads that reflect their interests, they even see more such ads. As the eye scans the page, it is unconsciously drawn from the edges of vision to those items that are relevant to the reader. The eye avoids the irrelevant. The eye and brain together are engaged in a constant and rapid filtering process.

Key Elements to Ad Success

A report published by Standard Rate & Data Service, Inc. (SRDS), confirms that the qualities that most strongly influence ad readership are the ad layout, the ad's ability to key into the reader's interests, and the freshness of the advertising message. The report states that these key elements "should be considered as carefully as placement. Even the best placement or 'media buy' cannot guarantee an ad will be read."

The study, which produced the results quoted by SRDS, was conducted by Starch Inra Hooper, and addressed such issues as why two ads placed in the same publication produce different results.

"It's no secret that basic human needs and interests are the prime movers in human behavior," says the SRDS report, and "they are also, of course, the basic motivations behind what people read."

One finding showed that ads with a dominant single picture and caption (as compared to those with several line drawings and multiple sections of copy, none of which dominate), scored approximately one-and-a-half times higher.

"A dominant focal center, however, does not necessarily assure a high noting score," states the SRDS report. As many as 4 out of 10 advertisements with dominant focal centers did not secure high noting scores, which "points to the presence of a second important factor in determining the size of the observer audience. It is the operation of a quick perceptual-meaning interaction." The SRDS report explains that a "perceptual-meaning interaction" is the ad's ability to provide a momentary challenge to the curiosity or self-interest of the reader.

In summarizing the high success requirements, the SRDS report states, "The physical impact of a dominant focal center is highly important in attracting a reading audience. [However] the psychological impact of a challenge to curiosity, self interest or cue to a meaningful explanation is equally important. To create an ad with a dominant focal center, but without a perceptual cue to curiosity, self interest or unexpected explanations can cut down the reader audience considerably."

The Effectiveness of Advertising

The American Association of Advertising Agencies (AAAA), in a full-page advertisement in *The New York Times*, unequivocally states that "Advertising almost doubles your return on investment"—and offers a depth study to confirm it.

AAAA cites an extensive study from the Strategic Planning Institute in Cambridge, Massachusetts, that determines "the extent to which advertising levels influence a product's 'perceived value,' and how this perception affects both a product's relative market share and also its relative market price."

> *Brands that advertise much more*
> *than their competitors, average returns-*
> *on-investment of 32 percent, while brands*
> *that advertise much less than their*
> *competitors average only 17 percent*
> *return-on-investment.*
>
> *In an era when productivity is*
> *often understood only in terms of cutting*
> *costs . . . even today, there is still no better*
> *way to build consumer perception of added*
> *value than with advertising.*

The Function of Advertising

John Wanamaker, one of America's early merchants, was known for saying: "Advertising doesn't jerk—it pulls. If it is continuous, it will exert an irresistible force." Then he would often add that advertising is no game for the quitter. The U.S. Small Business Administration, in one of its seminars, adds, "It's a game, though, in which you can't very well sit on the sidelines if you hope to run a successful business."

Advertising has three basic functions:

- Informing
- Persuading
- Reminding

Advertising's most important action probably is to sell the advertiser's products or services, but it performs other acts equally important to organizations:

- Building an image.
- Building a reputation for quality and service.
- Conveying an impression that your organization is dependable, versatile, and reliable; that you have credibility.
- Creating an understanding of and belief in your organization's purpose, efforts, and goals, which, in turn, builds support.

The Importance of Newspaper Advertising

It could be said that statistics are to this book what lumps are to mashed potatoes—the fewer the better. No one can make the decision for you as to where you should advertise. There are, however, impressive facts—some lumps in the mashed potatoes—that point to newspapers as being the primary choice of advertisers, large and small.

A 1990 advertising spending report published by the Public Relations Society of America, that reflects current media trends says that "Corporate advertisers continued their traditional preference for print media, primarily because it targets their important audiences."

Believability also is an important fact. According to a report from Henry Senft Research Associates, Inc. (1986) published in a booklet (*Key Facts 1987: Newspapers, Consumers, Advertising*) by the Newspaper Advertising Bureau, Inc., the public is inclined to trust newspaper advertising.

The following percentages rank public confidence in the truthfulness of newspaper advertising 15 percent higher than television, magazines, and radio combined.

Most Believable Advertising Medium	
Newspapers	48%
Television	21%
Magazines	8%
Radio	4%
All media equally believable	5%
No answer	6%

Today, when television seems to have an overwhelming clutch on our free time, it is not widely recognized that newspapers stand up well to that challenge. You can count on a majority of the public seeing your newspaper ad—if it is well constructed and well written. Newspaper readership confirms this fact.

More than 113 million American adults read a daily newspaper on an average weekday, and some 119 million read a Sunday or weekend newspaper. Weekly newspaper circulation has increased by more than 2 million to a high of 55 million. (The above statistics also support the extent of readership of your publicity that appears in newspapers.)

Newspaper as Advertising Leader

The figures in the preceding section make it easier to understand why daily newspapers continue to lead all other advertising media with 26.1 percent of the total 1990 U.S. advertising expenditures. Advertising expenditures in daily newspapers increased by 3.8 percent to a total of more than $32 billion—$5 billion more than all television services combined (network, spot, syndication, and cable). Radio accounts for 6.6 percent, and direct mail, for 17.9 percent.

With an added 7,550 weekly newspapers whose survival also depends on paid advertising, it is apparent that newspaper advertising is a highly productive medium. After all, advertisers do not put their dollars where the results aren't worthwhile.

Local News and Local Advertising

In this time of radio and television dominance, many people now depend on electronic-news media for national and international news. But people still want *local* information, whether it's about the city council's decision on redistricting or the best buys on food and back-to-school clothes.

The advertising in daily newspapers is largely from local advertisers. In weeklies, the advertising is almost entirely local. The reason for this is that most organizations depend almost exclusively on local or area people for their support.

Regardless of what you sell—a product, a service, or a message—advertising in a newspaper will reach people who live near you and who are logical purchasers and supporters.

Unique Benefits from Newspaper Advertising

The U.S. Small Business Administration (Office of Management Information and Training) gives some additional reasons for choosing newspaper advertising:

- Intensive coverage. (Most of a newspaper's readers are in a well-defined, compact geographical area.)
- Flexibility. You can let the paper insert your ad wherever there is a place for it, *R.O.P.* (Run Of Paper), or you can specify that it is to be put on a special-interest page that preselects your readers (business, sports, fashion, women's, gardening, real estate, arts, travel, or other specific interests).

  There also is flexibility in the size of your advertisement. You can illustrate what you are offering and describe it in as much detail as you wish; you can focus attention on one or a few items, or make a splash with many items.

  Color is available even in many small dailies and weeklies.
- Quick response. You can expect a response within hours after your ad appears, and results often will continue to show up for many days after.
- Quick changes. Because your ad can be submitted only two or three days before the publication date, sometimes even later, quick changes in your advertising plans are possible.

  A change in temperatures may call for changing a planned ad for a hot-weather product to an item for cooler weather. If insurance is your business, you can give instructions to run your ad for flood coverage as soon as heavy rains are predicted.

Cost-Effectiveness Determination

An axiom in the advertising business has existed for years because it has proved sound: 80 percent of your advertising budget should be allocated for media to get the message to the readers; 20 percent should be allocated for preparation of the message.

That rule of thumb assumes, of course, that you have set an advertising budget. Unless it is a one-time-only happening, a budget is the principal means you have, later, to determine the effectiveness of your expenditures.

In your quest to discover which publications you will use, seek out the help of the people at the newspapers. They have audited circulation statements showing the total number of subscribers and breakdowns by areas where those subscribers live. More than likely, the newspapers also have figures showing demographic breakdowns to identify various consumer, or reader, markets.

If your budget is extremely limited, you may only be able to afford running your ad in the weekly community newspaper. This newspaper is less likely to have data other than circulation figures.

Finally, you must decide the size of your ad, and your budget most likely will dictate this decision, too. Only a readership survey can provide reliable clues to a specific ad's attention value, but in the absence of a survey, the following average of reported readership for a large number of ads may be useful.

Percent of Ads Read on Opened Pages

Page Size of Ad	Percent Read
Less than one-quarter	12%
One-quarter to less than one-half	17%
One-half to less than full	25%
Full page or more	44%

Repetition of small ads is more profitable than running a single, large ad; use smaller ads frequently rather than spend your entire budget for one big splash. An ad now and then can get results, but real success requires continuity in your advertising.

There are two basic reasons why newspaper advertising is important:

- Organizations need to advertise so that people will know about the organization's goods and services.
- The reader needs advertising so he or she will know what is available, where it is available, and at what price.

"Advertorials"

At the 1990 annual convention of The Associated Press Managing Editors, the highly controversial subject of advertorials caused some heated discussion.

What is an *advertorial?* According to one editor's definition it is a special type of advertising, unique and differentiated from regular advertising, which generates additional revenues and is intended to instruct or entertain the reader. To translate, it is advertising and editorial matter jointly produced for the advertiser in separate sections of a publication. And the consensus at the convention was that advertorials are here to stay for a very good reason: In today's economic environment, anything that drives revenues will stay around.

The managing editors were challenged by advertising executives who were present to provide the checks and balances in the situation. The concern by newspeople was that advertorial sections contain "fluff," content that may be one-sided, in conflict with the main news sections, or just plain inaccurate or misleading.

"The news staff has to believe their newspaper will not sacrifice credibility," said an unidentified executive editor. "There should not be a conflict between what's right for the readers and what's right for the advertiser," the editor said.

This same editor told how a specific situation affected the people at his newspaper. The paper lost the business of its second-largest advertiser over the news coverage of the retailer's labor problems. What the editor found most gratifying, he said, was that "the people in the ad department didn't flinch."

Two Categories of Newspaper Ads

Basically, there are two types of advertising in newspapers—classified and display. This chapter deals only with display ads because that is the type most likely to be used to substitute for publicity that does not qualify as news.

Classified, or *want ads,* are gathered in a separate section of the newspaper and arranged by classifications: Real Estate, Employment, Rentals, Transportation, Merchandise, etc. Newspaper classified sections are direct people-to-people advertising; the only place where individuals can place very small ads for very little money to sell almost everything.

Display ads are scattered throughout newspapers and are the sales messages of local organizations that distribute products or services locally, or of large regional and national organizations.

History of Classified Ads. The first ads in an American newspaper appeared in the third issue of the first regularly published newspaper, the *Boston News-Letter* in 1704.

There were three ads. One was a real estate sale ad and the remaining two offered a reward for the return of "stollen" goods.

Richard W. Sears met Alvah C. Roebuck through a classified ad in the *Chicago Daily News* in 1887. Sears placed a classified ad for a watchmaker, and young Roebuck answered the ad and got the job. The two men started selling watches and jewelry by mail, then branched out to develop one of the world's greatest merchandising operations.

This ad was the "want ad" that brought Sears and Roebuck together:

> **WANTED—Watchmaker with references, who can furnish tools. State age, experience, salary.**
>
> **R. W. Sears, Jeweler.**

Earlier newspapers carried want ads scattered throughout the paper, even on front pages, but the small want ad is essentially the same today as it was then, and it serves basically the same purposes.

The First Display Ad. The forerunner of display advertising was a store ad, and the first one appeared in the seventeenth issue of the *Boston News-Letter*. There were no illustrations or graphics such as the ones advertisers now use in display sales messages to attract reader's attention.

Truth in Advertising

Criticism of advertising ethics has been a constant companion of media through the years, going back to long before the popular, current "consumer-protection" cry by politicians.

"Promise—large promise—is the soul of advertising," stated Dr. Samuel Johnson in a 1758 edition of a British newspaper, *The Idler*. "Advertisements are now so numerous that they are very negligently perused, and it has therefore become necessary to gain attention by magnificense of promises and by eloquence, sometimes sublime and sometimes pathetic."

It is important that the public, who buys products as a result of advertising, be able to determine when the "magnificense of promises" outweighs the solid facts within advertisements.

Advertisers in Dr. Samuel Johnson's time knew, as do advertiser's today, that emotional appeals to universal desires meant increased sales. It is essential for consumers to be aware of and to be able to analyze the methods, devices, and terms advertisers use in their bids for increased sales.

It is unfortunate that the very trade organization—the American Association of Advertising Agencies (AAAA)—whose responsibility it should be to act as watchdog over advertising practices (or at least to institute vigorous educational campaigns to inform media about how to deal with false or deceptive advertising) is specifically prohibited from doing so by United States antitrust laws.

16

Anatomy of a Newspaper
How the newspaper
business works

Newspapers Are Unique

Most people feel they understand newspapers because they have read them all their lives. Actually, newspapers are complex and complicated free enterprise operations that in many ways are unlike other businesses. Moreover, newspaper people perform some almost unbelievable feats. For one, each day, every day, for each average-size newspaper, enough information is gathered to fill a full-size book. And although newspapers are strictly profit making operations, they disregard some basic business canons, such as selling their products for less than their manufacturing costs, and giving free delivery for less than their cash-and-carry prices.

Understanding how newspapers operate is interesting, but more significantly, that understanding can help you learn and practice better publicity skills.

The Many Purposes of Newspapers

Of all media available, only the newspaper serves so many different educational levels, ages, personalities, interests, and concerns.

Even after it has informed, educated, enlightened, entertained, amused, instructed, enriched, enlivened, stimulated, convinced, activated, involved, saddened, gladdened, and perhaps angered, the newspaper still makes the reader think.

Anna Quindlen, a reporter from *The New York Times*, describes the newspapers' function this way: A newspaper is "portable and reusable. If you don't get the gist the first time, you can reread. If you don't care about one gist, you can turn to another.

"And when you're through with gist," she says, "you can pack up old dishes and line bird cages." She neglected to say that the newspaper also is useful for swatting flies, covering schoolbooks, wiping paintbrushes, training puppies, and, of course, wrapping fish.

Newspapers Serve Many Needs

Almost everyone reads a newspaper, even in these days of time dominance by television and radio. Newspapers are the key to jobs, housing, movies, television shows, bargains, sports events, and such close-to-home questions as why the fire sirens sounded during the night.

Jeff Greenfield, Universal Press Syndicate columnist, describes it in his own way. "An old adage about news consumers goes like this: When someone wakes up in the morning, the first questions she asks are, 'Am I OK? Is my family OK? Is my neighborhood OK?' Then she will permit herself to think about bigger things."

People count on radio to find out about immediate things such as whether to take an umbrella or whether the interstate is backed up for miles. And even though people may witness events firsthand or see them on television, the first thing they do the next morning is reach for the newspaper. Why? Because the newspaper fills in the gaps. It explains, reports, narrates, and reviews. In short, it interprets the scene by answering people's questions about the event. Newspapers try to tell the reader the *why* of what has happened, since he or she has already learned the *what* from the television screen.

Newspapers as Information Factories

Today's newspaper is the biggest information factory in the world! And it offers many kinds of information—from front-page news that presents current history and becomes tomorrow's past, to biographical data supplied in obituaries and feature stories.

People turn to newspapers to be able to make valid judgments after being given both sides of an issue and to analyze for themselves what has been read so they can draw their own conclusions.

But you can ask any group of people—including newspaper people—the question, What is a newspaper? Then look up the word in a dictionary and in an encyclopedia. Chances are there won't be one answer exactly like another. This is because a daily newspaper is so many things, and it is different things to different people. It is uniquely different from other communication media (magazines, television, radio). It also is different from other businesses.

Fulfillment of Individual Needs

The *Centre Daily Times* in State College, Pennsylvania, told its readers that it believes a newspaper serves different purposes for different readers:

- To opinion searchers, it stimulates thought.
- To the voter, it is guidance; to a politician, friend or foe.
- To the seller, it means a quick response; to buyers, many selections.
- To some, it brings good news; to others, sad tidings.
- To front porch sitters, it describes life beyond the horizon.
- To the immigrant, it is a schoolbook that helps him [or her] learn English; to hunters of truth, it translates the customs from which the immigrant fled.
- To the living, it is a source of freedom and hope; for the dead, a tribute to their virtues.
- To the homemaker, it is ideas for new menus and new clothes and sensible buying.
- To the mother, it is suggestions for raising the youngsters.
- To the teacher, it is an incredible aid in teaching any subject to any age students regardless of their learning abilities.
- To the lonely diner, it is a companion; around the family dinner table, a topic of conversation.
- To sports and theater lovers, it's who and what is playing, when and where.
- To athletes and actors, it's scrapbook material.
- To an unknown, it brings fame; to a well-known, it furthers his [or her] name.
- To the publicity seeker, it is a haven; to the publicity shy, a source of annoyance.
- To friends and neighbors, it tells about promotions, school achievements and who got married, who was born, who died.

- To all who read the newspaper, it means uncensored news; in some countries—fewer and fewer, as the iron curtain has been lifted—it means censored propaganda.

The Newspaper Paradox

A newspaper is a private business enterprise that makes a product and sells it for a profit. But the kinds of material it sells—information and news—make it a quasi-public utility. Actually, it could be described as a private business that performs as a public institution.

A newspaper has five basic responsibilities. The first is selfish; the remaining four are social:

- To preserve itself
- To provide information
- To offer guidance and advice
- To entertain
- To serve and represent the public

The People's First Right

Uniquely, the newspaper carries the distinctive honor of being one of the four major freedoms guaranteed by the Constitution of the United States; it is the only private business mentioned in the Constitution. It is the people's first right in the Bill of Rights.

However, the First Amendment to the Constitution does not say it protects only the "responsible" press. Recognizing this, many years ago, the American Society of Newspaper Editors set down what it believed were the obligations of a responsible press in its "Canons of Journalism: A Code of Ethics."

> To be truthful, accurate, and thorough.
> To be fair, decent, and impartial.
> To defend the public's right to know without invading individual privacy under a guise of public curiosity.
> The role of the press is to report events and what they mean; to provide leadership with responsibility and integrity.

Service to All

Each newspaper has what seems an insurmountable task—to furnish its services for all of the people, no matter how varied their ages, personalities, interests, and concerns.

A book is written in one style and is often read by many people for the same kinds of reasons; in addition, those people usually have similar levels of education. This is not true with a newspaper.

A newspaper is written for a wide variety of audiences and in a variety of writing styles. It is written for people who like sports; people who only read the comics; people who want to know who is divorcing whom; people who follow the stock market; and people who want to know the really important things that have happened in the last 24 hours. To make it even more difficult, these readers may have education levels that range from minimal to scholarly.

It also is written for people who want to be informed, but who don't have much reading time; for people who have plenty of time and demand everything in depth; for people who cannot comfortably begin their day until they know what the stars say; and for people who must feed and outfit a family for school on a limited budget and need to know where food and clothes cost the least. It must satisfy people who want pro and con opinions; people who want details about products; people who want to be entertained; people who want to know what's playing at the movies and what each movie is about; and people who want to find new jobs, buy second-hand cars, or give away puppies.

Almost unbelievably, each edition of an average daily newspaper contains as many words (not including advertising) as a full-sized novel or a couple of paperbacks. And it all comes together and is in the hands of its readers within a matter of hours. It seems like an impossible job, but it is done day in and day out, usually every day of the year.

Information for Pennies a Day

Where today can you get the world on a platter, for 25 cents or even 35 cents? Those are the single-copy sales prices charged by almost 9 out of 10 (87.5 percent) of the country's dailies.

There's not much available these days for only 35 cents. Even Snoopy's brother Spike acknowledges this in one of the "Peanuts" cartoon strips. In the strip, he's flanked by paintings and a sign that says, "Western Paintings For

Sale," and he is remarking, "Did I tell you I got a grant from the National Endowment For the Arts?" Then he adds, "You can't do much, though, with thirty-five cents."

Try giving yourself an allowance of 35 cents a day, and see what you get. You can't buy a Coke from a Coke machine for 35 cents. And where in a metropolitan area are there bus rides under 50 cents one way? (This doesn't even consider the return trip!)

The astonishing thing is that those 25 or 35 pennies don't begin to cover the cost of producing a newspaper, let alone give the owners some margin of profit. The paper and ink alone that go into a daily newspaper cost more than the price of the newspaper. Actually, the sale of the product is only about one-third of a newspaper's revenue.

Business and Competition

A newspaper is the only product, other than a magazine, that is sold to the consumer for less than the cost of manufacturing it. Top that with a newspaper's practice of delivering its product daily with no charge for the delivery, and often for *less* than when sold on a cash-and-carry basis at a newsstand.

Be it a weekly or a daily serving a small community, a major megalopolis, or even the entire country, as in the case of such newspapers as the *The Wall Street Journal*, *The New York Times* and *USA Today*, every newspaper operates under the checks and balances inherent in a competitive economy. If, for long, a newspaper irritates its clientele, it writes its own obituary. If it offends morals or mores, it loses favor. If it caters to special interests, it risks loss of confidence, respect, and integrity. If it grows meek and fails to champion what benefits the people it serves—in the community, the state, or the nation—it may be replaced by a more courageous competitor.

So, how does a *business* not subsidized by government or any funding agency continue to operate under a process that is completely contrary to the market formula for business success (that retail sales price must include all costs of manufacture and distribution and still allow for profit)?

Advertising as Financial Mainstay

Advertising provides the largest chunk of a newspaper's revenue—about two-thirds of it for most newspapers. Advertising revenue is imperative so that newspapers can retain their freedom from government control of news content. Without it, newspapers would fail or be forced to accept government funding, which would remove their private-interest status and make them merely voices for government.

And why are advertisers willing to carry this lopsided cost burden? In reality, it is not so one-sided. Newspapers and advertisers are dependent on each other.

- Newspapers provide an editorial setting for advertising to enable it to do its best job.
- Advertising provides product news and other information readers want that is so necessary to the success of a newspaper. The importance to readers of advertising has been tested and proven over and over whenever there have been newspaper shutdowns or strikes.

Impressive Facts

Numerical data sometimes make dull reading, but when statistics present important information that translates to dollars in the cash register, they become a little more interesting. The following data about readership and advertising expenditures are given because they are factual testimonials for the compelling power of *publicity*—and advertising—placed in newspapers. The data are gathered and presented by the American Newspaper Publishers Association (ANPA).

General Statistics

Approximately 84 percent of all reading done by adults who did not go to college is done in the newspaper. In other words, for some people, newspapers are their *only* reading material.

Even more impressive figures exist. Newspapers are read in 74 percent of all U.S. households; almost 7 out of 10 (67 percent) American adults read at least one daily newspaper each week; more than 6 of 10 (63 percent) read a daily paper every weekday. There are 1,626 daily newspapers and 7,550 weeklies with a combined circulation of more than 117 million. Research shows that 2.138 persons read more than 62 million U.S. daily newspapers sold each weekday.

It is a fact of commerce that for-profit organizations will not put advertising dollars where they cannot produce results. In 1990, newspaper advertising expenditures *increased* to $32 billion—$5 billion more than all television services combined. Daily newspapers continue to lead all other

U.S. advertising media, with 26 percent of total U.S. advertising expenditures.

To be productive, publicity and advertising must be seen and read. Proof that newspapers are read and that they are a potent medium is in their share of advertising expenditures. (According to ANPA, in 1990 the percentage of advertising dollar disbursement was as follows:

Medium	Percentage Disbursement
Daily Newspapers	26.1%
Television	21.7%
Direct Mail	17.7%
Radio	6.8%
Other	27.7%

Facts for Your Cash Register

There are other benefits from printed publicity in newspapers:

- A cumulative effect can occur that builds recognition for a name or a program.
- The reader can read the newspaper at his or her convenience, rather than at a specified time.
- The reader can clip and save information in which he or she is interested.
- The act of reading forces attentiveness and attention, as opposed to the lack of concentration and attention required for television and radio. (This is one of the compelling reasons educators have embraced the "Newspaper In Education" program with such enthusiasm.)

Readership Statistics

People buy more newspapers every day than cartons of milk or loaves of bread.

As income and education increase, newspaper reading increases, according to the following W. H. Simmons study reported by ANPA:

Percent Coverage of Weekday Newspaper Audience

Education	Readership
Graduated college	87%
Attended college 1–3 years	87%

Percent Coverage of Weekday Newspaper Audience (Continued)

Education	Readership
Graduated high school	83%
Attended high school 1–3 years	75%
Did not attend high school	64%

Age	Readership
18–19	72%
20–24	73%
25–34	74%
35–49	82%
50–64	79%
65 or older	72%

Facts for Your Interest

The following list contains the top 10 daily and Sunday newspapers in the United States by rank, according to circulation figures from the Audit Bureau of Circulations, reported by ANPA.

Daily	Sunday
The Wall Street Journal (national edition)	The New York Times
USA Today (national edition)	Los Angeles Times
Los Angeles Times	Detroit News & Free Press
The New York Times	The Washington Post
The Washington Post	Chicago Tribune
Chicago Tribune	Philadelphia Inquirer
Newsday	Boston Globe
Detroit Free Press	Newsday
San Francisco Chronicle	San Francisco Examiner & Chronicle

Sometimes *only* newspapers have the information. Back in 1940, a dozen or so newspapers throughout the country stumbled onto a dramatic circulation booster. For two days, they published the list of Selective Service numbers chosen by lottery. Copy sales increased from 15 percent to 25 percent, and, in some cases, they skyrocketed to 90 percent. Newspapers were the only medium to publish the information.

Newspapers Then and Now

In 1690, Ben Harris probably could have collected most of the news he needed for the first newspaper published in the colonies, *Publick Occurrences, Both Foreign and Domestick,* from a centrally situated bench on Boston Common. In fact, Harris found the news for his paper from Bostonians who gathered in his coffeehouse to read the London papers and "to converse and argue as well as sip."

Later, in 1704, when John Campbell published the first regular weekly newspaper, *The Boston News-Letter,* he could have gathered the information without ever leaving his post as postmaster. Either man alone could have converted the news into the publications they published.

Today's newspaper staffs may roam counties, countries, and continents to find and report daily news. Additionally, newspapers have access to wire services and syndicate agencies for features and news analysis. And all newspapers receive additional important information from publicity releases distributed to them from organizations and publicity agencies.

Newspaper Operations

Newspaper practices and mechanics vary greatly, according to the size of the city, the newspaper's circulation, and its frequency of publication. *The New York Times, The Los Angeles Times,* and the *Rocky Mountain News* in Colorado, for example, are as dissimilar as the Army, the Navy, and the Marine Corps—or as Neiman Marcus, Lord & Taylor, and Marshall Field. Because of this, any generalized picture of newspaper operations is subject to some distortion by omission. A broad picture can be drawn, however.

Even a small newspaper requires a relatively large capital outlay; some of the largest newspapers are multimillion-dollar corporations. All must be well organized if they are to be financially successful and, although they generally do not have a rigid method of organization, all generally consist of five departments:

1. Editorial
2. Advertising
3. Circulation
4. Business
5. Production

Chain of Command

Generally, a flow chart for a newspaper would be as follows:

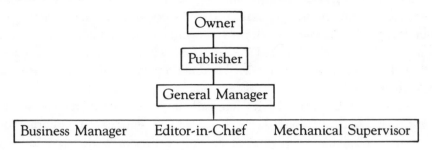

Publisher

In many cases, the owner is the *publisher.* (Although most daily newspapers are incorporated, and may have a president and chairman of the board of directors, the publisher often functions somewhat as chairman, president, chief executive officer, and chief operating officer.)

On larger papers, the publisher is hired to supervise the many details of publishing. He or she is responsible for operating the newspaper so as to make a profit, for seeing that it is accepted by the readers, and for ensuring that employees are satisfied with their working conditions. He or she is the authority with regard to decisions concerning advertising, circulation, business, and production departments.

On most newspapers, the publisher is the person who formulates broad policy. Generally, however, he has no part in day-to-day editorial matters.

The *general manager* is the publisher's assistant. Often he is the chief financial officer. He must have widespread knowledge of all departments within the newspaper.

Editor

How does an editor handle the constant tightrope walk? (Bet you didn't know that Ann Franklin was the first female editor of an American newspaper, the Mercury, published in Newport, R.I., in 1762!)

The *editor-in-chief* is in charge of the editorial departments. (Note: The designation "editorial departments" does not cover merely the editorial and opinion page(s) section, where editorials, opinions, and so on appear. "Editorial departments" denotes all news departments and all printed content that is *not* advertising.)

Rarely is the editor-in-chief's entire title used; the simple title *editor,* most often denotes the highest news official in charge of the editorial departments.

The Wall Street Journal, in its "Pepper . . . and Salt" feature, calls an editor "a line tamer," but in reality, he or she is much more. The editor is responsible for everything that appears in the paper except advertising. He or she works closely with the business manager and the production manager; determines the amount of space to be allotted to local, state, and national news; and decides on the features and cartoons that are to run in the newspaper.

There probably is no other single person in town who knows more about what makes your community tick—past, present, and future—than the editor of your local newspaper. In many towns, nearly every significant act of every citizen from birth notice to obituary passes across the editor's desk.

Newspaper editors often walk a tight line on what to put in the paper and what to leave out. They know, for instance, that the reporting of certain disturbances may lead to more violence by leaders who like to see the disruption they cause. But when this is weighed against the right of the people to know what is going on, the latter usually wins out. Often newspapers are accused of printing such information for its sensation value. However, newspapers no longer have to print sensational news in order to sell papers because home-delivered papers are paid for in advance, and home deliveries make up about 75 to 85 percent of the sales of the majority of newspapers.

Reporters

News reporters are news gatherers not ventriloquists. Anna Quindlen, in *The New York Times* said that a newspaper is given its voice by the people who write and edit it, and then added, "Ventriloquists won't cut it."

Reporters are the heart of the news-gathering operation. Most editors, editorial writers, and columnists were once reporters.

A want ad that appeared in a publication of the American Newspaper Publishers Association spells out a reporter's qualifications:

WANTED: Individual with innate curiosity, intelligence, college education (not merely degree), writing ability, typing proficiency. Must have capacity to dig for news and to write it accurately, fully and intelligibly even under deadline pressure. Must possess interest, versatility and skill to reduce complex issues to lucid, simple English for demanding readers seeking not merely facts but comprehension in era of unparalleled complexity, perplexity, ferment, change.

A reporter's rewards and gratifications—or the opposite—are built into the job. He or she is on the "inside" of news and in the confidence of news makers. The reporter must demonstrate initiative, independence, and judgment. The unexpected is to be expected. The relentless pressure of a deadline rides like a monkey on the reporter's back, and, at times, personal plans give way to emergency job demands. His or her priceless prose may be slashed to accommodate space. Being accurate, factual, honest, and objective about a story and refusing to take no for an answer sometimes create enemies.

David Casstevens, a columnist for *The Dallas Morning News*, adds some thoughts of his own about his job as a reporter: "There are times I feel jealous of athletes. . . . A football player scores a touchdown, and the feedback, the roar of the crowd, is instantaneous and exhilarating. Writing is solitary work. If words born from one's keyboard touch a reader in a positive way, the response, whether it be an agreeing nod or a touch of a smile, goes unseen by the one who produced it."

However, for most, the greatest reward is seeing the results of the day's work in print almost immediately, sometimes even with a byline.

Revenue Producers

The advertising and circulation managers may report to the business manager or directly to the general manager or publisher. They are the revenue producers for the company.

The advertising manager is responsible for selling advertising space in the newspaper and for supervising all advertising copy. He or she may have assistants: a classified advertising manager and a national advertising manager. The advertising department, which produces about two-thirds of the company's revenue, has salespeople who have regular customers on whom they call to sell advertising.

The circulation manager is in charge of distribution of the newspapers by all methods. He or she is responsible for promoting sales campaigns and for overseeing the carrier salespeople and the newspaper-delivery functions. The circulation department produces about one-third of the revenue.

The circulation manager performs somewhat like the general of a small but highly efficient army of specialists. Under his or her command are drivers, carriers, district field managers, skilled clerical force, solicitors, trouble-shooters, and supervisors.

Distributing the newspaper is a daily triumph in logistics and over obstacles of geography, traffic, weather, and train, bus, air, and post-office schedules.

There is something of an irony here, though. No other business in the world functions at jet-age speed right up to the shipping dock and then turns its product over to be delivered by a boy or girl on a bicycle (or, at best, to someone in a car tossing it out the window onto your lawn). (It wasn't until 1972—210 years after Ann Franklin broke the gender barrier in the news-room—that federal and state laws permitted girls in the 10-to-16 age group to be newspaper deliverers, too.)

The circulation of many newspapers are now almost totally controlled by computer programs.

Editorial Content

A newspaper has two basic parts—editorial content and advertising. Editorial content is anything that is not advertising. The editorial department includes not only the editorial pages on which the policy of the paper is set forth, but every other kind of editorial matter.

Editorial content space is never for sale; advertising space is always for sale. If an ad looks like a news or feature story, it is carefully labeled as advertising so there shall be no mistake in interpretation.

Separation of Fact and Opinion

Within the editorial content of a newspaper, there are two main categories—fact and opinion. There is no place for opinion—unless it is labeled as such—in the news columns of a newspaper. Opinions of the newspaper, of its opinions writers, and of its readers go on the editorial and op-ed pages.

More and more interpretive reporting is appearing in newspapers, necessitated by the fact that radio and television get the big news first but provide merely a headline service in reporting it. However, the word *interpre-tive* is not a synonym for the word *opinion*. An opinion is a judgment; an interpretation is an explanation. This is a major reason that even the most loyal broadcast-media fan turns to newspapers. The reporter who has covered one particular *beat* (news area) for any length of time knows more about it than his or her readers or even his or her editors. The reporter's interpretation of events in the light of what he or she knows is invaluable to the reader entering the situation for the first time.

The difference between interpretive reporting and editorializing was brought into focus by Allen H. Neuharth while he was president of the Gannett Company, the largest newspaper chain in the world: "Interpretive reporting, if done well, explores all angles related to any part of a story, and then puts them in perspective as the story develops, without expressing the views of the writer. An editorial, however, must be opinionated; it must say whether something is good or bad . . . there is no 'on the other hand.' "

Individual Newspaper "Personality"

One of the editor's important jobs is to give the newspaper its "personality"— and every paper has its own. You might understand what this means when you visit other cities and read their hometown newspapers. They just aren't like the old "friends" you read at home. The arrangement of stories in the columns is distinctively different, and the typographical appearance also may be totally different. The format may be six columns to a page, or even five or eight columns. The paper's size may be unique. For instance, the *Rocky Mountain News* in Denver, Colorado, and The New York *Daily News*—both major metropolitan dailies—are tabloid size, while *The New York Times* and the *Los Angeles Times* are standard paper size.

News Placement

The newspaper is arranged to enable a reader to digest its contents within a reasonable time. *Placement* of news is the primary method used. News of universal interest goes on the front page. News of lesser importance or of more specific interest goes on inside pages. Commentary, analysis, and pros and cons of issues are gathered on the editorial and op-ed pages.

Usually sports news, women's and family news, business and financial news, comics, fashion, and food and cooking information can each be found in their same places in a newspaper—each day or on special days of the week. Familiarity with a newspaper cuts reading time because you know where to find the information of special interest to you.

In making up the newspaper's pages, the editor for a specific page or section works from the top of the page down. The last column to the right on page one is considered the position of greatest importance since the reader scans the *banner* head (the headline across several columns or that often runs across the entire page) from left to right, and then his or her eye naturally drops into the last column. The most important story of the day goes there.

Headlines tell you what each story is about. The lead—or first paragraph—of a news story contains the most important details. Each succeeding paragraph contains elaboration or addition of details to the information in the lead.

The editor of page one (as every other page or section editor) wants an orderly variety of stories and pictures on each page and not a jumble, so he or she usually follows a tested formula. The editor alternates the size and type styles of headlines and uses stories of varying lengths. Subheads and short paragraphs are used to break up the gray look of solid columns of regular size type. Pictures and drawings provide greater contrast and interest.

Makeup on inside pages is more complicated because of ads. Page by page, news and advertising space is worked out according to *dummy* sheets (miniature page layouts), which indicate the placement of each ad and the amount of space on each page to be filled by stories and pictures. The production department works from dummy instructions as to where to place ads and arrange heads, pictures, and columns of type.

Readability Aids

Readability aids for the readers may be either of a subtle nature or of an obvious nature. One readability aid is the placement of news by category (business, sports, family, and so forth).

Other readers' aids are of a more obvious nature:

- Cross references. *Reefers,* as they are called by newspaper people, appear across a column of type or possibly across several columns, and are set apart from body copy by lines. The following is an example of a reefer that directs a reader to page 33 in section A for a photo that relates to the news story in which the reefer appears.

          ⟨ ⟩ Related photo   33A

- Explanatory notes. These notes are called precedes, tags, or inserts. One type of precede might be an editor's note that explains the contents of the information that follows. It is enclosed in parentheses, usually is set in a different type style such as italics, and may be indented.)
  An example might be an editor's precede above a column in the business section:

(Editor's Note: This is the eighth in a series of 16 articles excerpted from The Publicity Kit: A Complete Guide for Entrepreneurs, Small Businesses, and Nonprofit Organizations.)

- Jumplines. These include the line that uses a key word from the headline to direct the reader to where the story is continued. Jumplines may be worded differently, according to an individual newspaper's style. One newspaper may set its jumplines in italics; another newspaper may use boldface type with the key referral words in capitals. Whatever style is used, that style is used consistently throughout the newspaper. The following examples show different wordings and type styles:

Please see 2 GROUPS on Page 16
Continued on Page 8, Column 1

A line at the top of the continued story, in the same style as the jumpline, tells the reader he or she has located the continuation. Following are examples of continued lines:

Continued from Page 1A
Continued from Page 1

Often newspapers help to make a story clearer by having pictures, charts, maps, and diagrams accompany the story. A more complete understanding of a story is possible for a reader who takes the time to read the chart, study the map, and scan the picture.

You will find many more readers' aids when you look for them.

Types of Writing

If a newspaper is to be read, it must please an enormous range of people with a vast assortment of interests. It must be read in order to remain in business. But, the newspaper is a public trust as well as a commercial enterprise. In other words, the newspaper must provide information that people want to know as well as information that people need to know.

Because audiences vary so much, the newspaper's writing must also vary. What appeals to some people will not be read by others. Sportswriting is completely different from the writing on the business and financial pages. It also is different from much of the straight-news writing that appears on the front page.

The Editorial Department

All reading material except advertising is assembled in the editorial department. Medium- and large-size newspapers generally have five divisions under the editorial department:

1. Newsroom
2. Copy desk
3. Editorial pages
4. Photo department and lab
5. Library, or morgue

News Flow

The typical flow of news follows this order:

Managing Editor. The managing editor is the editor's chief-of-staff. He or she may even serve in both capacities, as editor and managing editor. He or she hires and fires and makes innumerable production decisions throughout the working day. The managing editor's job might be described as the task of seeing that every day when readers receive their newspapers the package is complete.

City Desk. (Local and State News). City editors assign reporters and photographers to cover news events.

Wire Desk. (World News). Each editor (national, international, sports, family, business, and so forth) receives news and photos from wire services and syndicates and decides what to use and what not to use.

Copy Desk. Copy editors read copy for accuracy and sense, and they write headlines. Rewrite people have the responsibility for taking phone calls from reporters and writing their stories to meet deadlines.

Editorial, or Opinion, Pages. The editorial page is the place where the newspaper's opinions appear, along with "editorialized" cartoons expressing the cartoonists' opinions. Editorials present issues of interest to readers, take stands, make judgments, and present attitudes that would not be found in news stories. Op-ed pages contain the personal viewpoints of readers—through letters to the editor and local and syndicated opinion columns.

Photo Department and Lab. Photographers are assigned by the city editor or by a special photo editor, and they often accompany reporters on assignments. An on-premise photo lab permits rapid development of film and printing of photos for reproduction in the paper.

Library, or Morgue. The "final resting place" for news stories and photos that run in the newspaper is the *morgue*. The librarian's responsibility is to clip and file the news stories so that reporters may easily have access to information for background when writing about the same person or subject at later times. At many mid-size and large newspapers such information is filed and located by means of computers.

Special Departments. Other editors head special news departments: fashion, food, business, family, and entertainment. Each of these editors reports to the managing editor. The sports editor has a separate department with reporters working for him or her and is usually responsible for covering all sports events on the local, state, and national scene. Much of the national sports coverage, however, is available through wire services. The sports editor and other special-department editors may report to the managing editor or directly to the editor.

Columnists. Newspapers also employ columnists, chosen for a particular style of writing, to round out the content of the paper. These columnists are free to choose their own material, but they are responsible to the managing editor or editor.

Editorial Decisions

Newspapers' decisions about particular editorial positions vary from paper to paper. With some newspapers, the editor *is* management. He or she may be the owner or co-owner, or, often in the case of small papers, he or she serves as both editor and publisher. In these situations, the editor represents the thinking of the paper and is able to speak for it. Some large newspapers have editorial boards who meet each day like a committee and arrive at judgments in a formal manner.

"An editor, who must or should take vigorous editorial positions on the great issues of the day, is not to be loved," said John S. Knight, when he was Editorial Chairman of Knight-Ridder Newspapers, Inc. "If he seeks affection and popularity, he should be in public relations. Newspapers must base their conclusions upon the facts at hand. The unvarnished truth is frequently unpleasant reading since it so often differs from the reader's preconceived notions of what the truth should be."

Another publisher expressed it this way: "Newspapers that don't express strong editorial opinions that can cause some reader's emotions to explode like throwing fat into a fire, are like a dish of boiled oatmeal."

E. B. White, co-author with William Strunk, Jr. of *The Elements of Style*, said it in a simpler manner: "There are three things no one can do to the satisfaction of anyone else: Make love, poke the fire, and run a newspaper."

Yet, as still another editor asks, "Did you ever think about the fact that a newspaper is the only business that is expected to jeopardize its income from advertisers, and even its very existence, by taking strong stands on highly volatile public issues?"

Newspaper Duties

A newspaper should be expected to do the following things:

- Supply accurate, objective information about national, international, state, county, and local events.
- Provide factual information, as well as news commentary to help its readers evaluate the news.
- Include material to interest a wide variety of readers with an enormous assortment of interests and concerns.
- Take an active part in supporting worthwhile community projects by printing news stories and perhaps editorials about needed improvements or projects.
- Be attractive and easy to read; make a sincere effort to eliminate errors and misspelled words.
- Guard the freedom of the press: withholding news from the public makes for an ignorant public; sensationalizing the news makes for a cynical public.

Newspaper Rights

A newspaper should *not* be expected to do the following things:

- Support a private interest that is contrary to the general welfare.
- Suppress news that one person or a particular group does not wish to see

in print. (A person may support freedom of the press only until he or she becomes personally involved in a news story and feels that his or her privacy has been invaded.)

- Search out and publish details, of prominent persons' private lives, that do not directly concern or affect the public.
- Operate at a loss.

Some Famous Names in Journalism

Many people whose accomplishments made them legends served periods of their lives as newspaper publishers or reporters.

- Charles Dickens was a reporter for the *London Chronicle*.
- Rudyard Kipling was 17 years old when he launched his literary career as a reporter for a paper in India. According to the late newspaper columnist Walter Winchell, Kipling carried on in Sahara temperatures and covered everything from murder trials to sporting events. He had a remarkable memory and never bothered making notes while covering a story. Winchell wrote that Kipling said, "If a thing didn't stay in my memory, I believed it was hardly worth writing about."
- Carl Sandburg, Ben Hecht, and Vincent Sheean were reporters on the *Chicago Daily News*.
- Gail Borden, a newspaper publisher who invented canned milk, was the man whose headline in the *Telegraph & Texas Register* immortalized the cry, "Remember the Alamo."
- Charles H. Dana started as a $10-a-week reporter on Horace Greeley's *Tribune*.
- Don Knox, who is a graduate of the University of Kansas and a reporter for *The Dallas Morning News*, knows more than a little about Kansas' most influential journalist, William Allen White. "His writing somehow managed to leap off the pages of *The Emporia* (Kansas) *Gazette*. White knew the journalist's credo, keep it simple, stupid, according to Knox who says that White chiseled his commentaries to a manageable size, if only to ensure their wide distribution over wires of The Associated Press.
- Winston Churchill was a war correspondent when he was 21 and also Britain's highest paid newsman of that period.

- Authors Ernest Hemingway, Kenneth Roberts, and John P. Marquand once were news reporters.
- Few people are aware that novelist Irving Wallace learned his writing skills as a reporter and editor for the *Wisconsin News & Southport Bugle*.
- Even the infamous once were reporters. Syndicated columnist L. M. Boyd wrote that it wasn't until after the famous Bat Masterson left the western frontier to return to New York City that he bought a gun in a pawn shop there, filed 22 notches in the handle, then manufactured his own legend while a reporter for the *New York Telegraph*.

OTHER FAMOUS JOURNALISTS

Robert Benchley	Horace Greeley	Dorothy Parker
Heywood Broun	Bret Harte	Edgar Allan Poe
William Cullen	William R.	Joseph Pulitzer
Bryant	Hearst	Ernie Pyle
Art Buchwald	O. Henry (W.	Will Rogers
Al Capp	Sydney Porter)	Damon Runyon
Marquise Childs	Thomas Jefferson	Jonathan Swift
Frank Irvin Cobb	Sinclair Lewis	Dorothy
Norman Cousins	Jack London	Thompson
Theodore Dreiser	Don Marquis	James Thurber
F. Scott	Christopher	Mark Twain
Fitzgerald	Morley	E. B. White
Benjamin Franklin	Thomas Paine	Walt Whitman

YESTERDAY'S NEWSPAPER CARRIERS
WHO BECAME HISTORY'S LEADERS

Entertainment
Art Linkletter
Danny Thomas
John Wayne
George Goebel
Dick Van Dyke
Joe E. Brown
Richard Boone
Frank Sinatra
Glenn Ford
Jack Webb
Emmett Kelley
Bing Crosby
Ernie Ford
Arthur Godfrey
Bob Hope
Fred MacMurray
Lauritz Melchoir
Red Skelton
Ed Sullivan

**Business
Leaders**
Walt Disney
Benjamin F.
Fairless
Crawford H.
Greenewalt
Eric A. Johnson
W. Alton Jones
Garvice D.
Kincaid
Mervin LeRoy
Elmer L.
Lindseth
George Eastman
David Sarnoff

Sports
Joe DiMaggio
Jack Dempsey
Rafer Johnson
Ben Hogan

Sam Snead
Ken Venturi
Gil Dodds
Yogi Berra
Stan Musial
Mickey Mantle
Rogers Hornsby
Knute Rockne
Willie Mays
Jackie Robinson
"Duke" Snider
Red Grange
Mike
McCormick

Statesmen
Lyndon B.
Johnson
Harry Truman
Dwight D.
Eisenhower
Herbert Hoover
Glenn H.
Anderson
Harold S.
Stassen
Ralph J. Bunche
Anthony J.
Celebreeze
Tom C. Clark
Jack G.
Diefenbacker
William O.
Douglas
Lester B. Pearson
Abraham A.
Ribicoff
Earl Warren

**Religious
Leaders**
Rabbi Edgar J.
Magnin

Francis Cardinal
Spellman
Dr. Norman
Vincent Peale

Military
Walter
Cunningham
John W. Glenn
John W. Young
Michael Collins
Gus Grissom
Alan Shephard,
Jr.
Scott Carpenter
Gen. James
Doolittle
Gen. Omar
Bradley
Gen. Nathan
Twining
Rear Adm. Jack
P. Monroe
Capt. Eddie
Rickenbacker

**Law
Enforcement**
J. Edgar Hoover
William H.
Parker

Education
Glenn T.
Seaborg
Roy E. Simpson
Robert Gordon
Sproul

Literary
Carl Sandburg

Fictional News Release Samples

Sample 1: New Executive Announcement Release

PAULLUS DEPARTMENT STORE

Street Address
City, State, Zip
Telephone, Fax Numbers

Contact: (Your name)

Release at your convenience

Paullus Department Store Names New COO

ST. LOUIS--Joseph P. Johnson, senior vice president of Paullus Department Store, was named president and chief operating officer, the company announced Monday (July 18).

Johnson, 48, will report to James W. Paullus, founder, formerly president and now chairman and chief executive officer.

As an experienced general merchandise manager at Paullus Department Store prior to his appointment as senior vice president in 1987, and at other companies throughout his 24-year career, Johnson said he will be able to bring to the store better coordination between manufacturers and buyers in addition to acting as operations manager.

Prior to joining Paullus Department Store in 1983, Johnson was general merchandise buyer for several stores, including Sullivan's and Geramee's, both headquartered in St. Louis.

Paullus Department Store is well known for its support of community-wide reading programs for children with learning disabilities.

# # #

Sample 2: Grant Award Release

HOUSING FOR ALL, INC.

Street Address
City, State, Zip
Telephone Number

Contact: (Your name)
            (Phone #, if not as above)
                                                    For Immediate Release

            (Alternate's name)
            (Phone number)

**Housing For All Receives
$75,000 Matching Funds Grant**

    Housing For All, a nonprofit organization that repairs and
restores abandoned housing, has received a matching grant of
$75,000 to help start a special development district in the
Wilson area of South Jackson.

    Joe Jones, executive director of Housing For All, said that
the funds, which come from a foundation set up in honor of the
late Natalie B. Gonzalez, mean that a new area can be developed.
"It means we can reach out to people we have been unable to
service before." Ultimately, the program will provide housing
for 20 families.

    Jones also makes it clear that raising the matching funds
will require enormous effort on the part of the organization.
"We must immediately put into action Housing For All's plans for
some special events to raise the required matching funds. And we
must enlarge our base of volunteers. We're also looking to
corporations for funding."

                            # # #

Sample 3: Planned Move Release

PAULLUS DEPARTMENT STORE

Street Address
City, State, Zip
Telephone, Fax Numbers

Contact: (Your name)   For Immediate Release

Specialty Clothing Store to Move

Paullus Department Store, a retailer of specialty clothing for women, plans to move its store at 28th and South Parkway to the River Road Shopping Center early next year.

Jim Paullus, owner and operator of the store, says the move is necessary because the store's lease cannot be renewed. The building's owner is planning construction of a 10-story office building at the location. Paullus Department Store has been at its present location for almost five years.

The new 1,400-square-foot store will offer a wide variety of women's apparel and will expand to include ski and swim wear.

Emmett Considine handled lease negotiations for ABC Management Co., owner and manager of River Road Shopping Center.

# # #

Sample 4: Award Recognition Release

RECOGNITION INSURANCE COMPANY

Street Address
City, State, Zip
Telephone, Fax Numbers

Contact: (Your name)   <u>For Immediate Release</u>

**Local Insurance Agency Owner
Wins Public Speaking Title**

KENSINGTON, Okla.--Hansen Wright, owner of Recognition Insurance Agency, took top honors in a state-level public speaking contest in Kensington Saturday evening.

Wright defeated contestants from eight other cities in Oklahoma at the annual semifinals of Speakers Unanimous, a service group that teaches public speaking skills. National finals will be conducted in Chicago next month.

The speech, entitled "One For the Low Road," focused on the humorous aspects of traveling by motorhome and the often difficult conditions that such travel entails. Wright said he picked up almost all of his humorous anecdotes from Recognition Insurance Co.'s clients, although he too owns a motorhome. "I must have always taken the high road, because I can't ever remember getting myself into the kinds of situations these people did."

- more -

Recognition Insurance Owner Wins Award - 2-2-2

His 10-minute presentation was enthusiastically received by
the audience of about 300 at the Convention Center Hotel.

Competitors' speeches ranged from professional to earthy,
down-home advice.

The second-place winner, from Lake Isabella, was Dennis
Dolman. Third place went to Joanna Williams of Southfork.

In discussing his speech after receiving the award, Wright
said that he loves selling insurance to motorhome owners because,
"I rarely have a chance to laugh as much with other clients as I
do with these people about the things that happen to them. So
often insurance deals with situations that are sad or of concern
to the buyer. This is different."

Recognition Insurance Company, owned by Hansen Wright, has
been recognized in past years for its contributions to the local
literacy program. Several of Recognition's agents are volunteers
who teach reading to inmates at the county prison facility.

# # #

Sample 5: Image Builder Release

WATERBURY SAVINGS & LOAN BANK

Street Address
City, State, Zip
Telephone, Fax Numbers

Contact: Your name   **For Immediate Release**

**Education Crisis Is Focus of
Waterbury Bank Ad Campaign**

DELTA, Ariz.--Waterbury Savings & Loan Bank announced today that
it will launch a one-year advertising campaign designed to
increase recognition of the growing county-wide education crisis.

The campaign will feature local high school dropouts from
around the county who have gone back to school because their lack
of education and vocational training has blocked their efforts to
find employment. Each will tell his or her difficulties, explain
what it was like to face failure at every turn, and describe how
going back to school has turned his or her life around.

The campaign is a departure from Waterbury Savings & Loan
Bank's traditional services-oriented consumer advertising.

- more -

Waterbury Ad Campaign Shifts Emphasis - 2-2-2

    Gary Dominick, president of Waterbury Savings & Loan Bank, cited several reasons for the shift in advertising direction. "Not only are students facing huge challenges in achieving success, but businesses face the near impossible task of finding competitent employees if there is not a significant increase in literate, trained young people to fill the variety of jobs this country offers. As technology improves, the need for a really smart generation of workers increases dramatically," he said.

    Waterbury Savings & Loan Bank's advertising campaign is timed to begin in mid-July to stimulate interest by potential dropouts in staying in school when it begins in the fall.

# # #

Sample 6: Merger Release

BENTLEY & ASSOCIATES

Street Address
City, State, Zip
Telephone Number

Contact: (Your name)   <u>For Immediate Release</u>

**Bentley & Associates Merges
with Bryan Evans Hughes**

Bentley & Associates, a Deerfield-based accounting firm, has merged with Bryan Evans Hughes, John Bentley announced today.

"Bryan Evans Hughes is a highly respected accounting firm within the city and throughout the county," said Bentley. "The merger will augment both group's capabilities. We are exceptionally strong in standard accounting while BEH adds strength through their tax capabilities."

Bentley & Associates, a 14-year-old accounting firm, represents a broad range of clientele, from individuals to retail firms and maufacturing companies. Bryan Evans Hughes, in business for almost 10 years, has concentrated on handling tax matters for large corporations.

As a result of the merger, the firm will be renamed Bentley, Bryan & Evans. John Bentley will continue as president, and George Bryan will assume the new position of chief executive officer.

# # #

Sample 7: Feature News Release

ALPHA-OMEGA TRAVEL AGENCY

Street Address
City, State, Zip
Telephone Number

Contact: (Your name)   For Release
                                       <u>At Your Convenience</u>

**Travel Agency Owner Will Go to
Any Lengths to Bring His Clients Home**

When Kenneth Ellison handed Mary Hutchison and Lance Killion their travel tickets, none of them had any idea what all three of them were in for.

Ken Ellison is owner of Alpha-Omega Travel Agency and has a reputation for putting together travel itineraries that are varied and vastly different. The one he put together this time lived up to his reputation, but because the couple wanted to include their wedding in trip plans and expressed a desire to really "get away from it all," Ken went out of his way to find them exactly what they wanted.

He guaranteed them, he said, that the trip he'd arranged would get them so far away from it all that no one could contact them until they were ready to be contacted.

- more -

Travel Agency Goes to Great Lengths - 2-2-2

    And then it happened. The couple had been gone less than a
week of their three week wedding-honeymoon-vacation when a family
member phoned Alpha-Omega Travel Agency in a high state of
excitement. Mary Hutchison (now Mary Hutchison Killion) had won
a special lottery for one million dollars, but Mary must present
her winning ticket within five days, the family member said, or
lose the money. "What do we do?" shouted the caller.

    You've guessed it. Alpha-Omega Travel Agency also is noted
for its exceptional service, so Ken Ellison figured he had no
other choice but to jump on a plane, then a train, and finally a
horse, to reach the Killions in their remote location.

    The couple was right where the itinerary said they'd be when
he found them. Although Ken offered to act as their emissary so
they could continue their trip, the couple decided to return
immediately and present Mary's ticket to the lottery board.

    Now, a few weeks later, the Killions have received their
first lottery installment and are looking forward to another
trip. This time, they say, they'll choose a location where
getting home can be a lot easier, just in case they win another
prize.

                              # # #

Sample 8: Obituary

FEDERAL HOME BLUEPRINT COMPANY

Street Address
City, State, Zip
Telephone Number

Contact: (Your name)   <u>For Immediate Release</u>

**William D. Carpenter, Blueprint
Firm President, Dies**

William Daniel Carpenter, president of Federal Home
Blueprint Co., died Sunday at Gateway Medical Center. He was 53.

A memorial service will be held at 11 a.m. Wednesday at
Interfaith Bible Church. Burial will follow at Sunset Shadows
Cemetery.

Mr. Carpenter, a New London native, attended Norwalk public
schools and earned his bachelor's degree in math from Blackman
State University in 1959. Four years later he earned a master's
degree in business management from BSU.

He began his career with Southwest Engineering Corp. in
Norwalk, as an assistant manager of the firm. In 1975 he
returned to New London to join Federal Home Blueprint Co., a
family-owned business. He became president, following his
father's death, and remained in that position until his own
death.

- more -

Blueprint Firm President dies -- 2-2-2

    Mr. Carpenter was a member of the social fraternity of Phi
Phi Phi and the New London Musical Society. He also belonged to
several professional organizations and the New London Chamber of
Commerce. He served as president of the latter.

    He is survived by his wife, Jean Bell Carpenter of New
London; a daughter, Maryanne Carpenter Longstreet of Templeton;
and a son, William Daniel Carpenter, Jr., also of New London, who
assumed the presidency of Federal Home Blueprint Co. upon his
father's death.

    Memorials may be made to the Blackman State University
Cancer Center.

                                # # #

Sample 9: Fact Sheet

NILSSON AVIATION SERVICES

Street Address
City, State, Zip
Telephone, Fax Numbers

(Date)

Contact: (Your name)   FACT SHEET

Nilsson Aviation Services Begins New Service

A three-times-weekly air service between Norman, Okla. and Brandon Springs, Colo. will begin at the start of the ski season in late November and continue through March.

The service will use a Skyjet 653-MK, an advanced-technology twin-jet plane with seating for 25 passengers.

"We have received so many requests for this special service, which no airline or charter service currently provides, that we decided to add this aircraft and make regular runs," said Joseph Lamata, owner of Nilsson Aviation Services. "This is an exciting prospect that we are very enthusiastic about."

Brandon Springs Mayor Jeremy Langton offered the following comments: "This new service will allow weekend skiers to enjoy our great powder snow and still be able to get back to work Monday mornings. Before Nilsson inaugurated this service, skiers could only get here by car or bus. Our merchants and resort people are really excited about it."

— more —

Nilsson Aviation Services Begins New Service —2-2-2

Nilsson Aviation Services was founded in 1980 and purchased by Joseph Lamata in 1986. (Additional company information is included in the attached annual report.)

Currently, the company runs a four-helicopter operation that specializes in agricultural helicopter flying and a charter service that uses smaller Skyjets that seat seven passengers.

# # #

Photo-Release Form
and Photo Guidelines

Photo-Release Form

I, _____, being of legal
  (photo subject's name)
age, hereby consent and authorize _____
                                  (name of your organization)
_____, its successors, legal

representative and assigns, to use and reproduce my name and photograph(s) (or

photographs of) _____ taken by _____ on
              (name of minor and relationship)   (photographer)
_____, and circulate the same for any and all purposes, including public
(date)
information of every description. Receipt of full consideration of \$_____ is

hereby acknowledged and no further claim of whatsoever nature will be made by me.

No representations have been made to me.

_____   _____
(signature)   (address)

_____   _____
(witness)   (address)

Guidelines for Color or B&W Still Photos

Following is a memo sent to agency staff members by an international advertising and public relations firm.

If you are going on a photo shoot or have any production activities that can be used for publicity purposes on behalf of the client or this agency, please bear in mind that the following points should be addressed:

- If the shot includes participants who are not agency staff or the agency's hired people, *get a signed release* from each "outsider."
- When the photo is taken, be sure that the people look presentable for a publicity release—particularly the agency's own representatives. (No cutoff tee shirts, untied shoes, or shorts, no matter how hot the temperature or how difficult the shoot.)
- Poses, too, should be of a "professional" quality;

  People doing something representative of the client's purpose for the shoot. (Please remember that the intent of the release is to publicize [agency's name]'s advertising professionalism—and to give the client added publicity exposure).

  No all-in-a-line-face-the-camera-and-grin shots, *please.* Have people *doing something.*

  No more than three—at the very most four—people in a photo.
- The format of most publications calls for vertical shots whenever possible. A horizontal shot most often must be cropped, which frequently cuts a person on the end or kills the shot entirely.
- If possible, take both black and white shots as well as color slides. Any standard b&w film is fine; but try to use a 100 or 200 ASA/ISO color slide film—not one of the new high-speed slide films.
- There is no need for the photographer to supply prints of the b&w shots; a contact sheet will be sufficient. But be sure to include the photographer's name and phone number, so that we may order the print(s) we require.
- All shots for publicity purposes should be made by a professional photographer, if possible. Otherwise, be sure that all publicity stills are made with a 35mm SLR [Single Lens Reflex] camera [not a point-and-shoot viewfinder camera]; with camera mounted on a tripod to achieve tack-sharp images that are acceptable for either newspaper or magazine reproduction.

(These guidelines are effective this date, and until further notice.)

How to Write Effective Publicity Goals and Objectives

Well-Defined Goals and Objectives

As the Cheshire Cat told Alice, "If you don't know where you are going, then any path will take you there."

Lack of well-defined goals create the kinds of problems in attaining success that you encounter with a map on which the names of the roads cannot be easily read. Or, as Ashleigh Brilliant unequivocally states in a "Pot-Shots" cartoon, "The greatest obstacle to achieving my goals is that I don't know what my goals are."

Every organization and every division or committee of that organization needs goals and objectives. Other terms, such as *targets, statement of purposes, strategies* and *tactics* (lumped under the current buzzwords *strategic planning*), may be used interchangeably by some. But everyone understands the old standby term: goals and objectives.

"Values determine needs;" says William F. Christopher in his book, *The Achieving Enterprise.* "needs determine goals; needs and goals together determine the function and the future of our business enterprises." This assertion is equally applicable to nonprofit enterprises.

You can achieve substantial, recognizable results if you know where you're going. Your publicity efforts will be much more effective if you set well-defined goals for what you wish to realize and specific objectives on how to get there.

Broad Participation

Who should establish your major goals with their objectives?

Some organizations adhere to the belief that goals and objectives should be handed down from on high, formulated by the board of directors or the company "czar." Even if you *are* the board of directors, you will achieve far greater success in accomplishing your goals and objectives if *everyone concerned* actively participates in planning and defining them. This includes the board, management, line staff, and volunteers.

An added bonus to broad participation is the insurance that everyone involved with the creation and execution of goals and objectives fully understands them and thereby trusts and is loyal to them.

The Necessity for Goals and Objectives

If you are wondering why you should bother with goals and objectives, the answer is this: Well-circulated and well-understood goals and objectives accomplish highly desirable results. No organization can operate efficiently, productively, and profitably without them. Nor will the results of your publicity be efficient, productive, and profitable without solid goals and objectives.

This is what well-defined goals and objectives can do for your publicity efforts:

- Cut down or eliminate much of the time and effort wasted on unproductive tasks.
- Set courses of action and stimulate performance.
- Guide efforts.
- Eliminate other goals or objectives that do not work to further the major purpose of your organization.

Definitions and Differences

The following sections clarify and explain the distinct differences between goals and their objectives and describe how to formulate them.

Goals

Goals are long-range plans. They are determined by *needs*. It is important that you set well-expressed publicity goals for a proposed plan—explicit specifications of the *results* that you are looking for.

Goals are the ends toward which efforts are directed. Though they may change as time requires, they are a necessary first step in the planning cycle.

Each goal should supplement other goals, and, at the very least, no cross-purposes should exist. More specifically, goals for your publicity program should be set to supplement the organization's goals as well as any other existing publicity goals. There must be no conflict between your publicity plans and overall organization plans.

Goals are general statements of end results.

Objectives

On the other hand, good objectives contain explicit, specified results. Goals can be lofty and visionary (but not unrealistic). Objectives, however, must be practical, specific, and attainable, but set to require some stretching and extending.

Side-by-Side Definitions and Differences

In order to make it easier to recognize the distinct differences between goals and objectives, they are defined here side by side. It's academic, my dear Watson—at least the definitions sound so.

A goal is a statement of broad direction or interest which is general and timeless and is not concerned with a particular achievement within a specified period. (Caution: It must be attainable.)

An objective is a devised plan for action that can be verified within a given time and under specific conditions that, if attained, advances the system toward a corresponding goal. (Caution: It must be measurable.)

Examples of Goals

Any one of the following are considered goals. Not one could be considered an objective.

- To devise and conduct a publicity campaign to achieve greater public recognition.
- To conduct a fund-raising program to finance organizational expansion.
- To increase the number of volunteers and the greater use of their donated time and participation in a nonprofit organization's activities and programs.
- To create public awareness of a for-profit organization's new service or product.

They are goals, not objectives, because none states precisely *what* is to be accomplished; *who* is to accomplish it; *when* it will be accomplished; or *how* it will be done.

Components of Objectives

A well-written objective should include the following components, in whatever order you prefer:

- *Who.* Specific statement as to the *individuals* who will perform the objective.
- *What.* Specific *accomplishment* when the objective has been achieved.
- *When.* Specific *point in time* when the objective is to be achieved.
- *How well:* Specific *criteria of success* to be obtained.

Measurable Words. Inexperienced writers of objectives often ensnare themselves in a common pitfall: They fail to state their objectives in measurable terms. They use words such as To *know,* To *understand,* To *appreciate,* To *enjoy,* and To *believe.*

How do you measure understanding, appreciation, or belief? Usually you can't, and when you can it is with great effort and difficulty! On the other hand, objectives are easier to measure when you use the following words in your statements:

To construct	To eliminate
To identify	To differentiate
To maintain	To solve
To increase	To compare
To decrease	To list
To reduce	To recognize
To improve	To lessen (the problem)
To develop	To better (a condition)

Five Objective Measurements.   Objectives formulated with words from the above list can be measured, and they will state the following:

- what will happen,
- to whom,
- to change them how much,
- by what time, and
- how we will know.

Sample Publicity Goal and Its Objectives

Goal: To devise and conduct a publicity campaign to achieve greater public awareness of and recognition for (your organization).
Objectives:
1. By (date), I (the publicity staffer or committee chairperson) will have gathered all data and pertinent information for a media fact sheet, including names, addresses, and phone numbers for the organization's headquarters, board of directors, and staff; brief descriptions of accomplishments and achievements of the organization to date; long-range goals; founders and founding date; a brief statement of philosophy of the group's purposes; and all other pertinent and important information about the organization.
2. By (date) I/staffer/chairman will have defined, listed, and personally contacted all news-media personnel who are important to furtherance of creating greater public awareness for the organization, and will have distributed to each the media fact sheet for his or her files, along with a letter introducing him- or herself and suggesting a future meeting to discuss publicity plans for the organization.

A goal as broad as the example shown above would require many more objectives to adequately create the plans for achieving it. But because goals and objectives must be customized to the individual organization, examples are difficult to offer.

Remember though, emphasis in objectives is always on *accomplishment*.

The SMAC and SMART Formulas

Here are some last suggestions. The following two memory crutches will help you write your objectives and test whether they will perform as they are meant.

First, SMAC 'em! SMAC stands for the following:

S Specific   A Attainable
M Measurable   C Compatible

Second, out-SMART 'em! SMART stands for the following:

S Specific   R Reasonable
M Measurable   T Time (frame)
A Achievable

Your objectives will fly, and they will return success to you, if you follow the SMAC and SMART formulas.

The Basics of Brainstorming

Some people might tell you not to call it *brainstorming*. Their argument is that the word is out of date. Today it's called problem solving or crisis management. But the technique of brainstorming isn't used exclusively on solving problems and overcoming crises. It is also a splendid, positive means of generating *ideas* that has been around for a very long time, and it holds great promise for being used productively for years and years to come.

The word *brainstorming* describes this technique best, but if it must be renamed, how about calling it creative thinking? Probably the greatest fear among businesspeople is that they will run out of the food that feeds their abilities—ideas! Your cupboard never will be bare if you brainstorm.

Brainstorming is a technique with which an issue, literally any issue, can be vigorously assailed—"stormed," if you will—by a volume of ideas.

The Mechanics of Brainstorming

1. Form your group. Involve as many individuals (up to 12) as can creatively contribute. You can even brainstorm by yourself, but the group process is far more productive as a rule.

2. Be the discussion chairperson, or facilitator, or appoint one. The chairperson's principal responsibilities are to see that the "rules" are followed and to get the process started. A good method for getting the flow of ideas started is to ask some questions. "What-if" and "how" questions are good ones with which to stimulate this creative-thinking process. Here is a word of caution: The *first* rule that must be followed is that anything goes. So if your strengths are inclined more toward logical, judicious thinking that, more or less, automatically suggests objections and says that something can't logically be done (as opposed to more creative, "far out" thinking), then make someone else the facilitator. This person should be able to ensure wideness of suggestions and be capable of blocking negative, inhibiting reactions. Robert P. Levoy, in *The Toastmaster*, explained the necessity when he quoted a plaque in the boardroom of one of America's largest corporations: Nothing will ever be accomplished if every possible objection must first be overcome.

3. Appoint someone to record ideas. This should be someone who is not part of the "think tank," but whose sole responsibility is to record *every* idea, even duplicates, and who does the job without editing of any kind.

4. Set time boundaries. This is important because there inevitably will be lulls in the session. When this happens, it is natural to assume that ideas have run out and to call an end to the meeting. However, a period of silence most often is followed by an explosion of ideas. The chairperson should be prepared, if the group becomes fidgety during these quiet times, to offer an idea to trigger further thinking.

Four Rules

1. Encourage freewheeling expression. The wilder the idea, the better. You can edit ideas later. Let free thinking flow, even if the ideas sound dumb, silly, crazy, or useless and even if the person submitting the idea is second only to Miss Piggy among deep thinkers. The "worst" or the wildest idea may be the very trigger on which someone else piggybacks to toss in one that works.

2. Do not criticize anyone's ideas. No adverse judgments are permitted. Anything goes.

3. Quantity—not quality—is desired. The more ideas you generate, the better are your odds for finding good, workable, profitable ideas.

4. Combine ideas for strength. Urge everyone not only to piggyback on others' ideas but to combine ideas to produce still other ideas.

Postsession Practices

After you have completed your brainstorming session, it is time for logical, rational, and sensible minds to take over.

Previously banned judgments now must be made about whether an idea is practical, which ones may have been tried before, what is too expensive, what is against policy, and so on. Common sense, experience, and sound judgment must take over. Stable, sensible evaluation of the ideas is *as important* as generating those ideas.

A Big Company Makes Brainstorming Pay Off Big

The Adolphe Coors Co. in Colorado has a special employee group called the Right Brainstorm (which takes its name from the theory that the right side of the brain is the creative side). This group has been saving the company large sums since 1980.

Members of the pioneer group acknowledged that they initially viewed the idea "as so much lunch meat" and signed up merely to ensure their next raise. "We knew our supervisor was real enthusiastic about this thing, so we just did it to get in good with him," said one Right Brain member.

Within the first two years, they produced ideas that saved thousands of dollars. One idea put into practice cost only $56 but resulted in annual savings to Coors of $38,000. Also within that two year period, they handed the company a "3-to-1 payout"—their suggestions saved three times more than they cost. Another idea was projected to cost $2,400, including the brainstorming meeting time, with a savings to the company of $17,000. In actuality, the savings amounted to $29,000. That idea was followed by one that cost $27,000 but produced a savings payout of $146,000.

The group claims that productivity, rather than financial gain, is their real goal. The financial aspect is "nice," said one group member, "but we're not out to prove that we can save so much money. Our goal is working together as a team to produce the highest quality ideas we can."

Right Brainstorm's "Code of Conduct"

The following 14 rules for conducting brainstorming sessions, as set by Right Brainstorm, can help you set forth your "Code of Conduct" for your group's sessions.

1. Encourage the ideas of others.

2. Make positive constructive comments.

3. Encourage the participation of all members.

4. Solicit input from others in the department.

5. Ensure that credit is given to those to whom it is due.

6. Maintain a friendly and enthusiastic atmosphere.

7. Attend all scheduled meetings.

8. Rotate tasks on a voluntary basis.

9. Mail the minutes of the meeting within a reasonable time.

10. Assist other group members as necessary.

11. Follow the rules of brainstorming.

12. Follow "Robert's Rules of Order."

13. Maintain equality among all members of the group.

14. Accept the decision of the majority.

So, if developing exciting, productive, new ideas makes you feel a little like you're sticking your finger in a pail of water and pulling it out to see what kind of a hole it leaves, you may want to try organizing a brainstorming group.

There is no attempt here to pass off Adolphe Coors Co. as a small-business enterprise or as a nonprofit organization. But if brainstorming works so handsomely for such a large corporation, think how much easier it can be applied by smaller organizations.

Brainstorming can also help you develop ideas for the staged events described in Chapter 12. Using it for such an event can also provide the practice and conditioning you will need to apply this technique throughout your operation.

A book first published in 1958, and revised and updated in 1988, can provide valuable information about brainstorming: *Brainstorming: The Dynamic New Way to Create Successful Ideas,* by Charles H. Clark.

Directories and Other Information

Directories

EDITOR & PUBLISHER INTERNATIONAL YEAR BOOK
Editor & Publisher Company, Inc.
11 W. 19th St.
New York, NY 10011   212/675-4380

This directory gives the most complete and reliable information about newspapers that is available. It is the encyclopedia of the newspaper industry and is presented in an easy-to-use format with section tabs.

It lists daily and Sunday newspapers (in the United States and Canada), and weekly newspapers; foreign daily newspapers, special-service newspapers; news services; industry, foreign-language, college, and Black newspapers (in the United States); news, picture, and press services; feature and news syndicates, clipping bureaus; and more.

For daily newspapers, the entries include publisher's name, address, and phone, as well as the names of executives and departmental editors (business, financial, book, food, etc.).

Also presented are circulation and advertising data and production information, including the format of the newspaper and the equipment used.

Editor & Publisher magazine issues a special edition each year in July, which is devoted to syndicates. It is a directory of newspaper columnists and can be purchased for under $10 or as part of any annual subscription to the magazine.

BACON'S PUBLICITY CHECKER
Bacon's Publishing Co., Inc.
332 S. Michigan Ave.
Chicago, IL 60604   800/621-0561 or 312/922-2400

Bacon's Publicity Checker is a comprehensive two-volume coil-bound guide to magazines and newspapers in the United States and Canada. It is published annually.

Volume 1—Magazines, lists more than 7,000 magazines and newspapers, organized into 195 market classifications and subgroups, from advertising through woodworking.

Volume 2—Newspapers, lists all daily, weekly, and semiweekly newspapers in the United States and all daily newspapers in Canada. Daily newspaper listings include the names of editors, managing editors and city editors, and some departmental editors.

Radio/TV Directory is a separate listing of more than 9,000 radio and 1,300 television stations. It is organized geographically and includes station call letters, phone numbers, formats, programming, target audiences, network affiliations, and more.

STANDARD RATE AND DATA SERVICE (SRDS)
Standard Rate & Data Service, Inc.
3004 Glenview Rd.
Wilmette, IL 60091 312/256-6067

SRDS publications are most useful when frequent rate and circulation updates are required. The Business Publications directory provides good information about business, professional, and trade magazines. Other than rates and circulation data, SRDS Newspapers directory provides little information about news operations.

SRDS Newspaper Rates and Data is published monthly, and, as for all SRDS publications, it primarily provides advertising and market data.

SRDS Business Publication Rates and Data also is published monthly, in two parts. Part 1 includes an index to business publications, while Part 2 includes an index to international publications and to direct-response advertising media.

SRDS Spot Television Rates and Data, published monthly, lists television stations in the United States, Guam, and the Virgin Islands.

DIRECTORIES IN PRINT
Gale Research, Inc., Dept. 77748
835 Penobscot Bldg.
Detroit, MI 48277-0748 313/961-2242

This is an annotated guide to approximately 10,000 business and industrial directories, professional and scientific rosters, directory databases, and other lists and guides of all kinds that are published in the United States or that are national or regional in scope or interest.

ULRICH'S INTERNATIONAL PERIODICAL DIRECTORY
Order Dept., Box 762
New York, NY 10011 800/521-8110

Listed is information on magazines, especially foreign publications, including publishers' and editors' names and data on circulation and frequency of publication.

GALE DIRECTORY OF PUBLICATIONS & BROADCAST MEDIA
(Formerly Ayer Directory of Publications)
Gale Research Inc., Dept, 77748
Detroit, MI 48277-0748 313/961-2242

O'DWYER'S DIRECTORY OF PUBLIC RELATIONS FIRMS
J. R. O'Dwyer Company
271 Madison Ave.
New York, NY 10016 212/679-2471

Basic data on more than 1,400 individual firms and more than a thousand individual public relations counselors are provided to give quick access to experts in public relations, public affairs, investor relations, employee communications, corporate advertising, all forms of product publicity, issues analysis and management, forecasting, lobbying, proxy solicitation, TV speech training, and international PR.

Stylebooks

THE UPI STYLEBOOK
United Press International
1400 I St. NW
Washington, DC 20005   202/898-8000

The UPI Stylebook is a standard reference for the communications field that is used by UPI editors and writers, newspaper reporters and editors, and PR personnel. It includes information about writing style, courtesy titles, usage, spelling, punctuation, nuclear terminology, and capitalization.

THE ASSOCIATED PRESS STYLEBOOK AND LIBEL MANUAL
Dell Publishing
666 Fifth Ave.
New York, NY 10103   800/255-4133 or 212/765-6500

The *AP Stylebook and Libel Manual* is more than the traditional stylebook. It aids in spelling place names and brand names, identifying the correct form for government agencies, military titles, ship names, and corporation names. It also verifies correct punctuation, capitalization, and abbreviations. In addition, it provides a libel section for people writing for newspapers, newsletters, or anything that goes to the public in print.

THE ELEMENTS OF STYLE
by William Strunk, Jr., and E. B. White
The Macmillan Company
866 Third Ave.
New York, NY 10022   212/702-2000

This tiny book is a result of the principal author's "attempt to cut the vast tangle of English rhetoric down to size and write its rules and principles on the head of a pin," says E. B. White, coauthor. The book is perhaps used by more writers than any other of its kind.

U.S. NEWS & WORLD REPORT STYLEBOOK FOR WRITERS AND EDITORS
by Robert Gover
U.S. News & World Report
2400 N St., NW
Washington, DC 20037   202/955-2000

This stylebook by *U.S. News & World Report* news desk deputy chief Robert Gover is listed for those who wish to extend their publicity programs to news magazines. This stylebook is unique inasmuch as most magazines do not publish this information. The information is applicable to other magazines of the same genre.

Clipping Bureaus

Listed below are clipping bureaus that read and clip nationally. The following paragraph provides you with a means of preserving those clippings, so they won't yellow or become brittle, thereby permitting you to reproduce them into promotional and advertising material or for any other purposes. The method was developed by Richard Smith, when he was an assistant professor at the University of Washington.

Rx FOR PRESERVING NEWSPAPERS: Dissolve a milk-of-magnesia tablet or one tablespoon of milk-of-magnesia emulsion in a quart of club soda, recap tightly, and let stand in the refrigerator overnight. Pour into a pan large enough to accommodate the flattened newspaper. Soak newspaper for one to two hours; remove and pat dry. The solution cannot be reused. Estimated life: 200 years. Chemically, the magnesium oxide combines with the carbon dioxide in the soda to form magnesium carbonate, which neutralizes acids in the paper that cause deterioration.

Editor & Publisher Yearbook for 1990 lists 30 news-clipping services. Some are primarily regional; others are national and international. The best known are as follows:

BACON'S CLIPPING BUREAU
332 S. Michigan Ave.
Chicago, IL 60604   800/621-0561 or 312/922-2400

LUCE PRESS CLIPPINGS, INC.
420 Lexington Ave., Suite 360
New York, NY 10170   212/889-6711

Note: Luce offers an additional service called "Impact," a monthly reporting system that tracks publicity efforts and results.

Nonprofit Information

SOCIAL SERVICE ORGANIZATIONS & AGENCIES DIRECTORY
Gale Research Co.
Book Tower
Detroit MI 48226   313/961-2242

This publication lists approximately 6500 national and regional social service organizations. Entries include publications which they publish. *Note:* THE DIRECTORY OF DIRECTORIES, published by Gale Research Co., lists other social services directories.

"How-to" Booklet for Radio and Television

"IF YOU WANT AIR TIME . . . "
NAB Services
1771 N St., NW
Washington, D.C. 20036   202/429-5300

The National Association of Broadcasters publishes a how-to booklet that is designed to help community leaders, civic groups, organizations, and individuals to use radio and television to get their message to the public. It contains specific advice, checklists, rules, "do's" and "don'ts," and examples on writing creative public service announcements (PSAs), producing news releases, appearing on-air, and more.

Glossary

ad   short for "advertising."

ADI   area of dominant influence: an area in which a TV station has a commandingly large share of the viewing audience. This phrase, like "designated marketing area," was coined by a market research firm.

advertising   messages printed in newspaper space paid for by the advertiser.

advertorials   a relatively new, controversial type of advertising intended to instruct or entertain readers and produce additional revenue for the publication. They consist of promotional and editorial material, jointly produced for the advertiser, and usually are contained in a separate section of the publication.

anchor   a person who anchors a television news broadcast, narrates news, and introduces reports presented by reporters.

assignment   a single or continuing story a reporter covers for his or her newspaper.

assignment editor   the person at a television or radio station who is responsible for dispatching camera crews and reporters to cover news events.

Associated Press (AP)   a cooperative news-gathering agency, encompassing more than 4,500 newspapers, TV, and radio stations worldwide.

audience   the number of people reading, watching, or listening to a particular medium.

backgrounder   a story or news release that summarizes the history or background of a current matter in the news; also, a meeting with the press in which a source gives information not for publication.

banner   a large headline that runs across the entire width or most of the newspaper page, used most frequently across the front pages of "street editions." They are large and bold, and written to attract the eye and interest of the street buyer who may be offered several choices in racks standing side by side.

beat   the reporter's regular assignment, such as the police or courthouse "beat."

bleed   an advertisement in which all or part of the graphic material runs to the edges of the page. There usually is a premium charged for a bleed advertisement.

body, body copy   all of an article that follows lead paragraphs.

body type   type used in the story, not in the headline.

bold face   applied to type, meaning heavy or dark type.

box   a story with a border around it, or a rectangular space marked off in a story.

break   a period when a broadcast is interrupted, such as when a commercial plays on the air—a commercial break.

breaking news   news that is developing at the moment.

Many of the definitions in this glossary are reproduced with permission from a booklet printed by American Newspaper Publishers Association Foundation. Additions have been made.

byline   the name of the writer printed at the head of a story.

b&w   black and white; usually refers to photos supplied to newspapers or to film for television.

call letters   a broadcast station's name. Usually four letters starting with W east of the Mississippi and starting with K west of the Mississippi.

camera cue light   a red light on the front of a TV camera indicating it is the one in use.

caps   abbreviation for capital letters.

caption   descriptive matter accompanying an illustration; sometimes referred to as a *cut line*; also sometimes used to signify a headline used over a picture or group of pictures.

center spread   two facing center pages, on one continuous page in a newspaper.

Chroma-key   An electronic process used in television for matting one picture into another.

city desk   the desk where the editor (often flanked by other editors and assistants) processes local news.

city news service   a syndicated news service that distributes only city or local news.

circulation   the total number of copies of the newspaper distributed to subscribers and news vendors in a single day.

classified advertising   advertising space usually purchased in small amounts by the public. The ads are "classified" into various categories such as jobs, autos, apartments for rent, etc. Also, sometimes referred to as the "want ads."

column   the arrangement of horizontal lines of type in a news story; also, an article appearing regularly written by a particular writer or "columnist."

compose   an old term meaning to set type.

commercial   a broadcast term that, when used technically, means an advertising message broadcast during a program the advertiser sponsors. Most of what people call commercials, are, in broadcast parlance, advertising spots.

composing room   where copy, headlines, advertising, and illustrations are set and assembled in preparation for printing.

contact proof print   a positive photographic trial print, to be "read" by an editor and marked to indicate content and size of the final print for in-paper use.

controlled circulation   for business papers this is now usually called *qualified circulation*. It is nonpaid. For suburban newspapers it means delivery of nonpaid copies to everyone in a specific area, regardless of whether they are subscribers or not.

copy   any written material to be published or reproduced; a single newspaper.

copy editor   assistant to city or national editor, edits reporter's copy and writes headlines.

copy desk   horseshoe-shaped desk at which copy editors sit.

copyright   legal protection to an author from unauthorized use of his or her work.

cover   to go and seek information for a story. "He covered the fire."

coverage   in print media, the number of copies (assumed to be greater than the "circulation") physically received by people in the mail, from carriers, at newsstands, and as pass-alongs. In broadcast, it's an engineering measurement of how far and where a station's signal can be received. Coverage describes only potential. It doesn't tell you how many people actually look into that publication or tune in to that station. There is *mass* coverage (for example, a TV network program with wide appeal) or *specific* coverage. Specific coverage may be directed geographically (state, region, locality, etc.) or toward selected groups of people assumed to have the same interests (teenagers, sports fans, and so forth)

created news   controlled news that comes from a created event or happening such as appointments or elections of individuals, meetings, performances, new product or new service announcements, new programs, and so on.

crop (photo)   trimming the edges of a photo to fit space.

CU   broadcast term: Close up . . . of announcer's face only . . . or, for a small item with a signature card and price card.

cue   a sound or action noting the start or conclusion of a show. The signal to someone to say or to do something.

cue card   a television term meaning a card placed out of camera range for someone to read from.

cume   a television term meaning as frequency increases, new people who have not seen or heard an advertisement are exposed to it. Reach, thus, increases. Cume is short for cumulative audience.

cut   to shorten newspaper copy, more often referred to as *trim*; also, another word for *illustration*, derived from the days when all newspaper illustrations were woodcuts.

cut   broadcast term used for an instant camera change . . . from one camera to another.

cutline   written text accompanying an illustration or "cut," more often called *caption*.

dateline   precedes the first sentence of the lead, telling the reader the location and often the date of the story.

deadline   the time a story must be ready; a reporter may have to hurry because he or she is "on deadline."

demographic   statistics about people: their occupations, incomes, educational levels, and the like to help you identify your prospects among the total population. If you know the kind of people you want as customers, demographic information can help you better target your advertising by helping you select the media that best reaches them. Demographic editions of publications are aimed at specific groups of people based on one or more of the above criteria.

desk   desk at which journalists edit local sports, national, fashion news, etc.

deskman   copy editor.

display advertising   large, frequently illustrated advertisements usually purchased by retail stores, manufacturers, and service companies.

dissolve   a slow take out of one camera as the other camera is slowly brought in. On this shot there is a momentary super. It is possible to use a fast dissolve, or a slow dissolve. With a slow dissolve, for example, you can seem to take a wrapper off a loaf of bread.

dolly   to move the camera in on the subject or away from the subject. However, to go from a long shot to a CU, it is advisable to change cameras.

double planting   to give the same photo or news release to more than one person at the same newspaper.

double truck   two full facing pages or a center spread.

drive time   the early morning and late afternoon/early evening hours when radio has its largest audiences and highest rates.

dummy   a diagram or layout of the newspaper page that shows the placement of headlines, stories, pictures, and advertisements.

ears   space at the top of the front page on each side of the paper's name; usually boxed in with weather news, index to pages, or an announcement of special features.

ECU   a television term meaning extreme close up. Indicates filling the screen with an item and is used primarily on small objects (watches, rings, small cans of food). As an example, it can be used on tires for a good look at the tread design. It also can be used for a face-only shot of a person.

edition   one day's run of the newspaper; "today's edition"; some newspapers print several editions per day, each containing news of a different locale, such as "city edition," "northeast edition"; large circulation papers break up long press runs with several numbered editions updating the news of preceding editions; the most recent news is contained in the "final edition."

editor   the person responsible for deciding what news goes in the paper and where it will appear; one who reviews, corrects, and, if necessary, rewrites the stories submitted by reporters.

editorial   an expression of opinion of the newspaper's editors, usually reflecting the opinion of the publisher or owner of the newspaper; also the department of the newspaper where news is gathered, written, edited, and readied for publication.

editorial cartoon   cartoon art that expresses opinions on the news.

ENG   electronic news gathering. Television coverage of news using minicams at remote locations.

face   the part of the type that comes in contact with the paper; also the style or family of the type, such as boldface or italic, Caslon, or Bodoni.

fact sheet   a set of data or information about a specific event or happening that contains all of the information from which a news story can be written. It replaces or amplifies a news release.

fade   one camera is faded out before the other is faded in. There is a fleeting moment of black on screen.

feature   a story that deals with something other than late-breaking news.

filler   a short piece of copy used to fill small spaces in news columns.

five W's   who, what, when, where, why (some people add "H" for how); the major questions answered in the "lead" of a well-written news story.

flag   the name of the newspaper appearing on page one.

flak   a disparaging out-of-date name given to publicists who create publicity by means of staged stunts.

flush left/right copy that is "justified" on either left, right, or both edges so that the copy is aligned evenly. Traditionally, newspaper columns are aligned flush left and right (justified) except at the beginning of a paragraph where the first word is indented.

First Amendment the first article of the Bill of Rights, granting freedom of religion, speech, press, assembly, and petition.

follow-up a story that adds more information to a story already printed.

font a complete alphabet of type in one size and style.

fourth estate an eighteenth century phrase describing the press. During a speech in Parliament, British statesman Edmund Burke pointed to the reporters' gallery saying, "There are three estates in Parliament, but yonder sits a fourth estate, more important than all of them." He was referring to the three classes of people recognized under British law: the clergy, the nobles, and the commons. Thus, newspapers became the Fourth Estate.

freedom of the press the freedom granted in Article 1 of the Bill of Rights, "Congress shall make no law respecting an establishment of religion or prohibiting the free exercise thereof: abridging the freedom of speech or of the press . . . ".

fringe time the periods immediately before and after TV "prime time": generally, 4:30 P.M. to 7:30 P.M. and after 11:00 P.M.

general assignment a reporter who covers a variety of stories rather than a single "beat."

glossy, glossy print a smooth, shiny-surfaced photograph required to produce a sharp clear reproduction on newsprint.

graf newsroom jargon meaning paragraph.

handout a press release; a prepared statement for the press. Also a free film clip or video tape of a news event, supplied to a television station.

hard copy copy that is in touchable form as opposed to verbal copy or copy on a computer screen before it is printed.

headline display type placed over a story summarizing the story for the reader.

home editions newspapers that go to subscribers; do not have to vie for the buyer's interests, so small headlines can be used, often with separate headlines topping each front page story. The banner-type headline usually is omitted, although the lead story may carry a three- or four-column head if the story is important.

human interest elements in a story that appeal to readers' emotions, that have to do with events in human life.

index table of contents of each newspaper, usually found on page one.

issue all copies of a newspaper produced in a day.

inverted pyramid a method of writing news stories in which the parts of the story are placed in descending order of importance.

jargon the special vocabulary of a particular business; the language of that business.

jump to continue a story from one page to another (usually from page one to inside).

jumpline the line that tells readers the page where a story is continued.

jumphead the headline used on a story continued from another page, which repeats key words from the original story.

justification   type set to fill the entire line so that margins are flush left and flush right—as different from "ragged right" margins.

kill   to discard all or parts of a story before it is printed.

l.c.   lower-case letters as opposed to capital letters.

lead   the first paragraph or two of a story, which usually contain(s) the "5W" information (pronounced "leed").

letter to the editor   a letter in a newspaper in which a reader expresses his or her views, frequently printed on the editorial page or the page opposite the editorial page.

libel   a false communication that injures the reputation of an individual.

library   file of stories, biographies, pictures, etc., available for reference at any time; the place where these materials are kept. Also called the *morgue*.

line   a line of type; uniform method of measuring the depth of an advertisement; newspapers sell advertising by either a line or column inch; there usually are 8 lines to the column inch; advertising men refer to the total amount of advertising sold in a given period as "lineage."

logo   short for "logotype"; a design bearing the trademark or name of a company or business, or of a newspaper feature.

long shot, cover shot, full shot   television terms: can be used interchangeably; takes in the complete set or a full shot of the announcer.

make-up   the arrangement of stories, headlines, pictures, and advertising on a page.

managing editor   the editor at most papers who directs the daily gathering, writing, and editing of news, and of the placement of news in the paper; working for him or her are the city editor, the national editor, etc.

masthead   the formal statement of a paper's name, officers, point of publication and other information, usually found on the editorial page.

media   plural of *medium*, a term used to depict the combination of a variety of communications including newspapers, television, radio, magazines, direct mail, etc.

media event   an event designed to create news that attracts media news coverage.

media kit   also known as media information kit; see press kit.

media list   a list of newspaper, radio, and television people to whom news releases and other information is sent for the purposes of acquiring publicity or goodwill.

MCU or MS   (medium closeup or medium shot) television terms: usually used interchangeably. It can be a bust shot of the announcer. Or it is used for larger items, such as a dryer where the top is shown, but not a close up of the controls.

mobile unit   television broadcast equipment used outside the studio.

monitoring   a television term used to indicate checks of competitors' programming, commercials, and transmission quality.

mug   a photograph of a person's face.

morgue   an old term for the newspaper's library where files of clippings, photos, microfilm of past issues, reference books, and other material are contained.

national editor   "wire" editor, in charge of selecting and editing the news of the nation outside the newspaper's circulation area.

network a link-up of many stations by cable or microwave for simultaneous broadcast on all from a single originating point. The stations may be owned by or affiliated with the network.

news director/news editor dispatches broadcast crews and field reporters; puts a newscast together.

news hole the space in a newspaper allocated to news or unpaid content as contrasted to advertising.

news peg the main element of a news story; the "peg" upon which the story is hung.

newsprint a grade of paper made of wood pulp, used primarily for printing newspaper, delivered in rolls weighing up to a ton.

news release see press release.

news services news-gathering agencies such as AP and UPI that gather and distribute news to subscribing newspapers.

obituary (obit) a biographical account of a person's life published at the time of his or her death.

off the record information given by a source that is not for publication.

on location broadcast programming produced outside of a studio.

on the air the time a program is being broadcast or recorded. Signified by signs in the studio and outside the studio doors.

op-ed page means "opposite the editorial page"; some newspapers use this page to print reader opinions, articles by columnists, and other nonnews features.

page one the first page of the newspaper; also, "important" as in "page-one news."

pan from the word panorama, meaning to move sideways from one item to another in the same shot. It means merely turning the camera . . . not necessarily to move the wheels.

pasteup prepared advertising copy and art for reproduction. All elements are in the proper position. Also called *mechanical* or *camera-ready art.*

penetration another term for "reach," it means the extent to which a publication or broadcast station has gotten audience attention in a given area (market). If a publication or station gets half a potential audience, it is said to have a penetration of 50 percent.

photo release signed permission from an individual giving permission to use his or her name and photo likeness for the purposes stated in the release.

pica unit of linear measurement of 12 points, equal to $1/6$-inch.

pica pole a ruler that measures in picas.

plant/double plant a term used to mean that a story has been placed—planted—with a particular news outlet. Double planting is a taboo practice, meaning to place the same news release with two editors or two sections within the same publication.

point designating the size of type, one point representing about $1/72$ of an inch.

position the location of an ad on a page.

precedes a reader's aid, an explanatory note, that precedes and explains, such as an "editor's note."

press association an organization that collects news from around the world and relays it to subscribers. Best known are The Associated Press, United Press International.

press conference   special meeting called to give information to the press.

press junket   an especially arranged trip for press/media only—a strictly media event.

press kit   a special package of information related to an event or to the purpose of a press conference; a collection of selected materials to help reporters write a more complete news story.

press release   a specially prepared statement for the press (see handout).

prime time   when television has its largest audiences and highest advertising rates. In the Eastern, Mountain, and Pacific time zones it is from 7:30 P.M. to 11:00 P.M. In the Central zone it is from 6:30 P.M. to 10:00 P.M.

professional paper   a classification of business papers edited for people who buy very little themselves, but whose recommendations influence the expenditure of large sums of money. Architects are an example.

proof   an impression of a printed page or story; a printer "pulls a proof" so the "proofreader" can check for errors before the final version is printed.

proofreader   one who reads proof and marks errors.

publicity   newsworthy information distributed to media to gain public notice or support.

publicity stunt   an unusual, preposterous, often inane event staged solely to attract public and media attention.

public relations   activities and attitudes of an organization intended to create and maintain worthwhile relations with the public.

public service announcement   see PSA.

public service time   free air time that broadcast stations must allot according to FCC definitions; includes public service announcements and special programming in the interests of the community.

publisher   the chief executive and often the owner of a newspaper or other publishing enterprise.

put to bed   printer's term for the final steps taken before the presses start to run.

PSA   a broadcast term standing for public service announcement; an announcement for which no charge is made and which promotes programs, activities, or services of nonprofit organizations and other announcements regarded as serving community interests.

quotes sheet   a page or more of fully attributed quotes by an organization official or outside person qualified to speak about the subject or purpose of a press conference or a news release; usually part of a press kit.

ragged right   type set in a newspaper column that is not "flush right."

reefer   a cross reference, referring a reader to a item or photo.

release   to specify the publication of a story on or after a specific date.

Reuters   the first news-gathering service, founded in Great Britain in 1849.

review   an account of an artistic event such as a concert or play that offers critical evaluation, the opinion of the writer.

rewrite man   a news person whose job is to write a news account from information supplied by reporters at or near the scene of the story.

ROP   run-of-paper news and advertising appears in any position convenient to the make-up of the paper.

set   type is set when it is arranged into words and lines.

shopper   what shopping guides are called. Consisting almost entirely of advertisements, they have nonpaid "controlled circulation" and are distributed in specific geographic areas to give complete coverage. Most are weeklies.

sidebar   a secondary story presenting sidelights on a major news story.

source   supplier of information, such as a person, book, survey, etc.

spot news   news obtained first-hand; fresh news.

stand-alone news release   a news release that provides all the essential principal facts or purposes (as for a news conference) and can stand alone to be used by recipients as presented.

still video   a new technology for newspapers that produces newspaper photos from a camera that records up to 50 images on a computer disk; requires no developing before the image can be seen on a video screen.

street editions   often have "ears"—small boxes on one of both sides of the "flag," nameplate—to give further information that is meant to attract the single-copy buyer. Only the top half of page one is visible in a street rack. The editor uses this portion to catch the interest of street buyers.

stringer   a part-time writer usually covering a particular area or subject, often paid according to the amount of his or her copy printed by the newspaper.

stunt   see publicity stunt.

style, stylebook, style manual, style sheet   the rules and rulebook governing writing, spelling, etc., which most newspapers provide their writers and editors.

subhead   a one- or two-line head used to divide sections of a story.

super   a television term often used to mean superimposing information such as an organization's name, telephone number, address, or other essential information on a slide, film, or video clip.

syndicate   a company that sells news, features, comics, drawings, and photos to newspapers, magazines, radio, trade journals, business newspapers, all for a fraction of the amount paid to the contributor; syndicated features material such as comics, advice columns, etc., supplied nationally to newspapers by news syndicates.

tabloid   a newspaper format that is a little larger than half the standard size, usually with five columns per page.

tear sheet   a sheet torn from a publication to prove insertion of an advertisement.

teaser   an announcement placed prominently in the newspaper, often on page one, which tells of an interesting story elsewhere in the paper.

Telephoto   the United Press International service that transmits pictures to subscribing newspapers

tip   an item of information that might lead to a news story.

trade publication   a publication edited specifically to reach members of a specific occupational group. Such newspapers (or magazines) contain articles and advertisements directed to the group's interests.

truck   means almost the same as dolly, except the camera is moved, as around a car or along a large set.

type   the physical letters used by the printer to produce readable material.

typo   short for "typographical error"; a mistake made during the production rather than the writing of a story.

u.c.   upper case, another term for capital letters.

United Press International (UPI)   one of several worldwide news services.

visuals   any and all visual elements in a television program.

want ads   classified advertisements.

widow   a single word or a partial line at the end of a paragraph that appears alone at the top of a column of type.

wire editor   edits news supplied by the news agencies or "wire services."

Wirephoto   The Associated Press service that transmits pictures to subscribing newspapers.

zone edition   an edition of a city newspaper for a specific geographic area, which may be within the city or a group of suburban communities. A zone edition is for both news and advertising. It may consist of localized pages, a separate section, or a tabloid insert. It may be published every day or only on certain days, but almost always on Sunday. Big city newspapers often use zone editions to meet competition from suburban newspapers both for readers and advertisers.

"30" or ###   signifies end of copy.

Index